Early Landowners of Maryland

Volume 9: Queen Anne's County

1640-1710

Robert W. Hall

Edited by

Sandra T. Hall

Colonial Roots
Lewes, Delaware
2011

COLONIAL ROOTS

17296 Coastal Highway
Lewes, Delaware 19958
1-800-576-8608

Visit our website at www.colonialroots.com to determine if we have researched your family during the colonial period. Search our surname index which includes our "Colonial Families" books and other family histories of Delaware, Maryland, New Jersey, Pennsylvania, and Virginia.

Catalog on request

Some of our other titles include:

Other Early Landowners of Maryland Books by the author:
  Volume 1: Anne Arundel County 1650-1704
  Volume 2: Prince George's County 1650-1710
  Volume 3: Calvert County 1640-1710
  Volume 4: Charles County 1640-1710
  Volume 5: St. Mary's County 1633-1712
  Volume 6: Kent County 1640-1710
  Volume 7: Baltimore County 1658-1710
  Volume 8: Talbot County 1650-1710

Other Maryland Books by the author:
  Land Grants in Anne Arundel County, South River Hundred
      1650-1704
  Land Grants in Anne Arundel County, Middle Neck Hundred
      1650-1704

Contents

Foreward

The Conditions of Plantation, and amendments thereto, were codified and established by Lord Baltimore, the Lord Proprietor of Maryland, to provide Maryland settlers with the opportunity to become land holders, an opportunity that was often not available in their native land. The Conditions had many provisions and exclusions but they basically established a head-right system that provided that warrants for land would be awarded to persons who transported immigrants (including themselves) at their own expense to this Province here to inhabit. This included persons from other provinces of the New World. The Conditions also established and maintained land-management policy, procedures, and features such as annual rent for property owned and penalties (alienation fees) when rents were not paid on time. A rent amount and a payment schedule for each tract was shown in the survey/patent document. A detailed fee schedule of these and most of the other Secretary's and Sheriff's fees can be found in the Acts of Assembly, 1650 (L7/33-35 SR7343).

Redemptioners or Indentured Servants were persons who entered agreements to work as servants for specific periods of time to redeem their passage costs. Indenture periods varied according to factors such as the age, sex, and skills of the persons involved. Land ownership in early Maryland featured most of the rights of present day ownership except that a fee (or rent) was required upon issuance of the patent and every year following. The "Conditions" were formally amended five times with some additional tinkering between amendments. The amendments usually augmented or supplemented the earlier versions except the "Fourth Conditions," which superseded and revoked all earlier versions. The following is a synopsis of the changes to the Conditions brought about by the amendments:

First Conditions (1633). Provided that a person transporting others to this Province here to inhabit received 200 acres of land within this Province for each man transported, 100 acres for each woman, and 50 acres for each child.

Second Conditions (1636). Every "adventurer" who transported five men between the ages of 16 and 50 received 2,000 acres (i.e., 400 acres per man). Persons transporting less than five people received 100 acres per adult and 50 acres per child (under 16 years of age) and per maid servant (under 40 years of age) transported.

Third Conditions (promulgated in 1641, but did not take effect until 1642). Provided that anyone of English or Irish descent who transported 20 able-bodied men, between the age of 16 and 50, with arms and ammunition, or women between the age of 14 and 40, received 100 acres per person transported. If less than 20 persons were transported, the rate dropped to 50 acres per person, and the rate for children under 14 years of age was 25 acres per child transported.

Fourth Conditions (1648). This amendment replaced all earlier versions. Provision was made for land ownership by persons of French, Dutch, and Italian descent. A requirement was included that every prospective landowner take an Oath of Fidelity to the Lord Proprietor. The ground rules and ratio of land per person transported were not changed. Redemptioners of English or Irish descent, upon completion of an indenture period of not less than three years, were now entitled to "Freedom Rights" of 50 acres of land. Corporations, societies, fraternities, guilds, spiritual organizations and other groups were now prohibited from "new" or additional land ownership without permission from the Lord Proprietor.

Fifth Conditions (1649). Initially, the ground rules and acreage per person remained unchanged at 100 acres per person. This was reduced to fifty acres on 6/20/1652, except for several regions where settlement was to be encouraged (i.e., the Eastern Shore and areas of Prince George's County). Persons entitled to land were prohibited from assigning or selling rights to organizations, societies, etc. Head rights now had to be exercised within one year.

On October 2, 1680, Lord Baltimore issued an order to John Lewellin, Clerk of the Land Office, requiring him to issue warrants only upon due proof of rights thereunto made according to the oaths established in the order. This order applied to all phases of the patent process, i.e., certifications, surveys, and patents that had not been completed prior to the date of the order. (LWC2/249 SR7340)

Oath for Probate of Rights

You do sweare that the severall persons herein mentioned (unless) their names are to be published in a list) are to the best of your knowledge of British or Irish descent and, by your cost and charge are imported into this Province to inhabit in the year _ _ _ _, or otherwise at the proper cost and charge of your friends transported and consigned to you to be disposed of. And that neither you nor any other person or persons whatsoever for you or by your consent, priority, or knowledge has before proved or made over of the rights for same to any other person whatsoever, so help you God.

Oath Where a Person Proves His Rights for Completion of Service

You doe sweare that you are to the best of your knowledge of British or Irish descent and that at your friends proper cost and charges you were transported into this Province to inhabit in the year _ _ _ _ , and that you have truly performed your time of service within this Province and that you never before proved or made over of the right due you thereupon neither assigned the same over to any other person or persons whatsoever, so help you God.

Note 1: I found nothing in the land records suggesting that any record of persons taking any of these oaths was maintained or even started. Note 2: Although the Conditions of Plantation provides for land ownership by persons of Dutch, French, and Italian descent as early as 1648, oaths developed as late as 1680 required that landowners be of British or Irish descent.

Tracts that were deserted for four years (unless owned by orphans under 16 years of age), or if rents/alienation fees were unpaid for three years, and tracts belonging to deceased persons with no heirs reverted to the Lord Proprietor through a process called "escheat." Such tracts would usually be renamed, resurveyed (often with new shapes, metes and bounds), and granted to new owners. Unfortunately, there is no consolidated record of *escheated* tracts. Occasionally, however, a survey or patent document will provide a clue of prior ownership and some detail may be included. Sales of tracts were extensive and immediate. Some sales were directly from one individual to another through a contract or indenture. Direct sales are recorded in the County Land Record Index (#73) held at the Maryland State Archives (MSA).

The patent process involved three steps beginning with the certification of the rights of an individual to a given number of unidentified acres. It included a brief explanation of how and when those rights were earned. Like survey and patent documents, the certification was usually recorded in one of the land record Libers and a copy may have been provided to the owner. The next step was a survey of a specific parcel of land in the amount of acreage certified. My experience has been that certification and surveys were often combined into one step. The third and final step is the "Letters Pattent" granting the tract to the individual named in the Survey. At some point in the late 1880s, the survey and patent steps were merged. Ownership rights began upon certification. A certificate of rights or a surveyed tract could be divided, sold, traded, or willed to an heir. Tracts could be inhabited on the basis of a survey with or without a patent. Many settlers built homes and lived on surveyed tracts for years before patenting and, perhaps due to the added expense, some tracts were settled but never patented.

A 1648 amendment to the Conditions of Plantation required that persons receiving Letters Pattent take an Oath of Fidelity to the Lord Proprietor. Oath taking was a prerequisite to the acceptance of public employment or service as a Burgess or Clerk in the General Assembly, and in the probation of wills and other situations including obtaining patents (but not surveys) for a tract of land. The taking of oaths or any form of acknowledgement of governmental authority was repugnant to some and in particular to he sizeable Maryland Puritan population. After October 1680, the requirement for oaths was confirmed as a part of the probate process and to claim Freedom Rights to fifty acres of land upon completion of service indenture periods. It is impossible to know how many tracts were surveyed and inhabited, but not patented for these and other reasons. We can never know with certainty whether a tract was not patented or the patent record was lost during the move of the Capitol to Annapolis or burned in the courthouse fire in 1704.

The early development of a class of "head-right brokers" was, I believe, a natural spin-off of the Maryland head-right system. Rights brokerage offered a needed career ladder for surveyors and others involved in the affairs of the land office. To other enterprising settlers it presented a unique opportunity to obtain wealth. Unlike modern real estate brokers these early businessmen sold rights to random vacant acreage rather than specific properties. Grant documents indicate that some individuals such as surveyors, land office personnel, and wealthy citizens held warrants for thousands of acres. These were usually obtained from individuals such as sea captains, former indentured servants, widows and orphans with inherited rights, wealthy citizens who "transported" settlers to this province, or anyone with accumulated land rights and no interest in obtaining land.

Remarks recorded in 1676 (L19/459) show that the Lord Proprietor, Charles Calvert, believed that the headright system was too expensive and that land titles were dubious and incomplete due to poor performance by his land office. He believed that he was losing a great deal of money and intended to abolish the system at the earliest opportunity. However, the practice continued for years until finally abolished in 1683. The Lord Proprietor then sold land to anyone willing to pay the required fees and rents. The mechanics of the process continued generally as before and it appears that "unused" headrights continued to be honored.

Initially, I restricted the scope of the project to actual patents. My purpose was to identify land that was owned and inhabited and to identify the owners during the period targeted. As indicated above, surveyed tracts could be lawfully inhabited without ever being patented. Also, tracts were added to the rent roles when surveyed. In order to produce a complete record of who owned what and when, I have included tracts surveyed but not known to have been patented, and tracts surveyed by one person and patented by another. Also included are "resurveys" and "regranted tracts" whether or not a change in acreage or ownership was involved. For convenience, I refer to all of these as "grants." In addition, a small number of patents occurring after the period addressed have been included for any of the following reasons:

  a. The process (i.e.,cert, survey, or patent) began prior to 1711

  b. The tract is a recent addition, enlargement, re-grant, or resurvey of a tract already included

  c. The tract location is an important key to the geographical location of a number of tracts already included.

Lord Baltimore adopted the "hundred system" in Maryland shortly after the establishment of St Mary's. Hundreds in Maryland are usually described as geographical subdivisions that served as voting districts until about 1671. Like the hundreds in England, there was a military aspect to the hundred. The Assembly of February/March 1638/9 established that each hundred be under the management of a commander empowered to appoint a high constable and a sergeant to train all able men to bear arms. Unfortunately the information surviving on the locations and boundaries of the hundreds is incomplete for some of the counties.

Queen Annes County, founded in 1706, is bounded on the west by the Chesapeake Bay, on the south by Talbot County on the southeast and west by Caroline County and the state of Delaware, and on the north the Chester River and Kent County. My goal is to identify all tracts patented by or located in Queen Annes County now or at any time during the targeted period. Queen Annes County land grants/certifications/resurveys were found in present day Kent, Talbot, Queen Annes, Kent, and St. Marys Counties. A total of 804 grants, as defined above, were found.

A number of these tracts do not identify the patenting authority i.e., county. I have assumed that patents for land within the current boundaries of a county that predate the establishment of that county were most likely patented by the geographically closest established county. I have footnoted such entries to indicate that the tract was *probably located* in the county specified in the note. The *"probably located"* designation is also used for tracts located on a county boundary (creek or river) without indicating on which side the land was located.

Occasionally, patent documents indicate the owner's home county and manor rather than the county of location. In fact, nearly all of the patents found in this volume are shown as being on land located in Baltimore Manor. Because this can apply to grants found in Baltimore, Cecil, Kent, Queen Annes, Talbot, Harford, Dorchester, and possibly other counties, this is not, in itself, a factor in identifying either the patent issuing county or present day location.

As indicated above, some informed *guesswork* has been necessary for a variety of reasons. Factors such as the location of adjoining tracts identified in the patent document or the location of the preponderance of a land owner's other tracts are considerations. To aid in the determination of tract location, I have developed a detailed index of landmarks (by county) referenced in the tract location areas of grant documents. I have included this index for Queen Annes County in this volume as the Index of Landmarks.

The following is a breakout of Queen Annes County grant statistics by decade:

Year*	No. Tracts	Acreage	Avg. Acreage
1640 – '49	39	11,244	288
1650 – '59	84	28,580	340
1660 - '69	112	82,978	741
1670 - '79	112	42,482	379
1680 - '89	329	90,211	274
1690 - '99	75	16,708	223
1700 - '10	51	11,001	216
1710 +	2	450	225
Total	804	283,654	353

None in 1641-1646, 1648-1649, 1653-1657, 1660, 1690-1693, 1704, 1710

A class of wealthy landowners emerged toward the end of the period covered. Discounting partnerships 19% of the certified acreage granted in or by Talbot County was owned by the ten individuals listed below:

	Number of Tracts Owned	Certified Acres
Robert Smith	10	10,614
Vincent Lowe	11	8,100
William Hemsley	19	7,075
Lord Baltimore	1	6,000
Peter Sayer	5	4,025
Richard Tilghman	5	3,773

Francis Sheppard	13	3,600
Henry Coursey	5	3,550
Stephen Tully	9	3,450
John Wright	7	3,040
Total	85	53,227

Land records of this era sometimes directly or indirectly reveal unexpected information involving personal and family relationships, burial sites, employer's names, trades, disputes, and religious and political involvement. The execution of a former tract owner for sedition is also mentioned (see Vol.5, St. Johns owned by Thomas Jenkins). Another execution, this time for murder, is also mentioned in St. Margarett's (also in Vol. 5, patented by Margarett Noble). Special instructions from the Lord Proprietor regarding matters such as suspended surveyors, gifts to his relatives and special friends, the location of special springs reserved for The Lord Proprietors use, and much more were found.

The marking of the boundary between Maryland and Virginia on the eastern side of the Chesapeake Bay is addressed in the land records in Liber 18 Folio177 (SR7359). The boundary was laid out jointly by Phillip Calvert and Col. Edmund Scarborough of Virginia. This task included an agreement that all persons with Virginia grants found later to be in the Province of Maryland could keep their land after making rights within the guidelines of the Maryland system and re-patenting their land. A number of such tracts initially granted by William Clayborn on Kent Island were found. Clayborn, a former Surveyor General of Virginia and a member of the Virginia Governors Council, established a trading settlement on Kent Island in 1631. Kent Island was included in the boundaries of the new Province of Maryland in 1632. When Maryland assumed control of the Kent Island settlement, grants issued by Clayborn were honored in accordance with the terms of the above-mentioned agreement.

The entire Acts of Assembly, 1650, were found in Liber 3 (folios 29-61) of the land records. These are well worth a read in themselves. Among the topics addressed are corporal punishment (i.e., the removal of ears or hands) for swearing, the collection of ransom to rescue hostages from the Indians, retaliation against the Indians, requirements that Indians provide 24-hour notification before visiting a settlement (and then only in limited numbers), and the refurbishment of the fort at St. Inegoes to control the behavior of the crews of foreign trading vessels while in port.

I have tried to retain the special flavor of the records by including many of the consistently misspelled words and some of the less wordy quaint phrasing found. I have tried to include interesting misspelled words exactly as found in each instance. There are many instances of names (persons, tracts, places) spelled in different ways. I have tried to spell names as spelled each time found. In some, but not all, instances patent records show the letters "es" added as a suffix to a name ending in a consonant to show ownership, e.g. Cox's became Coxes, Crouch's became Crouches, etc. Occasionally, when the same name was used in a non-possessive context, only the "s" was dropped thereby resulting in spellings such as Coxe or Crouche. It is possible that names such as Browne, Brooke, Greene, etc., could have originally been Brown, Brook, Green, etc.

An index of the names of all individuals named in the patent records is included as the Index of People. In this index I have highlighted the names of individuals mentioned in the records as having been transported to this country at the expense of others or themselves and subsequently claimed in establishing rights to land. At the risk of some redundancy other references to the same names in a non-immigrant context have also been included because it cannot be determined with certainty that "same name" references are to a single person.

Although nothing I could say would be adequate, I would like to express my appreciation and gratitude to my wife Sandy for editing this book and for everything else that she did to help and, especially, for her unlimited patience with me while we worked on this project.

Early Landowners of Maryland
Volume 9 - Queen Annes County
1640-1710

Abbott/Abott, John, Planter
Unnamed Patent 9/17/1640 – 50a's. L1/90 SR7341
Location: Queen Annes County on the western side of Kent Island on a branch of Beaver Neck Creek in Crayford Manor. Adjoins **Andrew Basha's** tract of land near Abbotts Swamp. *Note: The patent document does not specify the patenting county.*

Abbotts Ash 12/9/1640 - 50a's. L1/90 SR7341
Location: Queen Annes County on the eastern side of Kent Island in Crayford Manor on the northernmost branch of Beaver Neck Creek. Adjoins **Andrew Basha's** tract of land near Abbotts Swamp. *Note: This patent was issued by St. Marys County.*

Abington, Andrew
Abington Square 5/1/1684 – 300a's. L22/96 SR7363
Location: Queen Annes County on the southeast side of the Main Branch of the Chester River. Adjoins **James Hall's** tract of land called Halls Harbor. *Note 1: This is a certification. The tract was patented by **James Bowles** in 1707 (DSF/416 SR7373). Note 2: This certification was issued by Talbot County.*

Adams, Thomas
Priors Manor 3/8/1640 - 1,000a's. L1/95 SR7341
Location: Queen Annes County on Kent Island bounded by Priors Creek, Adams Bite, and the Chesapeake Bay.
Other persons mentioned: Adams transported **Henry Morgan, Edward Williams, John Phillips, Thomas Prosson,** and **Walter Road** into this Province here to inhabit as appears on record. *Note 1: A notation in the margin of the patent document says "surrendered". No explanation found. Note 2: This patent was issued by St. Marys County.*

Aldridge, George, Planter
Indian Neck 9/16/1668 - 350a's. L12/136 SR7354
Location: Queen Annes County.
Other persons mentioned: Aldridge transported **himself,** wife **Ann,** four **children,** and **John Cluner** into this Province here to inhabit as appears on

record. *Note 1: This is a seldom-used form of abbreviated patent document that minimizes or excludes location information. This is included in the certification which, in this instance, was not found. Note 2: The patent document does not specify the patenting county.*

Allen, Thomas
Allens Neck 12/9/1640 - 66a's L1/92 SR7341
Location: Queen Annes County on Kent Island in Kent Fort Manor on the southern side of the Northeast Creek of the Chesapeake Bay. *Note 1: This certification was issued by Kent County. No patent was found. Note 2: This was an original* **William Clayborn** *grant (see forward).*

Allen, William
Allens Neck 6/1/1686 – 200a's. NSBi/326 SR7370
Location: Queen Annes County on the southern side of the Chester River between Roland and Double Creeks beginning at a bound White Oak. Other persons mentioned: Land rights assigned by **George Robotham** assignee of **Rowland Vaughan.** *Note: This patent was issued by Talbot County.*

Ashbury, Francis
Pascos Adventure 2/27/1681 - 150a's. CD2i/375 SR7366
Location: Queen Annes County on Kent Island near the Eastern Bay beginning at a marked stake near the Wading Place. Adjoins **Phillip Connor's** tract of land.
Other persons mentioned; Land rights assigned by former owner **Pasco Dunn.** *Note: This patent was issued by Kent County.*

Sparkes Point 2/17/1681 - 50a's. CB2i/375 SR7366
Location: Queen Annes County on Kent Island on Wading Place Bay beginning at a marked Oak standing at the mouth of a creek.
Other persons mentioned: Land rights assigned by former owner **Pasco Dunn.** *Note: This patent was issued by Kent County.*

Ashley, Henry, Planter
Unnamed Patent 8/6/1650 - 100a's. AB&AH/334 SR7344
Location: Queen Annes County on the northeast side of Kent Island on Cox Creek adjoining **John Bushall's** tract of land.
Note 1: Land rights based on Ashley having transported **himself** *into this Province here to inhabit in 1649, as appears on record. Note 2: This is a seldom-used form of abbreviated patent document that minimizes or excludes location information. This is included in the certification which, in this instance, was not found. Note 3: This patent was issued in St. Marys County.*

Baltimore, Lord

His LOPs Manor 6/27/1684 – 6,000a's. L21/339 SR7362
Location: Queen Annes County on the southern side of the Chester River on the Southeast Branch. *Note 1: This is a certification. No patent was found. Note 2: This certification was issued by Talbot County.*

Barracliffe, Edward

Horne Island 6/1/1686 – 75a's. NSBi/367 SR7370
Location: Queen Annes County on the northmost end of **Michael Rinon Island** in the Wye River beginning at a bound tree standing on a point of marsh.
Other persons mentioned: Land rights assigned by **Robert Smith** assignee of **Thomas Collins.** *Note: The information in the patent document is not sufficient to determine the present day location of this tract. However, Maryland State Land Patent Index #55 indicates that it was patented in Talbot County. Based on the location description it was probably located in present day Queen Annes County.*

Basha, Andrew & Cloughton, James

Basha 11/6/1640 - 100a's. L1/91 SR7341
Location: Queen Annes County on Kent Island in Abbotts Swamp on Beaver Neck Creek in Crayford Manor. Adjoins **Robert Cooper's** tract of land called Cooper. *Note 1: This is a certification issued by Kent County. No patent was found. Note 2: This may have been an original* **William Clayborn** *grant (see forward).*

Unnamed Patent 12/7/1640 - 100a's. L1/91 SR7341
Location: Queen Annes County by the Chesapeake Bayside on the western side of Kent Island in Abotts Swamp on Beaver Neck Creek in Crayford Manor where they now dwell. Adjoins **Andrew Abbott's** tract of land called Abbotts Ash and **Robert Cooper's** unnamed 100-acre tract. *Note: This patent was issued by St. Marys County.*

Basha, Giles

Peares Plantation 9/7/1640 - 1,100a's. L1/88 SR7341
Location: Queen Annes County on Kent Island in the Manor of Kent Fort in the woods on a neck of land where the Mill now standeth. *Note 1: Land rights based on Basha having transported **himself** and several unnamed able bodied men into this Province here to inhabit as appears on record. Note 2: Another patent was found dated 5/7/1643 (L1/112 SR7341). The latter patent includes legal considerations that should be read by anyone specifically interested in this land or in the people named. Note 3: This patent was issued by St. Marys County.*

Little Thickett 12/9/1640 - 200a's. L1/93 SR7341
Location: Queen Annes County on Kent Island in Kent Fort Manor on the northern side of the Northwest Branch on Hogpen Creek. *Note 1: Land rights based on Basha having transported **himself** into this Province here to inhabit as appears on record. Note 2: This is an original **William Clayborn** grant (see forward). Note: This patent was issued by St. Marys County.*

Peares Plantation 5/7/1641 - 78a's. AB&H/94 SR7344
Location: Queen Annes County on Kent Island bounded by the Chesapeake Bay and Bashas Branch of Oyster Creek about 20 perches to the north of his dwelling house. *Note: This is a certification issued by St. Marys County. No patent was found.*

Bastin, Henry
Hammonton 9/1/1685 – 220a's. NS2i/159 SR7371
Location: Queen Annes County on the southern side of the Chester River beginning at a marked Oak standing by the mouth of Double Creek.
Other persons mentioned: Land rights assigned by **Henry Parker.** *Note: This patent was issued by Talbot County.*

Baxter, Roger, Planter
Upper Blunt Point 8/20/1650 - 200a's. AB&H/129 SR7344
Location: Queen Annes County on Kent Island on Blunt Point Creek extending from the eastern side of Cox Creek in the woods.
Other persons mentioned: Baxter transported **himself** and his **wife** into this Province here to inhabit in 1637, as appears on record. *Note: This patent was issued by Kent County.*

Beedle, Henry
Beedles Outlett 6/1/1673 – 400a's. L17/151 SR7358
Location: Queen Annes County on the marked road from the Chester River to the Wye River. Adjoins **Henry Coursey's** tract of land.
Other persons mentioned: Land rights assigned by **William Coursey** and **John Pitt.** *Note: This patent was issued by Talbot County.*

Belcher, Thomas, Planter
Belcher 1/29/1652 – 300a's. AB&H/309 SR7344
Location: Queen Annes County on Kent Island near the Eastern Bay in the woods.
Other persons mentioned: Belcher transported **himself,** wife **Mary,** and daughter **Mary** into this Province here to inhabit in 1649, as appears on record. *Note: The patent document does not specify the patenting county.*

Unnamed Patent 1/29/1652 - 300a's AB&H/309 SR7344
<u>Location</u>: Queen Annes County on the northern side of Kent Island near the
Eastern Bay.
<u>Other persons mentioned</u>: Belcher transported **himself,** wife **Mary,** and
daughter **Mary** into this Province here to inhabit in 1649, as appears on
record. *Note 1: This is a seldom-used form of abbreviated patent document
that minimizes or excludes location information. This is included in the
certification which, in this instance, was not found. Note 2: This patent was
issued by Kent County.*

Bennem/Bennham/Bounam, Matthew & Mason, Hugh
Buck Hill 9/10/1683 - 150a's. SDA/49 SR7369
<u>Location</u>: Queen Annes County on Red Lyon Creek of the Chester River
beginning at a bound Red Oak standing by the creek side beginning at the
westernmost bound tree of **Thomas Norris'** tract of land called Presbury.
Also adjoins **William Peirce's** tract called Benjamins Lott.
<u>Other persons mentioned</u>: Land rights assigned by **William Hemsley, Jr.**
*Note 1: The patent document spells Matthew's surname as Bennem and
Bennham. Note 2: This patent was issued by Kent County.*

Bennett, Desborough
Bennetts Addition 9/17/1668 – 150a's. L12/137 SR7354
<u>Location</u>: Queen Annes County.
<u>Other persons mentioned</u>: Land rights assigned by **Daniel Jenifer** assignee
of **John England** due him for transporting **James Cartwright, William,
Sealy,** and **Thomas Mayor** into this Province here to inhabit as appears on
record. *Note 1: This is a seldom-used abbreviated form of patent document
that minimizes or excludes location information. This is included in the
certification which, in this instance was not found. Note 2: The patent
document does not specify the patenting county.*

Bennett, Richard
Stagwell 12/6/1706 - 526a's. DD5i/260 SR7378
<u>Location</u>: Queen Annes County by the riverside on the eastern side of the
Back Wye River formerly called Morgans Creek beginning at a bound tree of
Robert Smith's tract of land called Smeath.
<u>Other persons mentioned</u>: Land rights assigned by former owner **Andrew
Price.** *Note: This patent was issued by Talbot County.*

Bennett, Thomas
Bendon 1/15/1659 – 100a's. L4/316 SR7346
<u>Location</u>: Queen Annes County adjoining **Thomas Todd's** tract of land
called Todd Upon Darwin on the eastern side of Leeds Creek. Also adjoins
William Champe's tract called Champenham. *Note 1: Land rights based on*

*Bennett having transported **himself** into this Province here to inhabit as appears on record. Note: This patent was issued by Kent County.*

Bishop, Richard

The Mistake 11/10/1695 – 400a's. BB3B/500 SR7374
<u>Location</u>: Queen Annes County on the southern side of the Chester River on the northern side of Courseys Creek adjoining **Henry Coursey's** tract of land called Courseys Point. Also adjoins **Andrew Elina's** tract called Sintra.
<u>Other persons mentioned</u>: Land rights assigned by **Robert Smith.** *Note: This patent was issued by Talbot County.*

Bishop/Bishopp, William

Bishops Addition 5/1/1662 - 200a's. L16/616 SR7357
<u>Location</u>: Queen Annes County on the southern side of the Chester River on the Southwest Branch of Corsica Creek. Begins at a bound Red Oak of **Henry Coursey's** tract of land called Courseys Point. Also adjoins **William Hemsley's** tract called Brampton, and his own tract called Bishops Outlett. *Note: This patent was issued by Talbot County.*

Bishops Field 4/10/1677 – 400a's. L19/479 SR7360
<u>Location</u>: Queen Annes County on the southern side of the Chester River at the head of the northernmost branch at the dividing of the s'd river. *Note: This patent was issued by Talbot County.*

Bishopton 4/10/1677 - 350a's. L19/480 SR7360
<u>Location</u>: Queen Annes County on the southern side of the Chester River on the Northeast Fresh Runn of Dividing Creek adjoining **William Hemsley's** tract of land. *Note: This patent was issued by Talbot County.*

Mill Range Res. 3/20/1680 – 163a's. L21/343 SR7362
<u>Location</u>: Queen Annes County on the southern side of the Chester River on the western side of the Southern Branch of Corsica Creek convenient to his water mill beginning at a bound Beech.
<u>Other persons mentioned</u>: Land rights assigned by former owner **Henry Parker.** *Note: This patent was issued by Talbot County.*

Bishops Outlett 6/27/1681 – 800a's. CB3i/325 SR7367
<u>Location</u>: Queen Annes County on the southern side of the Chester River on the northern side of Courseys Creek beginning at a bound tree of **Henry Coursey's** tract of land called Courseys Point. Also adjoins **William Bishop's** tract called Bishops Addition and the land of **John Broadrib.** *Note: This patent was issued by Talbot County.*

Fox Hill 7/15/1684 – 170a's. L22/150 SR7363
Location: Queen Annes County on the southern side of the Chester River on a forke of Hambleton's Branch. *Note 1: This is a certification. No patent was found. Note 2: This certification was issued by Talbot County.*

The Outrange 7/15/1684 – 174a's. IB&ILC/150 SR7363
Location: Queen Annes County on the southern side of the Chester River on a forke of Hambletons Branch. *Note 1: This is a certification. No patent was found. Note 2: This certification was issued by Talbot County.*

Dangerfield 8/12/1684 – 200a's. L22/149 SR7363
Location: Queen Annes County on the Southeast Branch of the Chester River at the head of Hambleton's Branch. *Note 1: This is a certification. No patent was found. Note 2: This certification was issued by Talbot County.*

Blongy, Lewis
France 9/10/1683 - 100a's. SDA/197 SR7369
Location: Queen Annes County on Kent Island beginning at a bound tree of **Thomas Blunt's** tract of land. Also adjoins **John Wright's** tract called Tarr Kill and the land of **Thomas Broadnax** *(deceased)*. *Note: The patent document does not specify the patenting county.*

Blunt, Richard, Planter
Great Neck 8/8/1650 - 330a's. AB&AH/334 SR7344
Location: Queen Annes County on Kent Island on Martins Creek. Adjoins **Robert Martin's** tract of land called Martins Neck.
Other persons mentioned: Blunt transported **himself,** his **wife,** his daughter **Rebecca,** and **Thomas Head** into this Province here to inhabit in 1649, as appears on record. *Note 1: This is a seldom-used form of abbreviated patent document that minimizes or excludes location information. This is included in the certification which, in this instance, was not found. Note 2: This patent was issued by St. Marys County.*

Boage, John
Boagley 1/17/1658 - 350a's. LQ/307 SR7345
Location: Queen Annes County on the eastern side of the Chester River of Boages Branch of Corsica Creek beginning at a marked Oak standing by the branchside. Adjoins **Robert Macklin's** tract of land called the Reward.
Other persons mentioned: Land rights assigned by **Jane Fenwick** due her for transporting **Elizabeth Vaughan, John Hampton,** and **Ann Martin** into this Province here to inhabit as appears on record. *Note: This patent was issued by Kent County.*

Boddy, William/Will

Unnamed Patent 8/6/1650 – 200a's. AB&H/335 SR7344
Location: Queen Annes County on the eastern side of Kent Island.
Other persons mentioned: Boddy transported **himself** in 1650. Additional rights assigned by **Robert Dunn** due him for transporting himself into this Province here to inhabit in 1650, as appears on record. *Note: The patent document does not specify the patenting county.*

Great Neck 8/8/1650 - 330a's. AB&H/334 SR7344
Location: Queen Annes County on Kent Island.
Other persons mentioned: Boddy transported **himself,** his **wife,** his daughter **Rebecca,** and **Thomas Head** into this Province here to inhabit as appears on record. *Note 1: This is a seldom-used abbreviated form of patent document that minimizes or eliminates location information. This is included in the certification document which, in this instance, was not found. Note 2: This patent was issued in Kent County.*

Bodwell, Atwell

Bodwell 9/15/1664 – 200a's. L7/443 SR7349
Location: Queen Annes County on the Southeast Branch of the Wye River by a small marsh in the woods beginning at a bound tree of **Thomas Wilkenson's** tract of land.
Other persons mentioned: Land rights assigned by **Andrew Skinner** assignee of **William Leeds.** *Note: This patent was issued by Talbot County.*

Bonham, William

Barbers Delight 8/10/1684 - 170a's. NSBi/55 SR7370
Location: Queen Annes County beginning at a marked Red Oak standing by a branch of the Southeast Branch of the Chester River.
Other persons mentioned: Land rights assigned by **Soloman Wright** attorney of **Robert Smith.** *Note: This patent was issued by Talbot County.*

Bonnam, William

Bonnams Addition 10/1/1685 – 100a's. NSBi/366 SR7370
Location: Queen Annes County on the southern side of the Chester River in the woods on a branch of Island Creek.
Other persons mentioned: Land rights assigned by **Robert Smith.** *Note: This patent was issued by Talbot County.*

Boothby, Edward, Mariner

Boothbys Fortune 2/10/1685 – 500a's. NSBi/59 SR7370
Location: Queen Annes County on the southern side of the Chester River on the western side of Andover Branch adjoining his own tract of land called Pleasant Spring. Also adjoins **John Davis'** tract called Davis Phenelia.
Note: This patent was issued by Talbot County.

Pleasant Spring 6/10/1685 – 500a's. L22/174 SR7363
Location: Queen Annes County on the southern side of the Chester River between the **Lord Proprietor's** tract of land called His LOPs Manor and a tract called Daniel Jenifers Manor. *Note 1: This is a certification. The tract was made over (assigned) to **Thomas Jenkins** on 12/28/1685 (same reference). No patent was found. Note 2: This patent was issued by Talbot County.*

Boulen, James, Planter
Boulingley 5/6/1662 - 250a's. L5/71 SR7347
Location: Queen Annes County on the Eastern Bay next to Kent Island on the eastern side of Courseys Creek at Boulens Cove. *Note 1: A notation in the margin of the patent document spells the owner's name as Bowling and the tract name as Bowlingsley. Note 2: The patent document does not specify the patenting county. The tract is included because MSA Patent Index #55 places it in Queen Annes County.*

Boulton, William
Suttons Delight 11/7/1709 - 140a's. DD5i/554 SR7378
Location: Queen Annes County on the southern side of the Chester River beginning at a bound tree of **Michael Hackett's** tract of land called Highgate. Also adjoins **John Tulley's** tract called Tulleys Delight and a tract called Bakers Lott.
Other persons mentioned: Land rights assigned by **Giles Bond.** *Note: This patent was issued by Kent County.*

Bowes, George
Bowes Range 4/1/1687 - 227a's. CC4i/61 SR7375
Location: Queen Annes County on the western side of Tuckahoe Creek at the head of Gibson's Branch in Pyney Swamp. Adjoins **Jacob Broadway's** tract of land called Jacobs Beginning. *Note: This patent was issued by Talbot County.*

Bowles, James
Abington Square 6/18/1702 - 300a's. DSF/416 SR7373
Location: Queen Annes County on the eastern side of a branch of the Chester River in Lord Phillips Forrest. Begins at a bound tree of **James Hall's** tract of land called Halls Harbour. Also adjoins **John Reynolds** tract called Chesterton.
Other persons mentioned: Land rights assigned by former owner **Andrew Abington.** *Note: The patent document does not specify the patenting county.*

Bowling, James
Bowlingsley 1/7/1658 - 150a's. LQ/254 SR7345

Location: Queen Annes County on the southern side of the Chester River on the eastern side of Courseys Creek beginning at a marked Cedar standing by Bowlings Cove. Adjoins **Robert Macklin's** tract of land called Macklin. Other persons mentioned: Bowling transported **himself** into this Province here to inhabit as appears on record. Additional land rights assigned by **Arthur Ludford** and **Alexander Abraham.** *Note: This patent was issued by Kent County.*

Bradnox, Thomas, Planter

Unnamed Patent 8/1/1650 - 600a's. AB&H/127 SR7344
Location: Queen Annes County on Kent Island.
Other persons mentioned: Bradnox transported **himself,** wife **Mary, John Phillips,** and **Edward Williams** in 1644 and since, **Anthony Callaway** and **Thomas Smith,** into this Province here to inhabit as appears on record. *Note 1: This is a seldom-used form of abbreviated patent document that minimizes or excludes location information. This is included in the certification which, in this instance, was not found. Note 2: This patent was issued by St. Marys County.*

Unnamed Certification 8/6/1650 - 200a's. AB&H/105 SR7344
Location: Queen Annes County on Kent Island in the Chesapeake Bay. Adjoins **Elizabeth Commins'** tract of land called Point Love and the land of **Phillip Connor.** *Note 1: This is a certification. No patent was found. Note 2: This certification was issued by St. Marys County.*

Unnamed Patent 1/24/1652 - 400a's. AB&H/314 SR7344
Location: Queen Annes County on the western side of Kent Island on Broad Creek in the woods. Adjoins **Phillip Connor's** unnamed 100-acre tract of land. *Note: This patent was issued by St. Marys County.*

Broad Oak 1/20/1658 - 500a's. LQ/326 SR7345
Location: Queen Annes County on the eastern side of Kent Island at the mouth of the Eastern Creek. *Note 1: Land rights based on Bradnox having transported "diverse persons" into this Province here to inhabit in 1658, as appears on record. Note 2: This patent was issued by Kent County.*

Cedar Bradnox 1/22/1658 - 300a's. LQ/344 SR7345
Location: Queen Annes County on the eastern side of the St. Michaels River on the eastern side at the mouth of Morgans Creek respecting Parsons Point beginning at a marked Cedar.
Other persons mentioned: Bradnox transported **John Pritchard** and **Nicholas Williams** into this Province here to inhabit as appears on record. *Note: This patent was issued by Kent County.*

Breme, John
    Jamaica 10/1/1681 - 150a's. CB3i/189 SR7367
    <u>Location</u>: Queen Annes County on the southern side of the Chester River on
    Hambleton Creek in the woods beginning at a marked Oak.
    <u>Other persons mentioned</u>: Breme transported **himself,** wife **Mary,** and son
    Nicholas into this Province here to inhabit as appears on record. *Note: This*
    patent was issued by Talbot County.

Brent, Giles
    Kent Fort Manor 9/7/1640 - 1,000a's. L1/47 SR7341
    <u>Location</u>: Queen Annes County in Kent Fort Manor on Kent Island on a neck
    of land nearest Kent Fort bounded by the Northwest Creek, the Chesapeake
    Bay, and a swamp. *Note 1: Another patent was found (AB&H/70 SR7344).*
    Note 2: This patent was issued by St. Marys County.

Bridges, Richard, Planter
    Detteridge 9/1/1665 – 500a's. L8/196 SR7350
    <u>Location</u>: Queen Annes County at the head of the Northeast Branch of the
    Wye River. Adjoins **George Prowse's** tract of land called Prowses Park and
    William Young's tract called Youngs Adventure.
    <u>Other persons mentioned</u>: Land rights assigned by **Richard Tilghman** due
    him for transporting **himself,** wife **Mary,** son **William, Richard Lane, Ann**
    Greene, Lewis Evans, Andrew Cunning, John Price, and **Rachell**
    Higgens into this Province here to inhabit as appears on record. *Note: This*
    patent was issued by Talbot County.

Bright, Francis
    The Saw Pitt 8/10/1695 - 78a's. C3i/4 SR7377
    <u>Location</u>: Queen Annes County on Kent Island at the head of Stints Creek
    extending to the head of Little Piney Creek.
    <u>Other persons mentioned</u>: Land rights assigned by **Simon Wilmer.** *Note:*
    This patent was issued by Talbot County.

Broadrib, John
    Freshford 9/11/1674 – 500a's. L15/292 SR4327
    <u>Location</u>: Queen Annes County on the southern side of the Chester River on
    Island Creek beginning at a bound Poplar.
    <u>Other persons mentioned</u>: Land rights assigned by **William Hemsley**
    assignee of **John Griggs** assignee of **John Baker** assignee of **John Rainey**
    due Rainey for transporting **himself,** wife **Mary, John Mellson, Elizabeth**
    Mellson *(no relationship indicated),* **Henry Allen, Warren Dye,** and **John**
    Reiney. Also, Broadrib transported **himself, Thomas Cox,** and **Larrane**
    Bennett into this Province here to inhabit as appears on record. *Note: This*
    patent was issued by Talbot County.

Bath 5/10/1676 – 500a's. L19/358 SR7360
Location: Queen Annes County on the southern side of the Chester River on the eastern side of Rousebys Creek beginning at a bound Poplar.
Other persons mentioned: Broadrib transported **himself, MaryWarren, John Paine,** and **Ralph Blackhall** into this Province here to inhabit as appears on record. Additional rights assigned by **Thomas Jones, Henry Gill, Thomas Wigley, Thomas Young, John Simmins, Benjamin Bennett, George Hayes,** and **Robert Marmaduke** due each of them for completion of their time of service in this Province. *Note: This patent was issued by Talbot County.*

Stoke 5/6/1679 - 200a's. L21/45 SR7362
Location: Queen Annes County on the southern side of the Chester River beginning at a bound tree of **Samuel Winslow** and **Henry Parker's** tract of land called Tottenham now in the possession of **John Broadrib.**
Other persons mentioned: Land rights assigned by **Robert Smith.** *Note: This patent was issued by Kent County.*

Bradford 5/7/1679 - 100a's. L21/119 SR7362
Location: Queen Annes County on the southern side of the Chester River on the northern side of Elletts Branch in the woods beginning at a marked Oak.
Other persons mentioned: Land rights assigned by **Robert Smith.** *Note: This patent was issued by Kent County.*

Warminister 5/7/1679 - 200a's. L21/19 SR7362
Location: Queen Annes County on the southern side of the Chester River on the Southwest Branch of Island Creek beginning at a marked Red Oak. Adjoins **James Heath's** tract of land called Upper Heathworth.
Other persons mentioned: Land rights assigned by **Robert Smith.** *Note 1: This tract was formerly called Heaths Forrest. Note 2: This patent was issued by Kent County.*

Larrington 6/17/1679 - 250a's. L21/120 SR7362
Location: Queen Annes County on the southern side of the Chester River on the Southwest Branch of Island Creek.
Other persons mentioned: Land rights assigned by **Thomas Tasker, Robert Enson, Richard Brown, Thomas Wilkenson,** and **Mick Phillips** due each of them for completing their time of service in this Province. *Note: This patent was issued by Kent County.*

Broadway, Nicholas, Planter
Broad Neck 10/9/1667 - 100a's. L11/76 SR7353
Location: Queen Annes County on the Eastern Branch of the Wye River by the bayside.

Other persons mentioned: Land rights assigned by **Henry Parker** assignee of **John Wright**. *Note: This patent was issued by Talbot County.*

Broadway, Robert
    Hazard 3/20/1695 – 75a's.BB3B/392 SR7374
    Location: Queen Annes County on the southern side of the Chester River on Wallsey Creek adjoining **Peter Sayer's** tract of land called Sayers Forrest. Also adjoins **Edmond Burton's** tract called Burton Upon Wallsey, and **Samuel Wright's** tract called Wrights Chance.
    Other persons mentioned: Land rights assigned by **Philemon Hemsley.** *Note: This patent was issued by Talbot County.*

    The Plaines 11/10/1695 – 100a's. BB3B/345 SR7374
    Location: Queen Annes County on the northern side of the northmost branch of the Wye River on Broadways Cove. Adjoins **Henry Coursey's** tract of land called Courseys Range.
    Other persons mentioned: Land rights assigned by **Philemon Hemsley.** *Note: This patent was issued by Talbot County.*

    Musketoe Range 1/12/1696 - 51a's. CC4i/48 SR7375
    Location: Queen Annes County at the head of Marshy Creek near the Wading Place. Adjoins **Peter Sayers'** tract of land called Sayers Forrest and the land of **Winchester.**
    Other persons mentioned: Land rights assigned by **Richard Skinner.** *Note: This patent was issued by Talbot County.*

Brostrick, Thomas
    Northumberland 4/11/1709 - 100a's. DD5i/526 SR7378
    Location: Queen Annes County on the southern side of the Chester River in Green Swamp between Red Lyon and Unicorn Branches. Begins at a bound tree of **John Lancaster's** tract of land called Lancaster.
    Other persons mentioned: Land rights assigned by **Elias King.** *Note: This patent was issued by Kent County.*

Bruer, Elizabeth
    Widdows Chance 9/16/1664 – 640a's. L7/453 SR7349
    Location: Queen Annes County at the head of the Eastern Branch of the Wye River on Cabbin Branch in the woods. Adjoins **James Scott's** tract of land called Old Mill, **John Wright's** tract called Skipton, **Edward Winckles'** tract called The Virgin Inn, and **Moses Harris'** tract called Ramsays Forrest. *Note: This patent was issued by Talbot County.*

Burk, Richard
    Readbourne 2/3/1684 - 1,000a's. SDA 508 SR7369

Location: Queen Annes County on the eastern side of the Chester River beginning at a marked Oak standing by a marsh on Herring Creek at Sewells Point. *Note 1: This tract was originally patented by **George Read** in 1659, and escheated to the Lord Proprietor for lack of heirs. Note 2: This patent was issued by Kent County.*

Burroughs, John
Burroughs Bridge 3/9/1685 – 100a's. L22/212 SR7363
Location: Queen Annes County on a run of the Southeast Branch of Island Creek of the Chester River. Adjoins **John Broadrib's** tract of land called Freshford and Burroughs own tract called Distinction Hall.
Other persons mentioned: Land rights assigned by **Richard Royston.** *Note 1: This is a certification. No patent was found. Note 2: This certification was issued by Talbot County.*

Burton, Edmond
Burton Upon Wallsey 1/18/1658 - 200a's. LQ/313 SR7345
Location: Queen Annes County on the southern side of the Eastern Bay on Wallsey Creek. Adjoins **Henry Coursey's** tract of land called Courseys Point.
Other persons mentioned: Burton transported **himself,** and his wife **Rebecca** into this Province here to inhabit as appears on record. *Note: This patent was issued by Kent County.*

Burton, Edward, Planter
Burtons Lott 9/1/1670 - 200a's. L14/61 SR7356
Location: Queen Annes County on the eastern side of Kent Island beginning at a bound Oak standing at the mouth of Greens Creek by the bayside and extends to the southernmost branch of the Northeast Creek at the head of a marsh. Bounded on the east by the Eastern Bay.
Other persons mentioned: Land rights assigned by **William Hemsley.** *Note: The patent document does not identify the patenting county.*

Butler, John
Butlers Neck 12/9/1640 - 200a's. LAB&H/88 SR7344
Location: Queen Annes County between Thickety Neck Creek, the Chesapeake Bay, and a pathway. *Note 1: This certification was issued by Kent County. No patent was found. Note 2: This was an original **William Clayborn** grant (see Forward). Note 3: Another patent was found, dated 12/9/1640 (L1/092 SR7344)and issued by St. Marys County. A notation in the margin of the patent document states that "this patent not delivered". No explanation found.*

Unnamed Certification 12/9/1640 - 200a's. L1/92 SR7341
Location: Queen Annes County on Kent Island in Crayford Manor between Beaver Neck Creek and the Chesapeake Bay. *Note 1: This certification was issued by Kent County. No patent was found. Note 2: This was an original* **William Clayborn** *grant (see Forward).*

Butler, Thomas, Planter
Butlers Marsh 12/9/1647 - 50a's. L1/87 SR7341
Location: Queen Annes County on the eastern side of Kent Island on Bathers Creek extending to Jones Branch of Coxes Bay in Crayford Manor where he is now seated. Adjoins the land of **Captain Cross**. *Note: This patent was issued by St. Marys County.*

Butter, Gyles
Butterfield 2/16/1673 – 200a's. L17/431 SR7358
Location: Queen Annes County on a fresh runn of the Wye River on the eastern side of the Main Branch beginning at a marked Oak. Adjoins **Arthur Emery's** tract of land called Neglect and **Hugh Paxton's** tract called Paxtons Lott.
Other persons mentioned: Land rights assigned by **William Hemsley**. *Note 1: This is a certification. No patent was found. Note 2: This certification was issued by Talbot County.*

Carmen, Thomas & Burton, William
Carmen and Burton 8/2/1683 – 150a's. SDA/250 SR7369
Location: Queen Annes County on the southern side of the Chester River beginning at the first bound tree of **Daniel Jenefer's** tract of land called Spread Eagle. Also adjoins **Thomas Collins'** tract called Collington.
Other persons mentioned: Land rights assigned by **Michael Turbutt**. *Note: This patent was issued by Talbot County.*

Carpenter, Simon
Carpenters Meadow 11/2/1668 - 50a's. L12/165 SR7354
Location: Queen Annes County on the southern side of the Chester River beginning at a marked Cedar standing by a marsh. Adjoins **Thomas Spriggs'** tract of land called Sprigley.
Other persons mentioned: Land rights assigned by **John Morgan**. *Note: This patent was issued by Talbot County.*

Carpenter, William
Carpenters Outlett 8/10/1685 - 136a's. NSBi/116 SR7370
Location: Queen Annes County at the head of Spriggs Creek of the Chester River. Begins at a bound Oak of **John Coursey's** tract of land. Also adjoins the land of **Thomas Spriggs**. *Note: This patent was issued by Talbot County.*

Carter, Henry

The Chance 8/10/1695 - 50a's. C3i/10 SR7377
Location: Queen Annes County on Kent Island on Coxes Branch in the woods. Adjoins **John Wright** and **Thomas Collins'** tract of land called Wallnutt Ridge. *Note: This patent was issued by Talbot County.*

Carters Addition 10/5/1695 - 50a's. C3i/30 SR7377
Location: Queen Annes County on the eastern end of Kent Isle in a swamp adjoining **William Boddy's** tract of land called Boddy.
Other persons mentioned: Land rights assigned by **John Jones.** *Note: This patent was issued by Kent County.*

Carter, Richard

Carters Inheritance 11/12/1667 – 300a's. L11/133 SR7353
Location: Queen Annes County on the eastern side of the Wye River on Indian Creek in the woods.
Other persons mentioned: Land rights assigned by **Thomas Wilkinson** and **Henry Parker.** Additional rights assigned by **John Whaley** due him for completing his time of service in this Province. *Note: This patent was issued by Talbot County.*

Carters Forrest 11/10/1695 - 326a's. C3i/462 SR7377
Location: Queen Annes County at the head of the Wye River on Williams Branch. Adjoins **Robert Noble's** tract of land called Nobles Range.
Other persons mentioned: Land rights assigned by **William Hemsley.** *Note: This patent was issued by Talbot County.*

Carters Addicon 10/10/1707 - 170a's. DD5i/406 SR7378
Location: Queen Annes County at the head of the westernmost branch of Tuckahoe Creek called French Womans Branch. Adjoins a tract of land called Vaughans Discovery.
Other persons mentioned: Land rights assigned by **William Coursey.** *Note: This patent was issued by Talbot County.*

Carter, Valentine & John

Copartnership 1699 - 104a's. CC4i/160 SR7375
Location: Queen Annes County on Kent Island in the woods on Coxes Creek.
Other persons mentioned: Land rights assigned by **Richard Skinner.** *Note: This patent was issued by Talbot County.*

Cary, Thomas

The Purchase 7/11/1664 – 1,000a's. L7/103 SR7349

Location: Queen Annes County on the northern side of the St. Michaels River on the eastern side of New Work Island in the Wye River extending to the Back Wye River. Adjoins tracts owned by **William Hemsley** and **William Stephens.** *Note 1: The patent document describes this as a "Special Patent". No explanation found. Note 2: The patent document does not specify the patenting county.*

Chaires, John, Cooper

Reareguard 6/25/1683– 400a's. SDA/301 SR7369
Location: Queen Annes County on the southern side of the Chester River on the southern side of Corsica Creek. Adjoins **Richard Bridges'** tract of land called Detteridge and his own tract called Chairs Addition. *Note: This patent was issued by Talbot County.*

Batchelors Adventure 5/4/1683 – 150a's. CB3i/486 SR7367
Location: Queen Annes County on the southern side of the Chester River on Corsica Creek near the road. Adjoins **John Bogues'** tract of land called Boagley.
Other persons mentioned: Land rights assigned by **Robert Smith.** *Note: This patent was issued by Talbot County.*

Chaires Addition 10/1/1687 - 100a's. NS2i/585 SR7371
Location: Queen Annes County on the southern side of the Chester River on a branch of Corsica Creek. Adjoins his own tract of land called Reareguard.
Other persons mentioned: Land rights assigned by **Thomas Smithson.** *Note: This patent was issued by Talbot County.*

Churnell, Joseph

Churnells Neck 5/20/1665 – 200a's. L7/570 SR7349
Location: Queen Annes County on the southern side of the Chester River on the Eastern Branch in the woods beginning at a marked Oak.
Other persons mentioned: Land rights assigned by **Thomas Gerard.** *Note: This patent was issued by Talbot County.*

Clapton, Edward, Planter

Unnamed Patent 8/20/1650 - 100a's. AB&H/126 SR7344
Location: Queen Annes County on the western side of Kent Island by the Chesapeake Bayside extending to Tarr Kill Creek. Adjoins **Phillip Connors'** unnamed 100-acre tract of land and **Robert Martin's** tract called Martins Neck. *Note 1: This is a seldom-used form of abbreviated patent document that minimizes or excludes location information. This is included in the certification which, in this instance, was not found. Note 2: This may have been an original* **William Clayborn** *grant (see Forward). Note 3: This patent was issued by St. Marys County.*

Clave, Nathaniell
>**Nathaniells Point** 9/16/1664 – 50a's. L7/457 SR7349
>Location: Queen Annes County on Woolmans Back Creek of the Wye River in the woods. Adjoins **William Hemsley's** tract of land called Hemsleys Arcadia and **Edward Lloyd's** tract called Meersgate Addition.
>Other persons mentioned: Land rights assigned by Edward Lloyd. *Note: This patent was issued by Talbot County.*

Clayland, James
>**Bridgewater** 6/12/1688 – 300a's. NS2i/661 SR7371
>Location: Queen Annes County on the southern side of the Chester River on the western side of Unicorn Branch by the Upper Road. Adjoins **Thomas Smithson's** tract of land called Reviving Springs. *Note: This patent was issued by Talbot County.*

Cleeve, Nathaniel
>**Mangy Porkey** 11/7/1709 - 100a's. DD5i/568 SR7378
>Location: Queen Annes County on the southern side of the Chester River beginning at a bound tree standing on the western side of Long Marsh of Tuckahoe Creek.
>Other persons mentioned: Land rights assigned by **Robert Smith.** *Note: This patent was issued by Kent County.*

Clocker, Daniel
>**Clockerton** 9/10/1674 - 200a's. L15/261 SR4327
>Location: Queen Annes County on the southern side of the Chester River beginning at a bound tree of **Richard Royston's** tract of land called Royston.
>Other persons mentioned: Land rights assigned by **Thomas Courtney** assignee of **William Thomas, Richard George, John Askin,** and **Richard Northorton** due each for completion of their time of service in this Province. *Note: This patent was issued by Talbot County.*

Cloud, Nicholas
>**Nollars Desire** 7/4/1665 – 198a's. L22/305 SR7363
>Location: Queen Annes County on the southern side of the Chester River beginning at a marked Oak of **William Bishop's** tract of land called Bishopton. Also adjoins his own tract called Clouds Adventure.
>Other persons mentioned: Land rights assigned by **Cornelius Comegys.** *Note 1: This is a certification. No patent was found. Note 2: This certification was issued by Talbot County.*

>**Clouds Adventure** 6/1/1685 – 500a's. NSBi/96 SR7370
>Location: Queen Annes County on the southern side of the Chester River at the head of Hambleton's Creek beginning at a bound tree of **John Hollingsworth's** tract of land called Fox Harbor. Also adjoins **William**

Hollingsworth's tract called The Beginning. *Note: This patent was issued by Talbot County.*

Salisbury 8/10/1685 – 500a's. NSBi/120 SR7370
Location: Queen Annes County on the southern side of the Chester River on the western side of Andover Branch on Salisbury Plaine. *Note: This patent was issued by Talbot County.*

Notlans Enjoyment 8/10/1685 – 500a's. NSBi/115 SR7370
Location: Queen Annes County on the southern side of the Chester River at the head on the northeast side of Andover Branch beginning at a marked Poplar. *Note: This patent was issued by Talbot County.*

Conquest 6/1/1686 - 394a's. NSBi/337 SR7370
Location: Queen Annes County on the southern side of the Chester River beginning at a marked White Oak standing in the southeast line of **William Coursey's** tract of land called Courseys Point. Also adjoins **Cornelius Comegys** tract called Newport and a tract called Beaverton.
Other persons mentioned: Land rights assigned by **Vincent Lowe.** Additional rights assigned by **Robert Smith** assignee of **Michael Miller.** *Note: This patent was issued by Talbot County.*

Notlans Delight 1695 - 150a's. BB3B/445 SR7374
Location: Queen Annes County on the southern side of the Chester River beginning at a bound tree of **William Bishop's** tract of land called Fox Hill. Also adjoins **William Bishop's** tract called Bishops Fields and **Henry Denton's** tract called Clowdent.
Other persons mentioned: Land rights assigned by **Robert Smith.** *Note: This patent was issued by Talbot County.*

Clouds Hermitage 10/10/1707 - 200a's. DD5i/383 SR7378
Location: Queen Annes County on a forke of Tuckahoe Creek on Long Neck Branch in Beaver Dams Marsh. *Note: This patent was issued by Kent County.*

Clouds Range 10/10/1707 - 100a's. DD5i/381 SR7378
Location: Queen Annes County in the forke of Tuckahoe Creek called Long Neck beginning at a bound Hickory standing by an Indian Path. *Note: This patent was issued by Kent County.*

Clymer, John
Grantham 4/18/1683 – 200a's. CB3i/230 SR7367
Location: Queen Annes County on Dividing Branch of the Wye River by the roadside. Adjoins **Thomas Williams'** tract of land called Wilton.

Other persons mentioned: Clymer transported **himself** into this Province here to inhabit as appears on record. Additional rights assigned by **John Longon, John Dunn, Robert Hankshaw,** and **William Claveter** due each of them for completing their time of service in this Province. *Note: This patent was issued by Talbot County.*

Collins, Richard

Collins His Lott 6/1/1684 - 200a's. NSBi/203 SR7370
Location: Queen Annes County on the southern side of the Chester River in the woods on a branch of Hambleton's Creek.
Other persons mentioned: Land rights assigned by **Philemon Loyd.**
Note: This patent was issued by Talbot County.

Freshford Addition 6/1/1684 - 100a's. NSBi/166 SR7370
Location: Queen Annes County on the southern side of the Chester River by the roadside beginning at a bound tree of **John Broadrib's** tract of land called Freshford.
Other persons mentioned: Land rights assigned by **Philemon Loyd.** *Note: This patent was issued by Talbot County.*

Shotland 6/1/1684 - 200a's. NSBi/204 SR7370
Location: Queen Annes County on the southern side of the Chester River on the western side of Broadribs Branch. Adjoins **John Broadrib's** tract of land called Freshford. and **Andrew Price's** tract called The Good Increase.
Other persons mentioned: Land rights assigned by **Philemon Loyd.** *Note: This patent was issued by Talbot County.*

Collins, Thomas & Knowles, Robert

Discovery 11/10/1695 – 220a's. BB3B/288 SR7374
Location: Queen Annes County on the Southwest Branch of the Chester River beginning at a bound tree in the northwest line of **William Hemsley's** tract of land. Also adjoins **Thomas Collins'** tracts called Collington and Kellmanam Plaines. *Note: This patent was issued by Talbot County.*

Collins, Thomas, Planter

Collington 8/20/1670 – 300a's. L13/30 SR7355
Location: Queen Annes County at the head of the Southeast Branch of the Chester River adjoining **Henry Parker's** tract of land called Parkers Lott. Also adjoins **Thomas Carmen** and **William Burton's** tract called Carmen and Burton. *Note: This patent was issued by Talbot County.*

Collins Range 5/4/1683 – 300a's. CB3i/489 SR7367
Location: Queen Annes County on the southern side of the Chester River on the Eastern Branch of Herring Creek by Sassafras Road.

<u>Other persons mentioned</u>: Land rights assigned by **Henry Parker.** *Note: This patent was issued by Talbot County.*

Castle Miles 6/1/1685 - 200a's. DSF/157 SR7371
<u>Location</u>: Queen Annes County on the Southeast Branch of the Chester River adjoining **William Hambleton's** tract of land.
<u>Other persons mentioned</u>: Land rights assigned by **William Bishop.** *Note: This patent was issued by Talbot County.*

Corke House 6/1/1685 – 200a's. NS2i/144 SR7371
<u>Location</u>: Queen Annes County on the southern side of the Chester River adjoining **Robert Smith's** tract of land called Pleasant Spring. Also adjoins **Thomas Todd's** tract called Todley.
<u>Other persons mentioned</u>: Land rights assigned by **Robert Smith.** *Note: This patent was issued by Talbot County.*

Kille Kenney 9/10/1685 – 200a's. NSBi/214 SR7370
<u>Location</u>: Queen Annes County on the southern side of the Chester River on the eastern side of Andover Branch beginning at a bound tree of **Robert Smith's** tract of land. *Note: This patent was issued by Talbot County.*

Frankford 3/7/1686 – 200a's. L22/308 SR7363
<u>Location</u>: Queen Annes County on the southern side of the Chester River on the eastern side of Andover Branch. Adjoins **Robert Smith's** tract of land called Forlorn Hope.
<u>Other persons mentioned</u>: Land rights assigned by **Robert Ellis.** *Note 1: This is a certification. No patent was found. Note 2: This certification was issued by Talbot County.*

Rings End 7/28/1686 – 100a's. L22/245 SR7363
<u>Location</u>: Queen Annes County on the southern side of the Chester River on the Upper Point at the mouth of Unicorn Creek.
<u>Other persons mentioned</u>: Land rights assigned by **Vincent Lowe.** *Note 1: This is a certification. No patent was found. Note 2: This certification was issued by Talbot County.*

Rings 6/1/1687 – 100a's. IB&ILC/325 SR7368
<u>Location</u>: Queen Annes County on the southern side of the Chester River on the upper point of the mouth of Unicorn Branch.
<u>Other persons mentioned</u>: Land rights assigned by **Vincent Lowe.** *Note: This patent was issued by Talbot County.*

Kelmannan Plaines 7/24/1687 – 500a's. L22/341 SR7363
<u>Location</u>: Queen Annes County on the southern side of the Chester River on the eastern side of Unicorn Branch. Adjoins **Lawrence Knowles'** tract of land called Knowles Range and **Robert Smith's** tract called Smith's Range. <u>Other persons mentioned</u>: Land rights assigned by Robert Smith. *Note 1: This is a certification. No patent was found. Note 2: This certification was issued by Talbot County.*

Colliston 1688 - 120a's. NS2i/626 SR7371
<u>Location</u>: Queen Annes County between the branches of Island and Coursegall Creeks. Begins at a bound tree of **Richard Jones'** tract of land called Jones Park. Also adjoins his own tract called Corke House. <u>Other persons mentioned</u>: Land rights assigned by **Thomas Smithson.** *Note: The patent document does not specify the patenting county.*

Kelmanan Plaines 6/12/1688 – 300a's. NS2i/641 SR7371
<u>Location</u>: Queen Annes County on the southern side of the Chester River on the upper side of Unicorn Branch adjoining **George Robotham's** tract of land called Robothams Parke. Also adjoins **John Lundy's** tract called Batchellors Plaines. *Note: This patent was issued by Talbot County.*

Collins Own 11/13/1694 – 91a's. WD/84 SR7372
<u>Location</u>: Queen Annes County on the southern side of the Chester River between the Southeast Branch and Cabbin Branch. Adjoins **Daniel Jenefer's** tract of land called Spread Eagle. <u>Other persons mentioned</u>: Land rights assigned by **Lawrence Knowles.** *Note 1: Another patent was found that shows the tract name as Collins His Own and the patent date as 11/10/1695 (C3i/178 SR7377. Note 2: This patent was issued by Talbot County.*

Foole Play 11/10/1695 - 500a's. BB3B/287 SR7374
<u>Location</u>: Queen Annes County on the southern side of the Chester River at the head of the Southeast Branch. Adjoins a tract of land called Loyd Parke. <u>Other persons mentioned</u>: Land rights assigned by **Lawrence Knowles.** *Note: This patent was issued by Talbot County.*

Comegys, Cornelius
Timber Forke 3/10/1685 – 500a's. NSBi/124 SR7370
<u>Location</u>: Queen Annes County in a forke on the northeast side of Andover Branch beginning at a marked Chesnutt. *Note: This patent was issued by Talbot County.*

Andover 8/10/1685 – 500a's. NSBi/119 SR7370
Location: Queen Annes County on the southern side of the Chester River on Andover Branch at Salisbury Plaine beginning at a bound Poplar. *Note: This patent was issued by Talbot County.*

Poplar Plaine 8/10/1685 – 500a's. NSBi/123 SR7370
Location: Queen Annes County on the southern side of the Chester River on the eastern side of Andover Branch beginning at a marked White Oak. *Note: This patent was issued by Talbot County.*

Comegys, William
Glocester 8/10/1685 - 400a's. NSBi/109 SR7370
Location: Queen Annes County on the easternmost branch of the Southwest Branch of the Chester River at the head of Andover Branch. *Note: This patent was issued by Talbot County.*

Winters Field 10/10/1708 - 50a's. DD5i/491 SR7378
Location: Queen Annes County on the northern side of Tappanhanna Marsh of the Great Choptank River near a path from the head of the Chester River to St. Jonses.
Other persons mentioned: Land rights assigned by **Richard Bennett.** *Note 1: MSA Patent Index #55 places this tract in Queen Annes County. Note 2: This patent was issued by Kent County.*

Comins, Edward, Planter
Unnamed Patent 9/8/1640 - 100a's. L1/77 SR7341
Location: Queen Annes County on Kent Island in Crayford Manor between **Robert Short's** tract of land called Merson Freehold and the Chesapeake Bay.
Other persons mentioned: Land rights assigned by **Thomas Pott.** *Note 1: This is an original **William Clayborn** grant to Thomas Pott and by him assigned to Comins. Note 2: This patent was issued by St. Marys County.*

Commins, Elizabeth, widow of Edward
Point Love 8/5/1650 - 600a's. AB&H/128 SR7344
Location: Queen Annes County on Kent Island adjoining **Robert Hewitt's** tract of land called Crany Neck. *Note 1: This is a seldom-used form of abbreviated patent document that minimizes or excludes location information. This is included in the certification which, in this instance, was not found. Note 2: This tract was patented in Kent County.*

Connor, Phillip
Connors Neck 9/25/1640 - 100a's. L1/79 SR7341
Location: Queen Annes County on Kent Island bounded on the north by Broad Creek, on the west by the Chesapeake Bay, and on the east by

Connors Creek. *Note 1: Land rights based on Connor having transported* **himself** *into this Province here to inhabit as appears on record. Note 2: This patent was issued by Talbot County.*

The Woodyard Thickett 8/1/1658 - 200a's. AB&H/105 SR7344
Location: Queen Annes County on Kent Island.
Other persons mentioned: **Connor** transported **himself** in 1636, and later transported **Edward Langford** and six unnamed servants into this Province here to inhabit as appears on record. *Note: This is a seldom-used form of abbreviated patent document that minimizes or excludes location information. This is included in the certification which, in this instance, was not found. Note 2: This patent was issued by St. Marys County.*

The Wading Place Neck 1/22/1658 - 300a's. L!/342 SR7345
Location: Queen Annes County on the eastern side of Kent Island beginning at a marked Pine standing at the mouth of Pine Creek.
Other persons mentioned: **Connor** transported **Edward Langford, Elizabeth Sheers,** and **John Dubb** into this Province here to inhabit as appears on record. *Note: This patent was issued by St. Marys County.*

Connor, Phillip, Jr. Son and Heir of **Phillip Connor Sr.**
Connors Neck 6/9/1670 - 280a's. L12/571 SR7354
Location: Queen Annes County on Kent Island on the southern side of Broadnax Creek extending to Connors Creek.
Other persons mentioned: Land rights assigned by **Phillip Connor, Sr.,** and **John Wright,** current husband of **Mary** the widow of Connors, Sr. *Note: The patent document does not specify the patenting county.*

The Woodyard Thickett Res. 6/9/1670 - 410a's. L12/571 SR7354
Location: Queen Annes County on Kent Island by the Chesapeake Bayside beginning at a bound Locust of **Thomas Broadnax's** tract of land now in the possession of **Toby Wells.**
Other persons mentioned: Land rights assigned by **Phillip Connor Sr.** (deceased). *Note: The patent document does not specify the patenting county.*

Cooper, Robert
Cooper 12/9/1640 - 80a's. L1/91 SR7341
Location: Queen Annes County on the western side of Kent Island in Crayford Manor on Beaver Neck Creek. Adjoins **Anderew Basha** and **John Cloughton' s** tract of land called Basha. *Note 1: This is a certification issued by Kent County. No patent was found. Note 2: This may have been an original **William Clayborn** grant (see Forward).*

Coppage, John
Coppages Ridge 7/24/1700 – 444a's. DD5i/30 SR7378

Location: Queen Annes County on Kent Island between Long Creek and Craney Creek on a cove on the northern side of Elder Branch of Long Creek. Adjoins **Robert Huitt's** tract of land called Craney Neck, **Michael Rowles'** tract called Oyer Maine, and **Thomas Stint's** tract called Crawford. Other persons mentioned: Land rights assigned by **Richard Skinner.** *Note: This patent was issued by Talbot County.*

Copping, Edward, Planter
Beaverton 10/17/1651 - 100a's. AB&H/196 SR7344
Location: Queen Annes County on Kent Island adjoining **John Phillips'** tract of land called Pigg Quarter. *Note 1: Land rights based on Copping transporting **himself** into this Province here to inhabit in 1650, as appears on record. Note 2: This is a seldom-used form of abbreviated patent document that minimizes or excludes location information. This is included in the certification which, in this instance, was not found. Note 3: This patent was issued by St. Marys County.*

Costin, Henry
Lambeth Fields 8/1/1673 – 200a's. L15/56 SR4327
Location: Queen Annes County at the head of the Wye River in the woods beginning at a bound tree of **Thomas Williams'** tract of land. *Note: This patent was issued by Talbot County.*

The Doctors Gift 9/12/1681 – 100a's. CB2i/272 SR7366
Location: Queen Annes County on Longbows Creek of the Wye River. Adjoins **Richard Woolman's** tract of land and a tract owned by **Edward Lloyd.**
Other persons mentioned: Land rights assigned by **Henry Parker** assignee of **Anthony Maile.** *Note 1: The information in the patent document is not sufficient to determine the present day location of this tract. It is included in this volume because it may have been in Queen Annes County. Note 2: This patent was issued by Talbot County.*

Sarahs Lott 9/22/1681 – 50a's. CB2i/227 SR7366
Location: Queen Annes County at the head of Long Toms Creek of the Wye River. Adjoins **Richard Carter's** tract of land.
Other persons mentioned: Land rights assigned by **Henry Parker** assignee of **Anthony Maile.** *Note 1: The information in the patent document is not sufficient to determine the present day location of this tract. It is included because it may have been in Queen Annes County. Note 2: This patent was issued by Talbot County.*

Lambeth 8/10/1684 – 279a's. IB&ILC/76 SR7368
Location: Queen Annes County on the southern side of the Chester River on the southern side of Williams Branch of the Wye River adjoining his own

tract of land called Dullidge. Also adjoins **Thomas Yewle's** tract called Lincolne and **Henry Parker's** tract called Broomly. *Note: This patent was issued by Talbot County.*

Lambeth 6/1/1685 – 200a's. NSBi/206 SR7370
<u>Location</u>: Queen Annes County on the Wye River beginning at a bound tree standing at the heads of Thomas Branch and Noble Branch. Adjoins **George Cowley's** tract of land called Normanton.
<u>Other persons mentioned</u>: Land rights assigned by **Henry Parker.** *Note: This patent was issued by Talbot County.*

Dullidge 4/28/1687 – 180a's. L22/324 SR7363
<u>Location</u>: Queen Annes County at the head of a glade of Williams Branch in the woods.
<u>Other persons mentioned</u>: Land rights assigned by **John Larkin** and **Woolman.** *Note 1: This is a certification. No patent was found. Note: This certification was issued by Talbot County.*

Coursey, Henry
Lords Gift 1/7/1658 - 1,050a's. LQ/257 SR7345
<u>Location</u>: Queen Annes County on the eastern side of the Eastern Bay beginning at a bound Oak standing at the mouth of Walseys Creek near Courseys Creek. Adjoins **George Copper's** tract of land called Williams Lott. *Note: This patent was issued by Kent County.*

Courseys Point 1/19/1658 - 1,350a's. LQ/318 SR7345
<u>Location</u>: Queen Annes County on the eastern side of the Chester River on the north side of Corsica Creek on Courseys Point. Adjoins **Edmond Burton's** tract of land called Burton upon Wallsey. *Note 1: Land rights based on Coursey having transported 15 unnamed persons into this Province here to inhabit as appears on record. Note 2: This patent was issued by Kent County.*

Courseys Rainge 6/19/1665 – 600a's. L7/618 SR7349
<u>Location</u>: Queen Annes County on the northern side of the Wye River beginning at a marked Red Oak. Adjoins **Henry Coursey, Jr.'s** tract of land called The Neglect and **Robert Broadway's** tract called The Plaines.
<u>Other persons mentioned</u>: Rights to 100 acres of land assigned by **Daniel Jenefer.** Also, Coursey transported 10 unnamed persons into this Province here to inhabit as appears on record. *Note: This patent was issued by Talbot County.*

The Neglect 8/25/1687 -400a's. L22/367 SR7363
Location: Queen Annes County on the western side of the Back Wye River
beginning at a marked tree of his own tract of land called Courseys Rainge.
Also adjoins **William Burton's** tract called Burton Upon Wallsey.
Other persons mentioned: Land rights assigned by **Thomas Smithson**
assignee of **Danielle Walker**. *Note 1: This is a certification. The tract was
patented by **Henry Coursey, Jr.** in 1688 (NS2i/639 SR7371). Note 2: This
certification was issued by Talbot County.*

Courseys Addition 6/10/1688 - 150a's. NS2i/628 SR7371
Location: Queen Annes County on the eastern side of the Back Wye River at
the head of a branch running into the Beaver Dams. Adjoins his own tract of
land called Courseys Choice. *Note: This patent was issued by Talbot County.*

Coursey, Henry, Jr.
The Neglect 6/1/1688 – 400a's. NS2i/639 SR7371
Location: Queen Annes County on the western side of the Back Wye River
adjoining **Henry Coursey, Sr.'s** tract of land called Courseys Rainge. Also
adjoins **Edmond Burton's** tract called Burton Upon Wallsey and **Stephen
Tully's** tract called Lords Guift.
Other persons mentioned: Land rights assigned by **Thomas Smithson**
assignee of **Daniel Walker**. *Note: This patent was issued by Talbot County.*

Coursey, John & William
Chester 2/13/1659 - 800a's. L4/293 SR7346
Location: Queen Annes County on the northern side of the St. Michaels
River on the eastern side of Morgans Creek beginning at a marked Oak
standing by Island Creek. Adjoins **William Coursey's** tract of land called
Coursey Upon Wye. *Note: This patent was issued by Kent County.*

Coursey, John
Cedar Branch 1/13/1658 - 400a's. LQ/290 SR7345
Location: Queen Annes County on Spriggs Creek of the Eastern Bay
beginning at a marked Cedar.
Other persons mentioned: Coursey transported **himself** into this Province
here to inhabit as appears on record. *Note: This patent was issued by Kent
County.*

Coursey, William
Courseys Neck 1/11/1658 - 140a's. LQ/275 SR7345
Location: Queen Annes County on the eastern side of the Eastern Bay at the
mouth of Courseys Creek. Adjoins **William Hemsley's** tract of land called
Hemsleys Choice and his own tract called Long Neglect.

Other persons mentioned: Land rights assigned by **Mark Benton** due him for transporting **himself** into this Province here to inhabit as appears on record. *Note: This patent was issued by Kent County.*

Unnamed Patent 2/28/1662 - 400a's. L5/150 SR7347
Location: Queen Annes County on the northern side of the St. Michaels River on Morgans Creek extending to Back River Creek. *Note: The patent document does not specify the patenting county. However, MSA Patent Index #55 for Queen Annes County does include this tract.*

Unnamed Patent 2/28/1662 - 250a's. L5/151 SR7347
Location: Queen Annes County on the northern side of the St. Michaels River on Russells Creek extending to the eastern side of the Wye River. Adjoins **John Russell's** tract of land. *Note: The patent document does not specify the patenting county. MSA Patent Index #55 for Queen Annes County includes this tract.*

Trustrum 9/14/1665 – 400a's. L8/260 SR7350
Location: Queen Annes County on the Northeast Branch of the Wye River in the woods. Adjoins **Robert Morris'** tract of land.
Other persons mentioned: **Coursey** transported **Christopher Thomas, Henry Bedell, Francis Parsons, Stephen Stansmore, John Glinding, Katherine Lawrence,** and **John Hawthorne** into this Province here to inhabit as appears on record. *Note: This patent was issued by Talbot County.*

Inclosure 8/10/1683 - 300a's. SDA/172 SR7369
Location: Queen Annes County on the western side of the Main Branch of Tuckahoe Creek. Begins at a bound White Oak of **Philemon Lloyd** and **Henry Parker's** tract of land called Loyds Parke. Also adjoins **William Digg's** tract called **Bramford** and a tract called Dawsons Neck.
Other persons mentioned: Land rights assigned by former owner **Thomas Vaughan.** *Note: This patent was issued by Talbot County.*

Vaughns Discovery 8/10/1683 – 400a's. SDA/280 SR7369
Location: Queen Annes County on the western side of the Main Branch of Tuckahoe Creek. Adjoins **Philemon Hemsley's** tract of land called Loyds Parke and **John Scott's** tract called Macwell. *Note: This patent was issued by Talbot County.*

Fare Play 9/12/1695 – 160a's. BB3B/520 SR7374
Location: Queen Annes County on the southern side of the Chester River on the eastern side of Hinson Haven Creek beginning at a bound tree of **Thomas Hinson's** tract of land called The Addition. Also adjoins **Robert Smith's** tracts called The Addition, **Richard Jones'** tract called Labor in

Vain, **Matthew Read's** tract called Reading, and **William Hinson's** tract called Hinsons Beginning.
Other persons mentioned: Land rights assigned by **Philemon Hemsley.** *Note 1: This is a certification. The tract was patented by* ***William Hemsley*** *in 1695 (SDA/521 SR7374). Note: This certification was issued by Talbot County.*

Coursey Upon Wye - 11/10/1695 - 920a's. BB3B/341 SR7374
Location: Queen Annes County on Island Creek in the woods beginning at a bound tree of his own tract of land called Chester.
Other persons mentioned: Land rights assigned by **Peter Sayer.** *Note: This patent was issued by Talbot County.*

Long Neglect 5/31/1696 - 60a's. BB3B/457 S7374
Location: Queen Annes County on the northern side of Carmens Branch of Coursey Creek beginning at a bound tree of his own tract of land called Courseys Neck. *Note: This patent was issued by Talbot County.*

Cowley, George
Normanton 12/8/1673 – 800a's. L15/196 SR4327
Location: Queen Annes County on Nobles Branch of the Wye River in the woods.
Other persons mentioned: Land rights assigned by **Thomas Todd.** *Note 1: This is a certification. The tract was patented by* ***Robert Smith*** *on 5/10/1677 (L20/60 SR7361). Note 2: This certification was issued by Talbot County.*

Cox, Edward
Coopers Quarter 8/18/1684 - 50a's. CB3i/520 SR7367
Location: Queen Annes County on Kent Island at the head of Howell's Branch in the woods.
Other persons mentioned: Land rights assigned by **Walter Kerby.** *Note: The patent document does not specify the patenting county.*

Cox, William
Coxs Neck 12/11/1640 – 1,000a's L1/94 SR7341
Location: Queen Annes County on Kent Island in Crayford Manor on Blunt Point Creek between Homes Byte and the Chesapeake Bay where he lives. *Note: This patent was issued by St. Marys County.*

Croft, Herbert & Mason, Matthew, Planters
Batchellors Chance 8/1/1673 – 300a's. L17/192 SR7358
Location: Queen Annes County on a fresh runn of the Wye River in the woods.
Other persons mentioned: Land rights assigned by **Bonhum Turner** assignee of **John Serjent** and **John Bullpitt, Simon Clayman,** and **Elizabeth**

Modbury due each of them for completing their time of service in this Province. Additional rights assigned by **Kathereine Turner** *(wife of **Bonhim Turner**) for transporting **herself** into this Province here to inhabit as appears on record. Note: This patent was issued by Talbot County.*

Cross, William

Leicester Fields 6/12/1688 - 200a's. NS2i/666 SR7371
Location: Queen Annes County between Wallnut Ridge and the head of French Womans Branch of Tuckahoe Creek. Begins at a bound tree of **Robert Bett's** tract of land called Rattlesnake Ridge.
Other persons mentioned: Land rights assigned by **Thomas Smithson.** *Note: This patent was issued by Talbot County.*

Crump, Nicholas

Plain Dealing 10/25/1682 – 200a's. L21/491 SR7362
Location: Queen Annes County on the southern side of the Chester River on the western side of Broadribs Branch of Island Creek.
Other persons mentioned: Land rights assigned by **Richard Peacocke.** *Note 1: This is a certification. The tract was patented by **William Crump** on 11/13/1683 (SDA/491 SR7369). Note 2: This patent was issued by Talbot County.*

Crump, William & Jones, Richard

Shrewsbury 12/10/1685 - 300a's. NSBi/463 SR7370
Location: Queen Annes County on the southern side of the Chester River on Island Creek beginning at a marked Poplar of **Charles Lowder's** tract of land called Constantinople.
Other persons mentioned: Land rights assigned by **Robert Suite.** *Note: This patent was issued by Talbot County.*

Crump, William

Crumpton 8/1/1683 – 50a's. CB3i/391 SR7367
Location: Queen Annes County on the southern side of the Chester River on the eastern side of Island Creek beginning at a marked Red Oak.
Other persons mentioned: Land rights assigned by **Michael Turbutt.** *Note: This patent was issued by Talbot County.*

Crumps Chance 9/10/1683 – 150a's. SDA/290 SR7369
Location: Queen Annes County on the southern side of the Chester River on Broadribs Branch of Island Creek beginning at a marked White Oak.
Other persons mentioned: Land rights assigned by **Richard Peacocke.** *Note: This patent was issued by Talbot County.*

Plaine Dealing 11/13/1683 - 200a's. SDA/529 SR7369
Location: Queen Annes County on the southern side of the Chester River on the western side of Broadribs Branch of Island Creek.
Other persons mentioned: Land rights assigned by **Richard Peacocke**. *Note: This patent was issued by Talbot County.*

The Triangle 6/1/1686 – 50a's. NSBi/343 SR7370
Location: Queen Annes County on the southern side of the Chester River on the northern side of Corsica Creek beginning at a marked Oak of **William Hemsley's** tract of land. Also adjoins the land of **Christopher Denny**.
Other persons mentioned: Land rights assigned by **Robert Smith**. *Note: This patent was issued by Talbot County.*

Crumps Forrest 6/12/1688 – 300a's. NS2i/644 SR7371
Location: Queen Annes County on the southern side of the Chester River on Island Creek by the branch side. Adjoins **James Heath's** tract of land called Heathworth.
Other persons mentioned: Land rights assigned by **Thomas Smith** assignee of **David Walker**. *Note: This patent was issued by Talbot County.*

Crunpton 6/12/1688 – 220a's. NSBi/622 SR7370
Location: Queen Annes County on the southern side of the Chester River on the western side of Red Lyon Branch beginning at a bound tree of **Cornelius Comegy's** tract of land called Newport.
Other persons mentioned: Land rights assigned by **Thomas Smithson**. *Note: This patent was issued by Talbot County.*

Dail, John, Planter
 Waxford 10/10/1707 - 100a's. DD5i/383 SR7378
Location: Queen Annes County on the southern side of the Chester River in the woods on Unicorn Branch beginning at a bound White Oak of **John Ponder's** tract of land called Ponderfield.
Other persons mentioned: Land rights assigned by **Nicholas Cloud**. *Note: This patent was issued by Kent County.*

Davenport, Humphrey
 Davenport 2/17/1678- 400a's. L15/697 SR4327
Location: Queen Annes County among the branches of Coursefield Creek of the Wye River.
Other persons mentioned: Land rights assigned by **Richard Royston** due him for transporting **Mary Royston** *(no relationship indicated),* **Ann Masterman, Ann Provinell, Anne Judith Goldsbury, Hester Fowkes, Robert Floyd, John Murry,** and **John Hare**. *Note: This patent was issued by Talbot County.*

Welsh Ridge Addition 6/11/1684 – 300a's. NS2i/389 SR7371
Location: Queen Annes County on the southern side of the Chester River beginning at a bound tree of **James Magregor's** tract of land called The Welsh Ridge. *Note: This patent was issued by Talbot County.*

Bath Addition 8/5/1684 – 300a's. IB&ILC/74 SR7368
Location: Queen Annes County on the southern side of the Chester River beginning at a bound tree of **John Broadrib's** tract of land called Bath. *Note: This patent was issued by Talbot County.*

Davis, John
Davis Outlett 8/10/1683 – 50a's. SDA/117 SR7369
Location: Queen Annes County on the eastern side of the Wye River beginning at a bound tree of **Stephen Whetstone's** tract of land called Whetstone.
Other persons mentioned: Land rights assigned by **Richard Peacocke**. *Note: This patent was issued by Talbot County.*

Davis Range 5/10/1685 – 600a's. NSBi/118 SR7370
Location: Queen Annes County on the southern side of the Chester River on the southern side of Red Lyon Branch beginning at a bound tree of **Peter Sayer's** tract of land called Sayers Range. *Note: This patent was issued by Talbot County.*

Davis Phenelia 5/31/1699 – 350a's. BB3B/447 SR7374
Location: Queen Annes County at the head of the Chester River on the southern side of Andover Branch. Adjoins **Edward Boothby's** tract of land called Boothbys Fortune. *Note: This patent was issued by Talbot County.*

Davis, Thomas
Providence 8/8/1683 - 100a's. L22/41 SR7363
Location: Queen Annes County on the eastern side of Kent Island beginning at a bound tree of **Edward Sparkes'** tract of land called Sparkes Point. Also adjoins **Christopher Granger's** tract called Chance and a tract called Workmans Hazard. *Note: This is a certification issued by Kent County. No patent was found.*

Dawson, William
Dawsons Neck 7/18/1665 – 400a's. L9/124 SR7351
Location: Queen Annes County on the northern side of the Choptank River on Tuckahoe Creek beginning at a bound tree of **Philemon Lloyd** and **Henry Parker's** tract of land called Lloyd Parke. *Note 1: This is a certification. No patent was found. Note 2: This certification was issued by Talbot County.*

Deane, William
    The Middle Branch 8/2/1686 - 200a's. L22/257 SR7363
    Location: Queen Annes County on the Eastern Branch of Swan Creek
    beginning at a marked Pokehikary. Also adjoins **James** and **John Ringold' s**
    tracts of land called The Middle Spring and Green Branch. *Note: This patent*
    was issued by Kent County.

Deer, John, Planter
    Pentregay 8/12/1650 - 200a's. AB&H/129 SR7344
    Location: Queen Annes County on Kent Island on the eastern side of Cox
    Creek in the woods. Adjoins **Roger Baxter's** tract of land called Upper
    Blunt Point.
    Other persons mentioned: Deer transported **himself** and his **wife** into this
    Province here to inhabit in 1647, as appears on record. *Note: This is a*
    certification issued by St. Marys County. No patent was found.

Denton, Henry
    Clowdent 9/18/1688 - 200a's. NSBi/164 SR7370
    Location: Queen Annes County on the southern side of the Chester River on
    Hambleton Branch beginning at a bound Oak of **William Bishop's** tract of
    land called Bishops Field. Also adjoins **Nicholas Cloud's** tract called
    Northers Delight. *Note 1: Another patent was found (NSBi/664 SR7370).*
    Note 2: This patent was issued by Talbot County.

Devenish, Robert
    Devenishs Chance 3/7/1688 – 500a's. NSBi/687 SR7370
    Location: Queen Annes County on the eastern side of the Chester River on
    the western side of Unicorn Branch beginning at a bound tree of **Francis**
    Sheppard's tract of land called Sheppards Fields. *Note: This patent was*
    issued by Talbot County.

    Lambeth 3/7/1688 – 250a's. NSBi/688 SR7370
    Location: Queen Annes County on the eastern side of the Chester River in a
    forke of Unicorn Branch in the woods. *Note: This patent was issued by*
    Talbot County.

Diggs, William
    Branford 5/10/1681 - 100a's. L21/341 SR7362
    Location: Queen Annes County on the western side of the Main Branch of
    Tuckahoe Creek. Adjoins **William Coursey's** tract of land called The
    Inclosure. *Note 1: This is a certification. No patent was found. Note 2: This*
    certification was issued by Talbot County.

Dine, John
    Limbuck 11/10/1695 - 100a's. C3i/105 SR7377

Location: Queen Annes County on Kent Island in the woods. Adjoins a tract of land called Barren Ridge.
Other persons mentioned: Land rights assigned by **Simon Wilmer** assignee of **Philemon Hemsley**. *Note: This patent was issued by Kent County.*

Dobbs, John

Bastable Hill 6/8/1682 - 100a's. L21/555 SR7362
Location: Queen Annes County on Kent Island on the eastern side of Great Hinkel Creek. Begins at a marked Hickory of **Arthur Gunn's** tract of land.
Other persons mentioned: Land rights assigned by **Henry Lawrence**. *Note 1: This is a certification. No patent was found. Note 2: This certification was issued by Kent County.*

Dobbs Adventure 11/10/1695 - 36a's. 7347/247
Location: Queen Annes County on Kent Isle near a point of marsh respecting Ericksons Island nearest to Poplar Neck.
Other persons mentioned: Land rights assigned by **Simon Wilmer** assignee of **Michael Miller**. *Note: The patent document does not specify the patenting county.*

Dodd, Peter

Doddington 6/12/1688– 200a's. NS2i/659 SR7371
Location: Queen Annes County on the western side of the second branch above Red Lyon Creek of the Chester River on the southeast side of the Lower Road.
Other persons mentioned: Land rights assigned by **Thomas Smithson**. *Note: This patent was issued by Talbot County.*

Downs, James

Downes Forrest 7/10/1683 – 300a's. SDA/186 SR7369
Location: Queen Annes County on the southern side of the Chester River on the western side of the northernmost branch of Tuckahoe Creek. Adjoins **Stephen Tully's** tract of land called Upper Deale. *Note: This patent was issued by Talbot County.*

Dun/Dunn, Pasco, Cooper

Duns Hazard 9/2/1664 - 150a's. L7/417 SR7349
Location: Queen Annes County on Kent Island on the western side of Thicketty Creek extending to Cox His Creek. Adjoins **William Body's** tract of land.
Other persons mentioned: Dun transported **Abraham Wiseback, Nicholas Marsay,** and **John Purser** into this Province here to inhabit as appears on record. *Note: The patent document does not specify the patenting county.*

Pascoes Adventure 9/2/1664 - 150a's. L7/415 SR7349
Location: Queen Annes County on Kent Island beginning at a marked stake by the Wading Place. Adjoins **Phillip Connor's** tract of land at the head of a creek running out of the Eastern Bay.
Other persons mentioned: **Dunn** transported **himself, Henry Carter,** and **John Crue** into this Province here to inhabit as appears on record. *Note: The patent document does not specify the patenting county.*

Parsons Neck 9/26/1665 - 200a's. L8/454 SR7350
Location: Queen Annes County on Kent Island in Crayford Manor on the eastern side of the island near Vaughans Bay. Adjoins **William Porter's** tract of land also called Parsons Neck.
Other persons mentioned: Land rights assigned by **Richard Skinner.** *Note: This patent was issued by Kent County.*

Dunn, John
   Dunns Range 4/22/1683 – 200a's. CB3i/244 SR7367
   Location: Queen Annes County at the head of a branch of Bruers Creek of the Wye River. Adjoins **Henry Parker's** tract of land called Dunns Range Addition, **William Vaughan** and **Alexander Moore's** tract called Morefields, and **John Morgan's** tract called Morgans Neglect.
   Other persons mentioned: Land rights assigned by **Richard Carter.** *Note: This patent was issued by Talbot County.*

Dunn, Robert, Planter
   Unnamed Certification 10/17/1651 - 100a's. AB&H/284 SR7344
   Location: Queen Annes County on Kent Island in the woods on Coxes Creek. Adjoins **John Phillips'** tract of land called Pigg Quarter. *Note: This is a certification issued by St, Marys County. No patent was found.*

Edenbrook, Edward, Mariner of London
   Crosscombes Pillar 5/3/1665 - 1,000a's. L9/91 SR7351
   Location: Queen Annes County on the southern side of the Chester River at the head of Courseys Creek at the dividing point in the woods. *Note 1: This is a certification. No patent was found. Note 2: This patent was issued by Talbot County.*

Elina, Andrew
   Sintra 1/31/1658 - 300a's. LQ/365 SR7345
   Location: Queen Annes County on the eastern side of the Chester River on the northern side of Corsica Creek. Adjoins **Henry Coursey's** tract of land.
   Other persons mentioned: Elina transported **Andrew Hanson, Anikeck Hanson, Fredrick Hanson, Catherine Hanson,** and **Hance Hanson** (*no relationships indicated*) into this Province here to inhabit as appears on record. *Note: The patent document does not specify the patenting county.*

Elliott, John
>**Elliotts Addition** 8/1/1683 – 100a's. SDA/287 SR7369
>Location: Queen Annes County on the southern side of the Chester River beginning at the second bound tree of **John Rawling's** tract of land called Rawlings Chance.
>Other persons mentioned: Land rights assigned by **Michael Turbutt.** *Note: This patent was issued by Talbot County.*

Elliott, William, Planter
>**Unnamed Certification** 1/30/1651 - 200a's. AB&H/297 SR7344
>Location: Queen Annes County on the northeast side of Kent Island beginning at a marked tree of **Henry Ashley's** unnamed 100-acre tract of land. *Note: This is a certification issued by St. Marys County. No patent was found.*

Ellis, Robert
>**Wrexains Plaines** 4/30/1683 – 560a's. CB3i/271 SR7367
>Location: Queen Annes County on the southern side of the Chester River on the western side of the Main Branch of Corsica Creek. Adjoins **James Magreggor's** tract of land called Welsh Ridge and **Robert Smith's** tract called Fishingham.
>Other persons mentioned: Land rights assigned by **John Dalton.** Additional rights assigned by **Richard Moss** *(husband of **Elizabeth Arrount** executrix of **James Arrount**). Note: This patent was issued by Talbot County.*

Emery, Arthur & Paxton, Hugh
>**Emery Paxton** 10/1/1687 – 372a's. NS2i/581 SR7371
>Location: Queen Annes County on a branch of a branch of the Wye River called Thomas Branch on the road to Wye Mill between **John Walker's** tract of land called Walkers Square and **Col. Lloyd's** land. Also adjoins Paxton's tract called Manchester.
>Other persons mentioned: Land rights assigned by **Thomas Smithson.** *Note: This patent was issued by Talbot County.*

Emery, Arthur, Planter
>**Emerys Neglect** 12/6/1682 – 125a's. L21/493 SR7362
>Location: Queen Annes County on the Main Branch of the Wye River beginning at a marked Oak of **Giles Butter's** tract of land called Butterfield. Also adjoins **Matthew Ward's** tract called Green Spring and **William Turlo's** tract called Emerys Fortune.
>Other persons mentioned: Land rights assigned by **Richard Peacocke.** *Note 1: This is a certification. No patent was found. Note 2: This certification was issued by Talbot County.*

Emerys Addition 6/1/1686 – 50a's. NSBi/348 SR7370
Location: Queen Annes County at the head of the Wye River by the side of a road beginning at a marked Hickory of his own tract of land Emerys Neglect. Also adjoins **Lewis Blongy's** tract of land.
Other persons mentioned: Land rights assigned by **Robert Smith.** *Note: This patent was issued by Talbot County.*

Emmerson, John

Kelding & Buckingham Res. 4/1/1697 – 393a's. CC4i/59 SR7375
Location: Queen Annes County on the road from Brewers Branch of the Wye River to Wye Mill by the old schoolhouse.
Other persons mentioned: Land rights assigned by former owner **Robert Carville.** *Note 1: The resurvey was undertaken to combine two tracts with a combined acreage believed to be 600 acres. The resurvey showed the combined acreage to be only 393 acres. Note 2: This warrant to resurvey was issued by Talbot County.*

Emmerson, Thomas, Planter

Long Point 9/4/1665 – 50a's. L8/226 SR7350
Location: Queen Annes County at the head of the Wye River on the Southeast Branch. Adjoins **Thomas Wilkerson's** tract of land.
Other persons mentioned: Land rights assigned by **Stephen Whitson** assignee of **Richard Preston.** *Note: This patent was issued by Talbot County.*

Erickson, John

Stinson Erickson 2/1/1658 - 200a's. LQ/369 SR7345
Location: Queen Annes County on the eastern side of Kent Island on the southern side of Stints Creek at the head of Ericksons Branch extending to Great Piny Creek on Coxes Bay.
Other persons mentioned: Erickson transported **himself** and wife **Elizabeth** into this Province here to inhabit as appears on record. *Note: This patent was issued by St. Marys County.*

Erickson, Matthew

Sarahs Portion 2/3/1681 - 150a's. CB2i/434 SR7366
Location: Queen Annes County on Kent Island near Goose Harbor extending to Phillpotts Creek. Adjoins **Thomas Hale's** tract of land.
Other persons mentioned: Land rights assigned by **Elizabeth Erickson,** administrator of **John Erickson** *(deceased),* due John for transporting **Mary Barefoote** and **Elizabeth Willoughby.** Also, Matthew Erickson transported **Martha Loverton** into this Province here to inhabit as appears on record. *Note: This patent was issued by Kent County.*

Ericksons Islands 4/17/1683 - 20a's. CB3i/235 SR7367
Location: Queen Annes County on Kent Island. Two "hummocks" of small islands at the mouth of the Eastern Creek of the Eastern Bay. Respects **Thomas Broadnax's** tract of land called Broad Oake now in the possession of **James Rigby.**
Other persons mentioned: Land rights assigned by former owner **Isaac Winchester.** *Note: This patent was issued by Kent County.*

Marys Portion 8/10/1684 - 150a's. SDA/479 SR7369
Location: Queen Annes County in the middle of Kent Island at the head of Tarr Hill Creek on Tarr Hill Field extending to Martins Creek beginning at a marked Oak. Adjoins **Richard Blunt's** tract of land called Great Neck and **Phillip Connor's** tract called Woodland Thickett. *Note: This patent was issued by Kent County.*

Matthews Enlargement 11/10/1695 - 155a's. C3i/104 SR7377
Location: Queen Annes County on Kent Island on Stints Creek in the woods. Begins at a bound tree of **John Erickson's** tract of land called Stinton Erickson.
Other persons mentioned: Land rights assigned by **Simon Wilmer.** *Note: This patent was issued by Kent County.*

Evetts, Nathaniel
Winton 1/15/1667 – 300a's. L11/244 SR7353
Location: Queen Annes County on the southern side of the Chester River on the western side of Corsica Creek on Macklins Branch.
Other persons mentioned: Land rights assigned by **Richard Dennis** due him for transporting **himself, Christopher Robinson,** his son **Christopher Hobson,** and **Edward Butteran** into this Province here to inhabit as appears on record. *Note: This patent was issued by Talbot County.*

Wintons Addition 1/17/1667 – 50a's. L11/243 SR7353
Location: Queen Annes County on the southern side of the Chester River on the northern side of Winchester Branch.
Other persons mentioned: Land rights assigned by **Edward Webb.** *Note: This patent was issued by Talbot County.*

Cove Point 1/15/1677 – 200a's. L11/242 SR7353
Location: Queen Annes County on the southern side of the Chester River on the western side of Corsica Creek adjoining a tract of land called Thomas His Cove.
Other persons mentioned: Land rights assigned by **James Webb.** *Note: This patent was issued by Talbot County.*

Farrington, Robert, Planter
    Farrington 8/1/1673 - 250a's. L15/103 SR4327
    <u>Location</u>: Queen Annes County on the southern side of the Chester River on
    Double Creek. Begins at a bound tree of **Matthew Ward's** tract of land
    called Wards Park.
    <u>Other persons mentioned</u>: Farrington transported his wife **Ann,** his daughter
    Jane, Joseph Billeter, and **Phillip Sutton** into this Province here to inhabit
    as appears on record. *Note: This patent was issued by Talbot County.*

Felton, John, Planter
    Drum Point 4/8/1662 - 400a's. L5/60 SR7347
    <u>Location</u>: Queen Annes County on the eastern side of an island in Morgans
    Creek beginning at a marked Oak of **Thomas Bradnox's** tract of land. Also
    adjoins **William Stevens'** tract called Stevens Choice. *Note: The patent*
    document does not specify the patenting county. The tract is included
    because MSA Patent Index #55 places it in Queen Annes County.

Finney, William
    Finneys Range 7/10/1671 - 225a's. L14/258 SR7356
    <u>Location</u>: Queen Annes County on a branch of the Back Wye River in a cove
    beginning at a bound tree of **Phillip Stevenson's** tract of land called
    Stevensons Purchase.
    <u>Other persons mentioned</u>: Land rights assigned by **Johnathan Hopkinson.**
    Note: This patent was issued by Talbot County.

    Finneys Hermitage 5/1/1672 – 400a's. L16/603 SR7357
    <u>Location</u>: Queen Annes County on Muddy Branch of the Wye River
    adjoining **John Wright's** tract of land called Skipton.
    <u>Other persons mentioned</u>: Finney transported **himself,** wife **Elizabeth,**
    daughters **Mary** and **Susanna, Nicholas Day, Nicholas Clarke,** and
    Margarett Burke into this Province here to inhabit as appears on record.
    Note 1: Another patent was found (L18/241 SR7359). Note 2: This patent
    was issued by Talbot County.

    Finneys Hermitage Res. 9/7/1674 – 400a's. L18/241 SR7359
    <u>Location</u>: Queen Annes County on Muddy Branch of the Wye River
    adjoining **John Wright's** tract of land called Skipton. *Note 1: The resurvey*
    was undertaken to correct errors in the original survey. Note 2: This patent
    was issued by Talbot County.

Fishborne, Ralph
    Mount Hope 8/15/1670 – 300a's. L13/2 SR7355
    <u>Location</u>: Queen Anne County on the southern side of the Chester River on
    the eastern side of the Southeast Branch of Island Creek. Adjoins **John**

Rawling's tract of land called Rawlings Chance and **Henry Wilcocks'** tract called Mount Hope Addition.
Other persons mentioned: Land rights assigned by **Samuel Winslow.** *Note: This patent was issued by Talbot County.*

Forbes, Alexander
Bonaventure 6/1/1700 – 77a's. DD5i/10 SR7378
Location: Queen Annes County on Barrons Neck of Kent Island beginning at a bound tree of **John Hawkins'** tract of land called Barron Necke. *Note: This patent was issued by Kent County.*

Primus 6/1/1700 – 95a's. CC4i/153 SR7375
Location: Kent Island on Wading Place Bay adjoining **John Meconkin's** tract of land called The Eastern Bay. Also adjoins **Henry Williams'** tract called Rotterdam. *Note: This patent was issued by Talbot County.*

Forrest, Patrick
Forrests Lodge 1/10/1658 - 100a's. LQ/271 SR7345
Location: Queen Annes County on the eastern side of the Eastern Bay on Marklins Branch of Courseys Creek beginning at a marked Oak standing on a point of land.
Other persons mentioned: Land rights assigned by **George Whitaker.** *Note: This patent was issued by Talbot County.*

Forsett, Thomas
Forsetts Planes 8/1/1673 - 150a's. L15/96 SR4327
Location: Queen Annes County between the Wye and Chester Rivers near the Horse Road.
Other persons mentioned: Land rights assigned by **Edward Cook** due him for completing his time of service in this Province. *Note: This patent was issued by Talbot County.*

Foster, Seth
Standishwood 8/10/1673 - 1,000a's. L15/160 SR4327
Location: Queen Annes County on the southern side of the Chester River beginning at a bound tree of **Richard Tilghman's** tract of land called Tilghmans Discovery.
Other persons mentioned: Land rights assigned by **Thomas Mountfort** due him for transporting **John Brown, Phinning Ottage,** and **Elizabeth West** into this Province here to inhabit as appears on record. *Note: This patent was issued by Talbot County.*

Francis, Thomas
The Planters Encrease 6/14/1676 – 100a's. L19/371 SR7360

Location: Queen Annes County at the head of the Wye River in the woods. Adjoins **William Jones** and **Peter Sides'** tract of land called Planters Delight.

Other persons mentioned: Land rights assigned by **Thomas Taylor** due him for transporting **Thomas Treare** and **Joseph Slaughter** into this Province here to inhabit as appears on record. *Note: This patent was issued by Talbot County.*

Gleaves, John
Gleaves Lott 8/10/1713 - 150a's. DD5i/817 SR7378
Location: Queen Annes County on Newells Branch beginning at a bound tree of **Vincent Lowe's** tract of land called Chesterfield.

Other persons mentioned: Land rights assigned by **Robert Lynch**. *Note 1: The certification date for this tract is 5/25/1710. Note 2: This patent was issued by Kent County.*

Glover, Daniel
The Hope 11/6/1684 – 200a's. L22/190 SR7363
Location: Queen Annes County on the southwest side of Mill Branch of Corsica Creek.

Other persons mentioned: Land rights assigned by **John Stevens** assignee of **Henry Parker**. *Note 1: This is a certification. No patent was found. Note 2: This certification was issued by Talbot County.*

Gouldhawke, George
Little Ease 8/12/1665 - 300a's. L8/155 SR7350
Location: Queen Annes County on Kent Island at the head of Coxes Creek extending to Smiths Creek. Adjoins his own tract of land.

Other persons mentioned: Land rights assigned by **William Chandler** assignee of **Thomas Bordley**. *Note: This patent was issued by Kent County.*

Granger, Christopher
Chance 8/10/1683 - 50a's. SDA/191 SR7369
Location: Queen Annes County on Kent Island at the Wading Place beginning at a marked Oak.

Other persons mentioned: Land rights assigned by **Walter Kerby**. *Note: This patent was issued by Kent County.*

Green, John
Greens Adventure 4/25/1683 – 300a's. CB3i/265 SR7367
Location: Queen Annes County at the head of Williams Branch of the Wye River beginning at a bound Hickory of **William Young's** tract of land called Carpenters Square. Also adjoins **Alice Lloyd's** tract called Lloyds Meadow and **Philemon Hemsley's** tract called Hemsleys Reserve.

Other persons mentioned: Land rights assigned by **Henry Barber** assignee of **James Barber** *(no relationship indicated)* assignee of **William Sharpe.** *Note: This patent was issued by Talbot County.*

Gresham, John
Unnamed Certification 9/7/1640 - 100a's. L1/80 SR7341
Location: Queen Annes County on Kent Island. *Note 1: Land rights based on Gresham having transported himself into this Province here to inhabit as appears on record. Note 2: This patent was issued by Talbot County.*

Griffin, Anthony
Prices Hill 1/5/1659 - 800a's. L4/305 SR7346
Location: Queen Annes County on the northern side of the Eastern Branch of the Chester River on Prices Hill.
Other persons mentioned: Griffin transported eight unnamed persons into this Province here to inhabit as appears on record. *Note 1: This tract was surveyed for **Richard Price** in 1659. Note 2: The patent document does not specify the patenting county.*

Griffin, Matthew
Griffins Adventure 6/10/1708 – 220a's. DD5i/514 SR7378
Location: Queen Annes County on Kent Island between Broad Creek and Coxes Creek by the main road to Broad Creek. Adjoins **John Wells'** tract of land.
Other persons mentioned: Land rights assigned by **Richard Bennett.** *Note: This patent was issued by Talbot County.*

Gross, Roger
Gross Coat 3/2/1658 – 300a's. LQ/380 SR7345
Location: Queen Annes County on the eastern side of the St. Michaels River on the northern side of Morgans Creek extending to the northern side of Lloyds Branch and Gross Branch.
Other persons mentioned: Gross transported **Joseph Salvage, John Drywood, Christopher Stopper, Lawrence Stephens, Francis Smith,** and **William Smith** *(no relationship indicated)* into this Province here to inhabit as appears on record. *Note: This patent was issued by Kent County.*

Abbington 9/12/1665 – 400a's. L8/245 SR7350
Location: Queen Annes County on the North Branch of the Wye River in the woods. Adjoins **William Jones** and **Peter Sides'** tract of land called Dobbs Creek and **John Wright's** tract. *Note: This patent was issued by Talbot County.*

Gross, William
Gross Addition 5/10/1685 – 24a's. IB&ILC/160 SR7368

Location: Queen Annes County on the Wye River on a point of land on Lloyds Creek beginning at a bound tree of his own tract of land called Gross Coat.
Other persons mentioned: Land rights assigned by **John Larkin.** *Note: This patent was issued by Talbot County.*

Guider, Thomas
Guiders Lott 11/6/1685 - 200a's. L22/221 SR7363
Location: Queen Annes County on the southern side of the Chester River on the western side of the Red Lyon Branch adjoining **William Guideth's** tract of land. *Note 1: This is a certification. No patent was found. Note 2: This certification was issued by Talbot County.*

Guiders Range 11/6/1685 - 500a's. L22/222 SR7363
Location: Queen Annes County on the southern side of the Chester River on the northern side of Red Lyon Creek in the first forke. *Note 1: This is a certification. No patent was found. Note 2: This certification was issued by Talbot County.*

Guither, Thomas
Guithers Lott 6/10/1686 - 250a's. NSBi/391 SR7370
Location: Queen Annes County on the southern side of the Chester River on the western side of Red Lyon Branch beginning at a bound tree of **William Gwyther's** tract of land called Gwythers Range. *Note: This patent was issued by Talbot County.*

Gwyther, William
Gwythers Range 10/10/1686 – 500a's. IB&ILC/171 SR7368
Location: Queen Anne County on a forke on the western side of Red Lyon Branch beginning at a bound White Oak. Adjoins **Thomas Guider's** tract of land called Guiders Lott. *Note: This patent was issued by Talbot County.*

Gynn, Arthur, Planter
Coney Hall 4/1/1672 - 100a's. L14/511 SR7356
Location: Queen Annes County on the western side of Kent Island at the head of Great Thickety Creek.
Other persons mentioned: Land rights assigned by **Isaac Winchester.** *Note: The patent document does not specify the patenting county.*

Hacker, John
Hackers Forrest 10/10/1707 - 200a's. DD5i/392 SR7378
Location: Queen Annes County on the western side of the Main Branch of Tuckahoe Creek beginning at a bound White Oak of **William Diggs'** tract of land called Branford.

Other persons mentioned: Land rights assigned by **William Connor** assignee of **Col. Hemsley.** *Note: This patent was issued by Talbot County.*

Hacket/Hackett, Michael/Michaell

Higate 5/4/1683 - 50a's. SDA/294 SR7369
Location: Queen Annes County on the southern side of the Chester River on the western side of Island Creek beginning at a marked Red Oak of **John Hawkins'** tract of land called Triangle.
Other persons mentioned: Land rights assigned by **Henry Parker.** *Note: This patent was issued by Talbot County.:*

Highgate Lane 1683 – 100a's. SDA/210 SR7369
Location: Queen Annes County on the southern side of the Chester River on the northern side of the Eastern Branch. Adjoins **Henry Parker's** tract of land called Parkers Lott.
Other persons mentioned: Land rights assigned by Henry Parker. *Note: This patent was issued by Talbot County.*

Hackets Delight 5/5/1683 – 150a's. SDA/283 SR7369
Location: Queen Annes County on the western side of the Delaware Road in the woods beginning at a marked Oak.
Other persons mentioned: Land rights assigned by **Henry Parker.** *Note: This patent was issued by Talbot County.*

Hacketts Chance 8/10/1683 – 250a's. CB3i/403 SR7367
Location: Queen Annes County on the southern side of the Chester River by the riverside beginning at a bound tree of **Robert Macklyn's** tract of land called Macklinburg.
Other persons mentioned: Land rights assigned by **Michael Miller** assignee of **Cornelius Comegys.** *Note: This patent was issued by Talbot County.*

Sparkes Choice 8/10/1683 – 450a's. SDA/114 SR7369
Location: Queen Annes County on the eastern side of the Chester River in the woods at the head of Island Creek.
Other persons mentioned: Land rights assigned by **Michael Miller.** *Note: This patent was issued by Talbot County.*

Hacketts Lott 4/1/1686 - 150a's. NS2i/190 SR7371
Location: Queen Annes County on the northern arm of a forke above the Southeast Branch of the Chester River on Hambletons Creek.
Other persons mentioned: Land rights assigned by **Henry Lyons.** *Note: The patent document does not specify the patenting county.*

Hackett, William

Barton 10/1/1682 - 150a's. CB3i/190 SR7367

Location: Queen Annes County on the southern side of the Chester River on a branch of Hambletons Creek beginning at a marked Red Oak of **Richard Collins'** tract of land called Collins Lott. Also adjoins **Steven Tully's** tract called Ashton.
Other persons mentioned: Land rights assigned by **Thomas Ford** due him for transporting **himself** and wife **Katherine** into this Province here to inhabit as appears on record. *Note: This patent was issued by Talbot County.*

Woolhampton 8/10/1683 – 200a's. CB3i/384 SR7367
Location: Queen Annes County on the southern side of the Chester River on the northern side of a small branch of Double Creek.
Other persons mentioned: Land rights assigned by **Richard Peacock** assignee of **John Edmondson**. *Note: This patent was issued by Talbot County.*

South Hampton 6/1/1687 – 150a's. IB&ILC/275 SR7368
Location: Queen Annes County on the Southeast Branch of the Chester River. Adjoins Stephen Tully's tract of land called Ashton.
Other persons mentioned: Land rights assigned by Henry Lines. *Note: This patent was issued by Talbot County.*

The Content 10/1/1687 – 50a's. NS2i/572 SR7371
Location: Queen Annes County on the northern side of Hambleton's Branch beginning at a bound tree of **Stephen Tulley's** tract of land called Ripely. Also adjoins tracts owned by **William Bishop** and **John Hollingsworth**.
Other persons mentioned: Land rights assigned by **Thomas Smithson**. *Note: This patent was issued by Talbot County.*

Hailings/Haillings, Thomas
    Batchellors Hope 4/26/1683 – 150a's. CB3i/250 SR7367
    Location: Queen Annes County on the southern side of the Chester River beginning at a bound Red Oak standing at the head of Fishing Creek in the woods. *Note: This patent was issued by Talbot County.*

    The Adventure 4/26/1683 – 200a's. CB3i/252 SR7367
    Location: Queen Annes County on the southern side of the Chester River on Matthew Reads Creek. Begins at a marked Red Oak of **Thomas Hinson's** tract of land. *Note: This patent was issued by Talbot County.*

Hales, Thomas
    Hales Neck 12/10/1640 - 50a's. L1/85 SR7341
    Location: Queen Annes County on Kent Island by Goose Harbor in Crayford Manor on Cedar Branch out of Pine Bay. *Note 1: Hales petitioned to have this land confirmed to him which he holds by gift of **Capt. William Clayborn**. Note: This patent was issued by St. Marys County.*

Hall, James

Halls Harbour 8/12/1685– 500a's. NSBi/104 SR7370
<u>Location</u>: Queen Annes County on the southeast side of the Main Branch of the Chester River adjoining **Andrew Abington's** tract of land called Abington Square.
<u>Other persons mentioned</u>: Land rights assigned by **Richard Royston.** *Note 1: This is a certification. No patent was found. Note 2: This certification was issued by Talbot County.*

Hambleton, William & Parker, Henry

Hambleton Parke 1667 - 400a's. L10/510 SR7352
<u>Location</u>: Queen Annes County on the Western Branch of the Wye River beginning at a bound tree of **John Wright's** tract of land called Skipton. Also adjoins **Thomas Stanwood's** tract called Back Branch. *Note: This patent was issued by Talbot County.*

Hambleton, William

Hambletons Hermitage 8/1/1673 - 500a's. L15/125 SR4327
<u>Location</u>: Queen Annes County on the southern side of the Chester River on the northern side of Dividing Creek. Begins at **Anthony Griffin's** tract of land called Prices Hill. *Note: This patent was issued by Talbot County.*

Hamer/Hammer, John

Hamers Choice 4/1/1685 – 200a's. NSBi/303 SR7370
<u>Location</u>: Queen Annes County on the southern side of the Chester River on the northern side of the Main Branch beginning at a marked Pokehikary.
<u>Other persons mentioned</u>: Land rights assigned by **Robert Smith.** *Note: This patent was issued by Talbot County.*

Hammers Lott 10/10/1708- 200a's. DD5i/504 SR7378
<u>Location</u>: Queen Annes County on the southern side of the Chester River on the Main Branch beginning at a bound Red Oak.
<u>Other persons mentioned</u>: Land rights assigned by **Giles Bond.** *Note: This patent was issued by Kent County.*

Harris, Moses

Harriss Range 6/1/1687 – 400a's. NS2i/351 SR7371
<u>Location</u>: Queen Annes County at the head of the Wye River adjoining **John Morgan's** tract of land called Morgans Neglect.
<u>Other persons mentioned</u>: Land rights assigned by **Richard Royston.** *Note: This patent was issued by Talbot County.*

Rumsey Forrest 3/1/1688 – 300a's. NSBi/681 SR7370

Location: Queen Annes County on the southernmost branch of Brewers Branch adjoining **Elizabeth Brewer's** tract of land called Widdows Chance. Adjoins **David Rogers'** tract of land called Marys Dower. *Note: This patent was issued by Talbot County.*

Harwood, Thomas
Harwoods Lyon 2/12/1663 – 400a's. L6/205 SR7348
Location: Queen Annes County on the eastern side of the Wye River up against an island on Harwoods Creek extending to the Northeast Branch. Other persons mentioned: Land rights assigned by **Henry Coursey**. *Note: This patent was issued by Talbot County.*

Hatton, William
Haddon 2/2/1658 - 500a's. LQ/372 SR7345
Location: Queen Annes County on Kent Island bounded by Hattons Branch and the Chesapeake Bay. Adjoins **Zachary Wade's** tract of land called Wades Point.
Other persons mentioned: Land rights assigned by **Thomas Hatton** *(uncle of William)*. *Note: The patent document does not specify the patenting county.*

Hawkins, Henry
The Addition 7/2/1668 – 100a's. L12/75 SR7354
Location: Queen Annes County on the Wye River beginning at marked Oak standing in the woods. Adjoins tracts owned by **John Marks** and **Nicholas Holmes.** *Note: This patent was issued by Talbot County.*

Poplar Hill 9/9/1677 – 200a's. L11/87 SR7353
Location: Queen Annes County on the eastern side of the Middle Branch of the Wye River extending to the Eastern Branch beginning at a marked Oak of **Peter Sides'** tract of land called Wisbitch. Also adjoins **John Wright's** tract called Middleton.
Other persons mentioned: Land rights assigned by **Edward Lloyd**. *Note: This patent was issued by Talbot County.*

Hawkins, John
Hawkins Farme 7/18/1679 - 300a's. L21/278 SR7362
Location: Queen Annes County on the eastern side of the southernmost branch of Courseys Creek. *Note 1: This is a certification. No patent was found. Note 2: This certification was issued by Talbot County.*

Contention 6/30/1681 – 150a's. L21/340 SR7362
Location: Queen Annes County on the southern side of the Chester River on the southern side of Red Lyon Branch. Adjoins **James Sedgwick's** tract of land called Stepney and **William Sparkes'** tract called Sparkes Outlett. *Note*

1: This is a certification. No patent was found. Note 2: This certification was issued by Talbot County.

Contention 9/2/1682 – 450a's. CB3i/179 SR7367
Location: Queen Annes County on the southern side of the Chester River on the southern side of the Red Lyon Branch.
Other persons mentioned: Land rights assigned by **Nicholas Sewell.** *Note: This patent was issued by Talbot County.*

Baron Necke 11/10/1695 – 227a's. BBeB/31 SR7374
Location: Queen Annes County on the southern side of the Chester River on Double Creek extending to Hawkinses Creek. Adjoins **Richard Tilghman's** tract of land called Tilghmans Discovery. *Note: This patent was issued by Talbot County.*

Braintons Addition 11/10/1695 – 314a's. C3i/170 SR7377
Location: Queen Annes County on the southern side of the Chester River on the northern side of Corsica Creek on a cove. Begins at a bound tree of **Nicholas Cloud's** tract of land called The Conquest. Also adjoins **William Bishop's** tract called Bishops Addition. *Note: This patent was issued by Talbot County.*

Jasper Lott 11/10/1695 – 770a's. BB3B/33 SR7374
Location: Queen Annes County on the southern side of the Chester River at the head of Red Lyon Branch. Adjoins **Robert Macklin's** tract of land called Macklins Beginning.
Other persons mentioned: Land rights assigned by **Robert Smith.** *Note: This patent was issued by Talbot County.*

Heath, James
Heathworth Res. 11/3/1700 – 533a's. DD5i/7 SR7378
Location: Queen Annes County on the southern side of the Chester River on Island Creek. *Note: The purpose of this resurvey was to consolidate tracts named Stoke and Tottenham and to include 10 acres of surplus land found between these tracts. Note 2: The authorizing county is not identified.*

Heaths Forrest Res. 11/8/1700 – 150a's. DD5i/8 SR7378
Location: Queen Annes County on the southern side of the Chester River on the southern side of Island Creek beginning at a marked Red Oak. Adjoins **Ruth Thomas'** tract of land called Ruths Gift. *Note 1: This is a resurvey of **John Broadrib's** tract called Warminster patented in 1679 (L21/19 SR7362). Note: This patent was issued by Talbot County.*

Heaths Discovery 11/01/1701 - 23a's. DD5i/40 SR7378

Location: Queen Annes County on the western side of the Southwest Branch of Island Creek. Begins at a marked Red Oak of **John Broadrib's** tract of land called Larrington. Also adjoins **Daniel Jenifer's** tract called Land of the Prophecy. *Note: This patent was issued by Kent County.*

Upper Heathworth 7/10/1702 - 690a's. DD5i/122 SR7378
Location: Queen Annes County between the Southeast and Southwest Branches of Island Creek of the Chester River beginning at a bound tree of **Samuel Winslow** and **Henry Parker's** tract of land called Tottingham. Also adjoins **John Broadrib's** tracts called Warrminster and Freshford and **William Crump's** tracts called Crampton, Crumps Chance and Crumps Forrest. *Note: This patent was issued by Kent County.*

Collins Refusal Res. 10/10/1703 – 129a's. DD5i/126 SR7378
Location: Queen Annes County on the southern side of the Chester River on Island Creek beginning at a bound tree of **Richard Collins'** tract of land called Tottingham. *Note 1: The purpose of the resurvey was to find surplus land within the existing boundaries of the adjoining tract Tottingham. One hundred twenty nine acres were found. Note: This patent was issued by Talbot County.*

Sandy Hurst 11/18/1703 - 500a's. DD5i/101 SR7378
Location: Queen Annes County in the freshes of the Chester River on the southern side near an island of marsh beginning at a bound Oak of **Richard Jones'** tract of land called Jones Fancy. *Note: This patent was issued by Kent County.*

Hemsley, Phillemon
  Fare Play 5/10/1695 – 160a's. BB3B/521 SR7374
  Location: Queen Annes County on the southern side of the Chester River beginning at a bound tree of **Thomas Hinson's** tract of land called The Addition. Also adjoins **William Galloway's** tract called Galloways Fancy and the land of **Robert Smith.**
  Other persons mentioned: Hemsley assigned land rights to **William Coursey** who assigned them back to Hemsley. *Note: This patent was issued by Talbot County.*

  Hemsleys Reserve 10/10/1707 – 231a's. DD5i/405 SR73778
  Location: Queen Annes County at the head of the Wye River between Williams Branch and Thomas Branch. Adjoins **John Trustram's** tract of land called Trustram Wells, **John Green's** tract called Greens Adventure, **Alice Lloyd's** tract called Lloyds Meadows, and a tract called Addicon. *Note: This patent was issued by Talbot County.*

Hemsley, William, Chyrugeon

Hemsleys Choice 6/19/1663 – 500a's. L5/332 SR7347
Location: Queen Annes County on the eastern side of the Eastern Bay on
Spriggs Creek by a marsh beginning at a bound White Oak of **William
Coursey's** tract of land called Courseys Neck. Also adjoins **John Coursey's**
tract called Cedar Branch.
Other persons mentioned: Coursey transported **himself,** wife **Judith,** and
Dan Penelope into this Province here to inhabit as appears on record. *Note:
The patent document does not specify the patenting county.*

Bromton 4/21/1669 – 225a's. L11/225 SR7354
Location: Queen Annes County on the southern side of the Chester River in
the woods beginning at a marked Oak. *Note 1: This is a certification. A note
in the margin of the certification document states that the tract was "lett
fall". Note 2: This certification was issued by Talbot County.*

Brampton 1/10/1670 - 250a's. L14/148 SR7356
Location: Queen Annes County on the southern side of the Chester River in
the woods. Adjoins **George Read's** tract of land called Reading. *Note: This
patent was issued by Talbot County.*

Chesterfield 1/10/1670 – 400a's. L14/149 SR7356
Location: Queen Annes County on the southern side of the Chester River on
the northern side of Corsica Creek extending to the mouth of Alder Branch.
Note: This patent was issued by Talbot County.

Chesterfield 5/1/1672 – 900a's. L14/471 SR7356
Location: Queen Annes County on the southern side of the Chester River on
Corsica Creek beginning at a marked Oak standing by a forke of the s'd
creek. *Note: This patent was issued by Talbot County.*

Hemsleys Britland 9/4/1674 - 500a's. L18/206 SR7359
Location: Queen Annes County on the eastern side of the Chester River
beginning at a marked Oak of **John** and **William Coursey's** tract of land
called Courseys Town. *Note: This patent was issued by Talbot County.*

Anthrapp 9/15/1674 - 400a's. L18/213 SR7359
Location: Queen Annes County on the eastern side of the Chester River on
the Eastern Branch at a forke on a point extending to Hambleton's Branch.
Note: This patent was issued by Talbot County.

Hemsley 7/12/1676 – 300a's. L19/407 SR7360
Location: Queen Annes County on the southern side of the Chester River on
a branch of Courseys Creek. Adjoins **Desborough Bennett's** tract of land

called Forrest Lodge. *Note 1: This is a certification. No patent was found. Note 2: This certification was issued by Talbot County.*

Plain Dealing 8/1681 - 600a's. L21/303 SR7362
Location: Queen Annes County on the eastern side of the Chester River at the head near the Lower Road going to Delaware.
Other persons mentioned: Land rights assigned by **Thomas Vaughan.**
Note 1: This is a certification. No patent was found. Note 2: This certification was issued by Talbot County.

Triangle 5/5/1694 - 55a's. B23i/138 SR7365
Location: Queen Annes County on the northern side of Bread and Cheese Branch of the Wye River near the Indian Bridge. Adjoins **Stephen Whetstones'** tract of land called Whetstone. *Note: This is a certification issued by Talbot County. No patent was found.*

The Farme 2/6/1688 – 348a's. NSBi/673 SR7370
Location: Queen Anne County at the head of the Wye River at the head of the Indian Bridge Branch. Adjoins **John Brownes'** tract of land. *Note: This patent was issued by Talbot County.*

The Addition 3/1/1688 – 63a's. NSBi/669 SR7370
Location: Queen Annes County at the head of the Wye River on the eastern side of Bread and Cheese Creek on the eastern side of Indian Bridge Branch. Adjoins **John Wright's** tract of land called Skipton. *Note: This patent was issued by Talbot County.*

Roadley 12/24/1694 - 200a's. B23i/35 SR7365
Location: Queen Annes County between the branches of Tuckahoe Creek beginning at a bound tree of **John Davis'** tract of land called Davis Range. *Note: This patent was issued by Talbot County.*

Hemsleys Britania 1694 - 600a's. C3i/197 SR7377
Location: Queen Annes County between Wye Branch of Tuckahoe Creek beginning at the first bound tree of a tract of land called Nobles Meadows. Also adjoins **Warner Suddall** and **Robert Smith's** tract called Normanton and tracts called Costins Choice and Botts Choice.
Other persons mentioned: Land rights assigned by **Joseph Green** assignee of **Vincent Lowe.** Additional rights assigned by **Philemon Hemsley.** *Note: The patent document does not specify the patenting county.*

Friendship 11/10/1695 – 89a's. BB3B/6 SR7374
Location: Queen Annes County on the southern side of the Chester River on the eastern side of Unicorn Branch. Adjoins **George Robotham's** tract of

land called Robothams Parke. *Note: This patent was issued by Talbot County.*

Hemsleys Arcadia 11/10/1695 – 1,030a's. BB3B/364 SR7374
Location: Queen Annes County on a branch of the Wye River called Williams Branch extending to the head of Hobbs Creek. Adjoins **Henry Costin's** tracts called Newington and Lambeth, **Philemon Lloyd** and Henry Costin's tract called Lloyds Costin, and a tract called Birdland. *Note: This patent was issued by Talbot County.*

Plain Dealing 11/10/1695 – 175a's. C3i/141 SR7377
Location: Queen Annes County on the western side of the Southeast Branch of the Chester River adjoining **Thomas Carmen** and **William Burton's** tract of land called Carmen and Burton. Also adjoins **Daniel Jenefer's** tract called Spread Eagle. *Note: This patent was issued by Talbot County.*

Hemsleys Brittland 5/3/1696 – 140a's. BB3B/4 SR7374
Location: Queen Annes County on the western side of the Back Wye River on the northern side of Smiths Cove. Adjoins a tract of land called Sadlers Necke. *Note: This patent was issued by Talbot County.*

Mears Gate 9/10/1714 - 300a's. PL4i/261 SR7463
Location: Queen Annes County on the eastern side of Morgans Creek in the woods. Adjoins **Robert Wilton's** tract of land. *Note: The patent document does not specify the patenting county.*

Hewit, Robert
  Crany Neck 10/16/1651 - 400a's. AB&H/143 SR7344
  Location: Queen Annes County on Kent Island on Crany Neck bounded by Crany Creek and the Chesapeake Bay. Adjoins **Edward Commins'** *(recently deceased)* tract of land called Point Love. *Note 1: This is a certification issued by St. Marys County. The tract was patented by **Hugh Lee** and his wife **Hannah** in 1651 (LAB&H/224 SR7344).*

Hill, William, Planter
  Hills Lott 1/10/1666 – 200a's. L9/443 SR7351
  Location: Queen Annes County on the southern side of the Chester River on Island Creek beginning at a marked Oak of **Samuel Winslow's** tract of land called Mount Hope. *Note: This patent was issued by Talbot County.*

Gunners Harbour 8/1/1672 - 100a's. L17/262 SR7358
Location: Queen Annes County on the southern side of the Chester River on the western side of Corsica Creek in the woods. *Note: This patent was issued by Talbot County.*

Himes, Isaac
Claypot Neck 12/22/1652 - 100a's. AB&H/295 SR7344
Location: Queen Annes County on the eastern side of Kent Island on Clay
Pot Neck of Coxes Creek beginning at a marked Pine standing at the head of
Hines Swamp. *Note: This is a certification issued by St. Marys County. No
patent was found.*

Hinson, John
Hinsons Towne Addition 5/27/1667 - 100a's. L10/518 SR7352
Location: Queen Annes County on the eastern side of Hinson Town Creek
adjoining **Thomas Hinson's** tract called Hinsontown.
Other persons mentioned: Land rights assigned by **Thomas Hinson**, father of
John. *Note: This patent was issued by Talbot County.*

Hinson, Nathaniel
Syllin 6/17/1698 - 200a's. CC4i/ 98 SR7375
Location: Queen Annes County on the eastern side of Kent Island bounded
on the west by the Chesapeake Bay. Adjoins **Phillip Conners'** tract of land
called The Woodland Thickett and **Elizabeth Commins'** tract called Point
Love. *Note: This patent was issued by Kent County. The patent document
contains legal details and should be read by anyone interested in this land or
in the people named including **George** and **Margaret Hall.***

Hinson, Thomas, Planter
Hinson Town 2/15/1659 – 400a's. L4/460 SR7346
Location: Queen Annes County on the eastern side of the Chester River on
the eastern side of Reeds Back Creek. *Note: The patent document does not
specify the patenting county.*

Shelington 4/20/1666 - 300a's. L9/339 SR7351
Location: Queen Annes County on the southern side of the Chester River on
the western side of Hinsontown Creek. Adjoins **Matthew Read's** tract of
land called Reading and **Thomas Hinson, Jr.'s** tract called Grays Inn.
Other persons mentioned: Land rights assigned by **Morgan Williams** due
him for transporting his wife **Dorothy, Richard Wyatt, Thomas Wingood,
Sarah Ranks***(could be Ramks),* **Edward Brown,** and **Richard Gray** into
this Province here to inhabit as appears on record. *Note: This patent was
issued by Talbot County.*

The Addition 6/30/1669 - 100a's. L12/398 SR7354
Location: Queen Annes County beginning at a bound tree of **Philemon
Hemsley's** tract of land called Fare Play.
Other persons mentioned; Land rights assigned by **Daniel Jenifer** assignee
of **Samuel Tilghman** due him for transporting **Ambrose Bally** and

Christopher Johnson into this Province here to inhabit as appears on record. *Note: This patent was issued by Talbot County.*

Hinsons Hills 9/6/1675 – 150a's. L19/167 SR7360
<u>Location</u>: Queen Annes County in the woods on the northern side of his own tract of land called Hinsons Addition. *Note 1: The location information is skimpy as it was for the adjoining tract. The tract is included because it may have been located in Queen Annes County. Note 2: This patent was issued by Talbot County.*

Hinson/Hynson, Thomas, Jr.
    Waltham 9/4/1665 – 100a's. L8/200 SR7350
    <u>Location</u>: Queen Annes County on the southern side of the Chester River on the southern side of Reeds Back Creek.
    <u>Other persons mentioned</u>: Land rights assigned by **John Singleton** and **Richard Jones.** *Note: This patent was issued by Talbot County.*

    Grayes Inn 5/29/1668 - 200a's. L11/451 SR7353
    <u>Location</u>: Queen Annes County on the southern side of the Chester River on the northern side of Winchester Creek beginning at a bound tree of **Daniell Walker's** tract of land called Cheshire.
    <u>Other persons mentioned</u>: Land rights assigned by **Thomas Hinson, Sr.** *Note: This patent was issued by Talbot County.*

Hollingsworth, Charles
    Smiths Forrest Addicon 11/10/1695 – 140a's. BB3B/354 SR7374
    <u>Location</u>: Queen Annes County on the southern side of the Chester River beginning at a bound tree of **Robert Smith's** tract of land called Smiths Forrest.
    <u>Other persons mentioned</u>: Land rights assigned by **Lawrence Knowles.** *Note: This patent was issued by Talbot County.*

Hollingsworth, John
    Clay Bankes 8/25/1664 – 50a's. SDA/385 SR7349
    <u>Location</u>: Queen Annes County on the eastern side of the Eastern Bay at the mouth of Gregory's Cove. *Note: This patent was issued by Talbot County.*

    Jerusalem 4/1/1686 – 400a's. NS2i/189 SR7371
    <u>Location</u>: Queen Annes County on the southern side of the Chester River beginning at a bound tree of **Thomas Impey's** tract of land called Kinvar Heath.
    <u>Other persons mentioned</u>: Land rights assigned by **Robert Smith.** *Note: This patent was issued by Talbot County.*

    Fox Harbor 5/8/1683 – 150a's. SDA/207 SR7369

Location: Queen Annes County on the southern side of the Chester River among the branches of Honeston Creek adjoining **Thomas Impey's** tract of land called Kinvar Heath, **William Bishop's** tract called Bishopton, and **Nicholas Cloud's** tracts called Clouds Adventure and Nollars Desire. Other persons mentioned: Land rights assigned by **Henry Parker.** *Note: This patent was issued by Talbot County.*

Hollingsworth, William, Planter
Solomans Friendship 5/14/1695 – 100a's. B23i/356 SR7365
Location: Queen Annes County on the southern side of Ellets Branch of the Chester River in the woods.
Other persons mentioned: Land rights assigned by **William Coursey.** *Note: This patent was issued by Talbot County.*

The Beginning 11/7/1709 - 100a's. DD5i/569 SR7378
Location: Queen Annes County on the southern side of the Chester River on Cabbin Branch. Adjoins **Nicholas Cloud's** tract of land called Clouds Adventure and **John Lillingston's** tract called Porters Lodge.
Other persons mentioned: Land rights assigned by **Robert Smith.** *Note: This patent was issued by Kent County.*

Hopkinson, Jonathan
Hopton 9/9/1668 - 320a's. L12/136 SR7354
Location: Queen Annes County
Other persons mentioned: Land rights assigned by **William Coursey.** *Note 1: This is a seldom-used form of abbreviated patent document that minimizes or excludes location information. This is included in the certification which, in this instance, was not found. Note 2: The patent document does not identify the patenting county.*

Horney, Geffrey
Dixon's Gift 11/7/1709 - 100a's. DD5i/569 SR7378
Location: Queen Annes County on the southern side of the Chester River on the western side of Unicorn Branch at Wilmers Fork. *Note: This patent was issued by Kent County.*

Houlton, Robert
Aulder Branch 1/20/1658 - 100a's. LQ/350 SR7345
Location: Queen Annes County on the eastern side of the Chester River on the eastern side of Corsica Creek at the mouth of Alder Branch.
Other persons mentioned: Houlton transported **himself** into this Province here to inhabit as appears on record. Additional acres assigned by **John Coursey.** *Note: The patent document does not specify the patenting county.*

Huett, Robert & Bellamy, Henry, Planters
Crany Neck 9/27/1640 - 400a's. L1/76 SR7341
Location: Kent Island between Crany Pond and Kent Mill in Crayford
Manor. *Note 1: This was an original **William Clayborn** grant (see forward).*
Note 2: This patent was issued by St. Marys County.

Hurlock, George & Costin, Henry, Planters
Costins Hope 3/10/1670 – 200a's. L14/192 SR7356
Location: Queen Annes County on the southern side of the Chester River on
the northern side of Corsica Creek beginning at a bound tree of **Henry
Coursey** and **Robert Hatton's** tract of land.
Other persons mentioned: Land rights assigned by **Francis Armstrong.**
Note: This patent was issued by Talbot County.

Hurlock, George
Yarntown 11/18/1685 – 200a's. L22/295 SR7363
Location: Queen Annes County on the southern side of the Chester River on
the northern side of Andover Branch adjoining **Nicholas Cloud's** tract of
land called Notlans Enjoyment. Also adjoins **Cornelius Comegys'** tract
called Timber Forke.
Other persons mentioned: Land rights assigned by **Robert Smith.** *Note 1:
This is a certification. No patent was found. Note 2: This certification was
issued by Talbot County.*

Husbands, Richard, Capt.
Elke Point Manor 1/20/1659 - 1,000a's. L4/303 SR7346
Location: Queen Annes County on the southern side of the Chester River on
the southern side of the easternmost branch on Elke Point. *Note 1: Land
rights based on Husbands transporting 21 unnamed persons into this
Province here to inhabit as appears on record. Note 2: The patent document
does not specify the patenting county.*

Impey, Thomas
Dellmore End 4/1/1686 – 500a's. NSBi/364 SR7370
Location: Queen Annes County on the southern side of the Chester River on
Salisbury Plaine by Andover Branch. *Note: This patent was issued by Talbot
County.*

Padan Aran 4/27/1686 – 500a's. L22/248 SR7363
Location: Queen Annes County on the southern side of the Chester River
between the Upper and Lower Fords. *Note 1: This is a certification. No
patent was found. Note 2: This certification was issued by Talbot County.*

Kinvar Heath 4/30/1686 – 500a's. L22/248 SR7363

Location: Queen Annes County on the southern side of the Main Branch of the Chester River above the Upper Ford. Adjoins **John Hollingsworth's** tracts of land called Fox Harbor and Jerusalem. *Note 1: This is a certification. No patent was found. Note 2: This certification was issued by Talbot County.*

Ingram, Thomas, Major
Ship Point 1/20/1668 - 100a's. L12/179 SR7354
Location: Queen Annes County on the southern side of Kent Island on the western side of Pickards Creek.
Other persons mentioned: Ingram transported **himself** and **Peter Walker** into this Province here to inhabit as appears on record. *Note: This patent was issued by Kent County.*

Jackson, John
Fortune 10/1/1683 – 100a's. SDA 243 SR7369
Location: Queen Annes County on the southern side of the Chester River in the woods beginning at a marked Oak of **Michael Powell Vandeford's** tract of land called Vandeford. Also adjoins **John Rodway** and **Walter Rowles'** tract called Bristoll Marsh and **Robert Smith's** tract called Smiths Reserve.
Other persons mentioned: Land rights assigned by **Richard Peacocke.**
Note: This patent was issued by Talbot County.

Jackson, Richard, Planter
Jacksons Choice 9/16/1664 - 300a's. L7/155 SR7349
Location: Queen Annes County. Two parcels on the Eastern Bay respecting Kent Island to the west on the northern side of Bugbyes Creek near two coves. Adjoins his own unnamed 100-acre tract of land. *Note: The patent document does not specify the patenting county. The tract is included in this volume because MSA Patent Index #55 places it in Queen Annes County.*

Unnamed Patent 9/16/1664 – 100a's. L7/455 SR7349
Location: Queen Annes County at the mouth of the Eastern Bay at the head of Bugbyes Creek. Adjoins his own tract of land called Jacksons Choice. *Note: The patent document does not specify the patenting county. The tract is included in this volume because MSA Patent Index #55 places it in Queen Annes County.*

Jacksons Choice 7/12/1677 – 100a's. L20/63 SR7361
Location: Queen Annes County at the head of Jenkins Creek beginning at a bound tree of **John Jenkins'** tract of land called Jenkins Neck. *Note: This patent was issued by Talbot County.*

Jackson, Thomas
Barbaras Choyce 9/10/1695 - 80a's. CC4i/62 SR7375

Location: Queen Annes County on the southern side of the Chester River at the mouth of Winchester Creek. Adjoins **Henry Parker's** tract of land called Winchester.

Other persons mentioned: Land rights assigned by **Philemon Lloyd.** *Note: This patent was issued by Talbot County.*

James, Edward
James Choice 1/1699 - 300a's. CC4i/134 SR7375
Location: Queen Annes County on the southern side of the Chester River at the head of the easternmost branch of Red Lyon Creek beginning at a bound Oak. Adjoins a tract of land called James Farme. *Note: This patent was issued by Kent County.*

Jenefer, Daniel
Land of the Prophecy 5/9/1666 – 500a's. L9/419 SR7351
Location: Queen Annes County on the southern side of the Chester River on the Southeast Branch of Dividing Creek *(also known as Island Creek)* beginning at a bound tree of **Andrew Skinner** and **Nathaniel Evetts'** tract of land called Waterford. Also adjoins **Robert Smith's** tract called Milland and **Joseph Smith's** tract called Heath's Discovery. *Note 1: Another patent dated 6/12/1688, was found ((NS2i/651 SR7371). Note 2: This patent was issued by Talbot County.*

Spread Eagle 6/10/1671 - 1,000a's. L15/187 SR7357
Location: Queen Annes County at the head of the Southeast Branch of the Chester River in the woods.
Other persons mentioned: Land rights assigned by **Charles Calvert** assignee of **Thomas Freeman** *(merchant)* due him for transporting **Daniell Holland, Desmond Meghend, Edmond Cannaday, Jeremiah Mahone, Charles Browne, Morris Welch, Jahaine Welch** *(no relationship indicated),* **Dernoot Deffecoate, Teague Callahone, Margarett Callahone** *(no relationship indicated),* **Ann Martin, Mortimer O'Brien, Delby Brian, John Hoolee, Jahain Sullivant, Darby Sullivant, James Sullivant** *(no relationship indicated),* **Dan Lynn, William Cinnisly,** and **James Kasey.** *Note: This patent was issued by Talbot County.*

Jenkins, John, Planter
Jenkins Neck 8/25/1665 – 250a's. L8/173 SR7350
Location: Queen Annes County to the north of Jenkins Creek to the east of the Chesapeake Bay respecting Parsons Point on Kent Island to the west. *Note: This patent was issued by Talbot County.*

Johnson, Albert
Alberts Delight 8/20/1683 – 200a's. SDA/326 SR7369

Location: Queen Anne County on the southern side of the Chester River on Hambletons Branch. Adjoins **John Breme's** tract of land called Jamaica. Other persons mentioned: Land rights assigned by **Richard Peacocke.** *Note: This patent was issued by Talbot County.*

Johnson, Henry
Johnsons Adventure 5/31/1696 – 100a's. BB3B/441 SR7374
Location: Queen Annes County on the southern side of the Chester River on a branch of Unicorn Branch.
Other persons mentioned: Land rights assigned by **Robert Smith.** *Note: This patent was issued by Talbot County.*

Johnson, John
Denbyes Addition 6/1/1687 – 27a's. NS2i/346 SR7371
Location: Queen Annes County on the southern side of Coursegalls Creek of the Chester River adjoining a tract of land called Denby. Also adjoins **Richard Jones'** tract called Jamaica and **Samuell Broadway's** tract called Ramah.
Other persons mentioned: Land rights assigned by **Vincent Lowe.** *Note: This patent was issued by Talbot County.*

Johnson, Odbert
Hope 5/2/1683 – 100a's. SDA/133 SR7369
Location: Queen Annes County on the southern side of the Chester River on Hamiltons Creek by the creekside.
Other persons mentioned: Land rights assigned by **Henry Parker.** *Note: This patent was issued by Talbot County.*

Jones, Daniel
The Lower Fords 10/1/1687 – 200a's. NS2i/586 SR7371
Location: Queen Annes County on the southern side of the Chester River at the mouth of Unicorn Branch on both sides of the Lower Road adjoining **Thomas Collins'** tract of land.
Other persons mentioned: Land rights assigned by **Richard Bennett.** *Note: This patent was issued by Talbot County.*

Jones, John
Barron Ridge Addition 8/1/1682 - 50a's. L22/16 SR7363
Location: Queen Annes County on Kent Island on the eastern side of Coxes Creek. Adjoins **John Wright's** tract of land called Barron Ridge and **Thomas Collins'** tract called Barron Range. *Note: This is a certification issued by Kent County. No patent was found.*

Jones Plott 5/10/1689 - 90a's. C3i/15 SR7377

Location: Queen Annes County on the eastern side of Kent Island on Great Thickety Creek extending to the eastern side of the Eastern Creek beginning at a bound Spanish Oak. Adjoins **William Joyner's** tract of land. *Note 1: This is a certification. The tract was patented by* **Francis Stevens** *on 10/5/1695 (C3i/16 SR7377). Note 2: This patent was issued by Kent County.*

Barron Ridge Addition 10/5/1695 - 60a's. C3i/9 SR7377
Location: Queen Annes County on Kent Island on Coxes Creek adjoining **Mark Benton's** tract of land. *Note 2: This patent was issued by Kent County.*

Jones Armour 10/5/1697 - 180a's. CC4i/31 SR7375
Location: Queen Annes County on the northern side of Williamses Branch of the Wye River by a road from Tuckahoe Bridge to Coar Sara Creek. Begins at a bound White Oak of **Phillemon Lloyd's** tract of land.
Other persons mentioned: Land rights assigned by **Richard Skinner.** *Note: This patent was issued by Talbot County.*

Jones, Richard
   Labor In Vain 10/1/1673 - 20a's. SDA 295 SR7369
   Location: Queen Annes County on the southern side of the Chester River on Hinsontown Creek. Adjoins **Robert Smith's** tract of land called Smiths Addition and his own tract called Jones Hall.
   Other persons mentioned: Land rights assigned by **Robert Smith.** *Note: This patent was issued by Talbot County.*

   Joanes Plackett 9/6/1675 -50a's. L19/179 SR7360
   Location: Queen Annes County in the woods near Hinsontown. Adjoins his own tract of land called Jones Addition. *Note 1: The certification L21/233 SR7362) shows the certified acres as 150. Note 2: This patent was issued by Talbot County.*

   Jones Plackett Addition 4/1679 - 150a's. L21/233 SR7362
   Location: Queen Annes County on the southern side of the Chester River near Hinson Towne. Adjoins his own tract of land called Jones Plackett, **Richard Tilghman's** tract called Tilghmans Addition, and the land of **Thomas Hinson.**
   Other persons mentioned: Land rights assigned by **Simon Wilmer.** *Note 1: This is a certification. No patent was found. Note 2: This certification was issued by Talbot County.*

   Jones Hall 8/16/1680 – 200a's. CB2i/30 SR7366
   Location: Queen Annes County on Hinsontown Branch of the Chester River. Adjoins **Richard Tilghman's** tract of land called Tilghmans Addition.

Other persons mentioned: Land rights assigned by **Mary Tilghman** executrix of the late Richard Tilghman. *Note: This patent was issued by Talbot County.*

Jones Addition 5/21/1681 – 50a's. L21/365 SR7362
Location: Queen Annes County on the southern side of the Chester River beginning at a bound tree of **David Fairbanks'** tract of land called Jones Hole. Also adjoins **Thomas Hinson's** tract called Hinsontown, **Soloman** and **Nathan Wright's** tract called Adventure, and his own tract called Jones Plackett.
Other persons mentioned: Land rights assigned by **Richard Peacock.** *Note 1: This is a certification. No patent was found. Note 2: This certification was issued by Talbot County.*

Adventure 5/24/1681 – 200a's. L21/339 SR7362
Location: Queen Annes County on the southern side of the Chester River on the northern side of Corsica Creek beginning at a bound tree of **Henry Green's** tract of land. Also adjoins the land of **Mathias Peterson.**
Other persons mentioned: Land rights assigned by **Thomas Jones.** *Note 1: This is a certification. The tract was patented by **Richard Jones, Jr.** on 10/5/1683 (CB3i/406 SR7367). Note: This certification was issued by Talbot County.*

Jones Fancy 8/9/1683 – 150a's. CB3i/326 SR7367
Location: Queen Annes County on the southern side of the Chester River in the woods beginning at a bound tree of **John Lillingstone's** tract of land called The Enjoyment.
Other persons mentioned: Land rights assigned by **Richard Peacock.** *Note: This patent was issued by Talbot County.*

Jones Park 8/10/1683 – 200a's. SDA/234 SR7369
Location: Queen Annes County on the southern side of the Chester River on the northern side of Corsica Creek in the woods beginning at a marked Red Oak. Adjoins **Robert Norris'** tract of land called Claxton Hills, **Robert Norrest's** tract called Norrests Addition, and **Thomas Collins'** tract called Colliston.
Other persons mentioned: Land rights assigned by **Richard Peacock.** *Note: This patent was issued by Talbot County.*

Spring Branch 8/10/1683 – 100a's. SDA/108 SR7369
Location: Queen Annes County on the southern side of the Chester River beginning at a marked White Oak of **John Rodway** and **Walter Rowells'** tract of land called Bristoll Marsh. Also adjoins **John Wilkenson's** tract called Waltham and **John Singleton** and **Robert Jones'** tract called Forlorn Hope.

<u>Other persons mentioned</u>: Land rights assigned by **Richard Peacocke.** *Note: This patent was issued by Talbot County.*

Denby 8/10/1683 – 250a's. SDA/123 SR7369
<u>Location</u>: Queen Annes County on the southern side of the Chester River in the woods adjoining **Henry Parker's** tract of land called Jamaica and **John Robinson's** tract called Jamaicas Addition.
<u>Other persons mentioned</u>: Land rights assigned by **Thomas Masterman.** *Note: This patent was issued by Talbot County.*

Jones Fortune 11/13/1683 – 100a's. IB&ILC/71 SR7368
<u>Location</u>: Queen Annes County on the southern side of the Chester River in the woods beginning at a bound tree of **Richard Tilghman's** tract of land called Tilghmans Addition. Also adjoins **Soloman** and **Nathaniel Wright's** tract called Adventure.
<u>Other persons mentioned</u>: Land rights assigned by **Richard Peacocke.** *Note: This patent was issued by Talbot County.*

Jamaica 3/1/1686 – 100a's. NSBi/309 SR7370
<u>Location</u>: Queen Annes County near a branch of Cousegall Creek in the woods beginning at a marked Red Oak. Adjoins **Robert Smith's** tract of land called Smithfield.
<u>Other persons mentioned</u>: Land rights assigned by Robert Smith. *Note: This patent was issued by Talbot County.*

Jones, Richard, Jr.
The Adventure 10/5/1683 - 200a's. CB3i/406 SR7367
<u>Location</u>: Queen Annes County on the southern side of the Chester River on the northern side of Corsica Creek adjoining tracts owned by **Henry Green** and **Mathias Peterson.**
<u>Other persons mentioned</u>: Land rights assigned by **Thomas Jones.** *Note: This patent was issued by Talbot County.*

Jones, Thomas
Jones Delight 1/18/1681 – 200a's. CB2i/441 SR7366
<u>Location</u>: Queen Annes County on the southern side of the Chester River in the woods at the head of a branch.
<u>Other persons mentioned</u>: Land rights assigned by **Robert Smith.** *Note: This patent was issued by Talbot County.*

Jones, William & Sides, Peter, Planters
Planters Delight 7/9/1665 – 200a's. L9/121 SR7351
<u>Location</u>: Queen Annes County at the head of the Wye River in the woods. Adjoins **Robert Noble's** tract of land called Nobles Addition. *Note 1: This*

is a certification. Issued by Talbot County, The tract was paten ed by William Jones on 8/1/1673(L15/126 SR4327).

Dobbs Creek 9/12/1665 – 550a's. L8/243 SR7350
Location: Queen Annes County on the North Branch of the Wye River adjoining **John Wright's** tract of land. Also adjoins **Roger Grosses** tract called Abbington and **Thomas Williams'** tract called Wilton.
Other persons mentioned: Land rights assigned by **Roger Gross.** Additional rights assigned by **John Watkins** due him for transporting **Samuel Birchfield, Robert Ward, Richard Harrisson,** and **Alice Fisher** into this Province here to inhabit as appears on record. *Note: This patent was issued by Talbot County.*

Jones, William, Planter
Planters Delight 8/1/1673 - 200a's. L15/126 SR4327
Location: Queen Annes County at the head of the Wye River one-half mile from the waterside.
Other persons mentioned: Land rights assigned by **Matthew Ward.** *Note: This patent was issued by Talbot County.*

Joyner, William
Coopers Hill 10/1680 - 100a's. L22/15 SR7363
Location: Queen Annes County on Kent Island on the southern side of Long Creek beginning at a marked Oak standing by the creekside. Adjoins **John Jones'** tract of land called Jones Plott.
Other persons mentioned: Land rights assigned by **Bryan Omaly.** *Note: This patent was issued by Kent County.*

Kent, Thomas
Unnamed Patent 5/7/1641 - 100a's. L1/112 SR7341
Location: Queen Annes County on the eastern side of Kent Island in Crayford Manor bounded by Shirts Branch of Coxes Bay near Butlers Marsh, where he now lives. *Note: This patent was issued by St. Marys County.*

Kerbey/Kerby, Walter
Ashford 10/29/1680 - 100a's. L22/15 SR7363
Location: Queen Annes County on Kent Island on the southern side of Long Creek extending to the Eastern Creek. Adjoins **William Joyner's** tract of land called Coopers Hiss and the land of **James Rigbie.**
Other persons mentioned: Land rights assigned by **Henry Parker.** *Note: This is a certification issued by Kent County. No patent was found.*

Kerbys Addition 6/10/1681 - 50a's. L22/15 SR7363
Location: Queen Annes County on Kent Island near the Main Branch of Long Creek running out of Wading Place Bay.

64

Other persons mentioned: Land rights assigned by **Henry Parker.** *Note: This is a certification issued by Kent County. No patent was found.*

Kerbeys Prevention 10/5/1695 - 50a's. B23i/360 SR7365
Location: Queen Annes County on Kent Island beginning at a marked Pine standing near the Wading Place.
Other persons mentioned: Land rights assigned by **Simon Williams.** *Note 1: The certification document does not specify the patenting county. Note 2: This is a certification. No patent was found.*

Keyne, Thomas
Hogpen Neck 12/10/1647 - 100a's. L1/78 SR7341
Location: Queen Annes Island on Kent Island in Crayford Manor on Hogpen Neck of Hogpen Creek extending to Thicketty Creek on the west. *Note: This patent was issued by St Marys County.*

Knowles, Lawrence & Collins, Thomas
Partners Help 11/10/1695 – 400a's. WD/98 SR7372
Location: Queen Annes County on the southern side of the Chester River in a forke of Unicorn Branch on the western side of the Main Branch. *Note: This patent was issued by Talbot County.*

The Partnership 11/10/1695 - 400a's. C3i/236 SR7377
Location: Queen Annes County on the eastern side of the Chester River on the western side of a forke of Unicorn Branch on Finnell Hill. *Note: This patent was issued by Talbot County.*

Knowles, Lawrence
Knowles Range 9/9/1685 - 500a's. Nsbi/253 SR7370
Location: Queen Annes County on the eastern side of the Chester River on the northern side of Unicorn Branch. Adjoins **Thomas Collins'** tract of land called Kellmanan Plaines and **George Robotham's** tract called Robothams Parke. *Note: This patent was issued by Talbot County.*

Lancaster, John
Lancaster 4/10/1709 - 119a's. DD5i/525 SR7378
Location: Queen Annes County on the southern side of the Chester River by Green Swamp beginning at a bound tree of **Thomas Brostrick's** tract of land called Northumberland.
Other persons mentioned: Land rights assigned by **Edward Elliott** assignee of **George Haddoway.** *Note: This patent was issued by Kent County.*

Land, Phillip & Fox Gregory, Planters
The Rich Neck 10/20/1651 - 1,000a's. AB&AH/397 SR7344

Location: Queen Annes County on Kent Island on Rich Neck beginning at a bound tree standing on Marshy Point adjoining a neck of land called The Wading Place.
Other persons mentioned: Land rights assigned by former owner **Will Mitchell**. *Note: This patent was issued by St. Marys County.*

The Wading Place 10/21/1651 - 1,000a's. AB&AH/397 SR7344
Location: Queen Annes County on the eastern side of Kent Island respecting a neck of land called The Wading Place.
Other persons mentioned: Land rights assigned by former owner **Will Mitchell**. *Note: This patent was issued by Kent County.*

Lane, John

Charleville 1/5/1681 – 150a's. CB2i/460 SR7366
Location: Queen Annes County on a branch of Tuckahoe Creek adjoining his own tract of land called Corke. *Note: This patent was issued by Talbot County.*

Corke 11/13/1683 – 100a's. NSBi/64 SR7370
Location: Queen Annes County on a branch of Tuckahoe Creek adjoining his own tract of land called Charleville.
Other persons mentioned: Land rights assigned by **Richard Peacock**. *Note: This patent was issued by Talbot County.*

Lawrance, William

Forlorn Hope 8/20/1683 - 100a's. SDA/55 SR7369
Location: Queen Annes County on Kent Island on Hogpen Creek near the mouth adjoining **William Ellet's** tract of land called Ellets Choice. Also adjoins **Brent Giles'** tract called Kent Point Manor and the land of **Edward Burton**.
Other persons mentioned: Land rights assigned by **Thomas Courtnay** assignee of **John Shingleton** due him for transporting **himself** and wife **Mary** into this Province here to inhabit as appears on record. *Note: The patent document does not specify the patenting county.*

Lee, Hugh & Hannah

Crany Neck 10/16/1651 - 400a's. AB&H/224 SR7344
Location: Queen Annes County on Kent Island on Crany Creek. Adjoins **Edward Commins'** unnamed 100-acre tract of land.
Other persons mentioned: Hannah Lee is the widow of former owner **Robert Hewett**. *Note 1: Another patent was found (AB&H/233 SR7344). Note 2: This patent was issued by St. Marys County.*

Legg, William

The Adventure 7/27/1680 - 50a's. L22/14 SR7363

Location: Queen Annes County on Kent Island on the eastern side of the Northeast Creek. *Note 1: This is a certification. The tract was assigned to* **Lewis Meredit** *(same reference). No patent was found. Note 2: This certification was issued by Kent County.*

Lewis, Thomas
Lewis Chance 10/1/1683 – 50a's. SDA/187 SR7369
Location: Queen Annes County on the southern side of the Chester River on the southern side of Corsica Creek on Bogues Branch beginning at a bound tree of **Robert Macklin's** tract of land called The Reward. Also adjoins **John Bogue's** tract called Boguely.
Other persons mentioned: Land rights assigned by **Richard Peacock** assignee of **Simon Wilmer.** *Note: This patent was issued by Talbot County.*

Lillingston/Lillingstone, John
Lillingstons Castle 4/27/1683 - 500a's. CB3i/253 SR 7367
Location: Queen Annes County on the southern side of the Chester River on the southern side of the Main Branch of Double Creek. Adjoins **Matthew Ward's** tract of land called Ward Park.
Other persons mentioned: Land rights assigned by **Robert Smith.** *Note: This patent was issued by Talbot County.*

Porters Lodge 10/1/1683 – 300a's. SDA/286 SR7369
Location: Queen Annes County on the southern side of the Chester River beginning at a bound tree of the **Lord Proprietor's** tract of land called His LOP's Manor. Also adjoins **William Hollingsworth's** tract called The Beginning. *Note: This patent was issued by Talbot County.*

Berkes 11/13/1683 - 200a's. NS2i/393 SR7371
Location: Queen Annes County on the southern side of the Chester River on the western side of Double Creek beginning at a bound tree of a tract of land called Wardes Park. *Note: This patent was issued by Talbot County.*

Lillingstons Castle Addition 8/10/1684 - 350a's. NSBi/49 SR7370
Location: Queen Annes County on the eastern side of the Chester River on Double Creek. Begins at a marked Red Oak of his own tract of land called Lillingstons Castle. *Note: This patent was issued by Talbot County.*

The Enjoyment 8/10/1684 – 300a's. NS2i/394 SR7371
Location: Queen Annes County on the southern side of the Chester River beginning at a marked Pokehikary in the south line of a tract of land called Mount Pleasant. Also adjoins **Richard Jones'** tract called Jones Fancy. *Note: This patent was issued by Talbot County.*

Lloyd, Alice
Lloyds Meadows 10/10/1703 – 334a's. DD5i/117 SR7378
Location: Queen Annes County at the head on the southern side of Thomas
Branch of the Wye River. Adjoins **John Green's** tract of land called Greens
Adventure and **Philemon Hemsley's** tract called Hemsleys Reserve.
Other persons mentioned: Land rights assigned by **William Coursey**. *Note:
This patent was issued by Talbot County.*

Lloyd, Edward
Long Neglect 11/10/1697 – 133a's. CDi/29 SR7376
Location: Queen Annes County on a cove of the Wye River adjoining
Christopher Santee's tract of land called Knaves Stand Off. Also adjoins
his own tract called Linton.
Other persons mentioned: Land rights assigned by **Philemon Lloyd** deceased
father of Edward. *Note: This patent was issued by Talbot County.*

Meersgate Addition 11/10/1697 – 267a's. CDi/28 SR7376
Location: Queen Annes County on Doctors Branch of the Wye River
beginning at a bound tree **Ennion Williams'** tract of land called Ennion's
Lott. Also adjoins **Nathaniel Cleve's** tract called Nathaniels Point and a tract
called Meersgate.
Other persons mentioned: Land rights assigned by **Philemon Lloyd** deceased
father of Edward. *Note: This patent was issued by Talbot County.*

Lloyd, Henrietta Maria
Batchellors Plaines 11/10/1695 – 216a's. C3i/408 SR7377
Location: Queen Annes County on the southern side of the Chester River on
the eastern side of Corsica Creek. Adjoins **Thomas Collins'** tract of land
called Kellmanan Plaines.
Other persons mentioned: Land rights assigned by **John Lundy,** deceased.
Note: This patent was issued by Talbot County.

Johns Forrest 11/10/1695 – 200a's. C3i/406 SR7377
Location: Queen Annes County on the southern side of the Chester River on
the western side of Unicorn Branch. Adjoins **Thomas Smithson's** tract of
land called Reviving Springs.
Other persons mentioned: Land rights assigned by **John Lundy,** deceased.
Note: This patent was issued by Talbot County.

Lloyd, Philemon & Costin, Henry
Loyds Costin 11/10/1685 – 500a's. NSBi/229 SR7370
Location: Queen Annes County on the Wye River between Dobbs Branch
and Williams Branch. Adjoins **William Hemsley's** tract of land called
Hemsleys Arcadia.

<u>Other persons mentioned</u>: Land rights assigned by **Henry Parker.** *Note: This patent was issued by Talbot County.*

Lloyd/Loyd, Philemon
  Loyds Freshes 3/8/1679 – 1,000a's. L21/232 SR7362
  <u>Location</u>: Queen Annes County on the southern side of the Chester River on the northern side of the Southeast Branch beginning at a bound tree of **John Walters'** tract of land. Also adjoins the Lord Proprietor's tract called His Lops Manor. *Note 1: This is a certification. No patent was found. Note 2: This certification was issued by Talbot County.*

  Loyds Meadows 10/22/1680 - 600a's. CB2i/106 SR7366
  <u>Location</u>: Queen Annes County among the branches of the Back Wye River on the Northeast Branch near the crossing of Tuckahoe and Coursefield Roads. *Note: The patent document does not specify the patenting county.*

  The Addition 10/22/1680 – 600a's. CB2i/106 SR7366
  <u>Location</u>: Queen Annes County among the branches at the head of the Wye River on the Northeast Branch at the crossing of Tuckahoe and Coursefield Roads. *Note: This patent was issued by Talbot County.*

  Rosseth 1681 – 350a's. CB2i/497 SR7366
  <u>Location</u>: Queen Annes County at the head of branches of the Wye River beginning at bound tree of **George Prowse's** tract of land called Prout Park. Also adjoins **William Smith's** tract called Kelding. *Note: This patent was issued by Talbot County.*

  Meersgate Addition 8/10/1684 – 69a's. L22/317 SR7363
  <u>Location</u>: Queen Annes County on the southern side of the Wye River in the woods adjoining **Nathaniel Clave's** tract of land called Nathaniel's Point. Also adjoins a tract called Meersgate. *Note 1: This is a certification. No patent was found. Note 2: This certification was issued by Talbot County.*

  Lloyd Town 10/11/1684 - 1,000a's. SDA/513 SR7369
  <u>Location</u>: Queen Annes County on the northern side of Manour Branch of the Chester River in the woods.
  <u>Other persons mentioned</u>: Land rights assigned by **Richard Swan** *(deceased). Note: This patent was issued by Talbot County.*

  Cedar Point 10/23/1684 – 48a's. L22/317 SR7363
  <u>Location</u>: Queen Annes County on the Wye River in the woods on Beare Point beginning at the first bound tree of **Edward Lloyd's** tract of land called Linton. *Note 1: This is a certification. No patent was found. Note 2: This certification was issued by Talbot County.*

Long Neglect 1687 – 133a's. L22/318 SR7363
Location: Queen Annes County beginning at a bound tree of **Christopher Santee's** tracts of land called Santee and Knaves Standoff. Also adjoins **Edward Lloyd's** tract called Linton. *Note 1: This is a certification. No patent was found. Note 2: This certification was issued by Talbot County.*

Darland 1/18/1681– 400a's. CB2i/427 SR7366
Location: Queen Annes County between the head of the Wye River and branches of Corsica Creek on Thomas His Branch. Adjoins **James Magregor's** tract of land called The Welch Ridge. *Note: This patent was issued by Talbot County.*

Carters Inheritance Res. 10/20/1709 – 400a's. DD5i/540 SR7378
Location: Queen Annes County on the southern side of the Wye River on the eastern side of Indian Creek. *Note 1: This tract was formerly patented by* ***Richard Carter*** *in 1667, for 300 acres (L22/133 SR7363). The resurvey resulted in an increase of 100 acres. Note: This resurvey was issued by Talbot County.*

Lombard, Francis & Jones, William, Planters
The Cabbin Neck 8/16/1650 – 350a's. AB&H/108 SR7344
Location: Queen Annes County on Kent Island in Alder Swamp on the western side at the head of Little Pine Creek extending to Cabbin Creek. Other persons mentioned: Lombard transported **himself** and **Captain Robert Vaughn** into this Province here to inhabit as appears on record. Additional rights assigned by **Mary Richbrooke.** *Note 1: This is a certification. No patent was found. Note 2: This certification was issued by St. Marys County.*

Londey, John
Waterford 3/2/1688 – 200a's. NSBi/676 SR73370
Location: Queen Annes County on the southern side of the Chester River on Pearles Creek. *Note: This patent was issued by Talbot County.*

Woodhouse 3/2/1688 – 300a's. NSBi/675 SR7370
Location: Queen Annes County in a small forke of Unicorn Branch on the southern side of the Chester River. Adjoins **Henry Costin's** tract of land called Lambeth. *Note: This patent was issued by Talbot County.*

Lovely, Deliverance, Planter
Lovely 2/15/1659 - 200a's. L4/469 SR7346
Location: Queen Annes County on the northern side of the St. Michaels River on the western side at the head of Morgans Creek by a marsh. *Note: The patent document does not specify the patenting county. The tract is included because MSA Patent Index #55 places it in Queen Annes County.*

Lowder, Charles

Constantinople 10/01/1701 - 100a's. WD/336 SR7372
<u>Location</u>: Queen Annes County on the southern side of the Chester River on the eastern side of Red Lyon Branch beginning at a bound Oak of **William Crump** and **Richard Jones'** tract of land called Shrewsbury.
<u>Other persons mentioned</u>: Land rights assigned by **David Teal.** *Note: This patent was issued by Kent County.*

The Forke 4/10/1709 - 200a's. DD5i/557 SR7378
<u>Location</u>: Queen Annes County on the southern side of the Chester River on a fork of Red Lyon Branch of Davenports Branch beginning at a bound tree of **Humphrey Davenport's** land.
<u>Other persons mentioned</u>: Land rights assigned by **Edward Elliott** and **George Haddoway.** *Note: This patent was issued by Kent County.*

Chance 11/7/1709 - 66a's. DD5i/556 SR73778
<u>Location</u>: Queen Annes County on the southern side of the Chester River on Red Lyon Branch adjoining a tract of land called James His Chance. Also adjoins his own tract called Constantinople.
<u>Other persons mentioned</u>: Land rights assigned by **Edward Elliott** assignee of **George Haddoway.** *Note: This patent was issued by Kent County.*

Lowe, Vincent

Okutharpe 2/12/1673 - 1,000a's. L17/432 SR7358
<u>Location</u>: Queen Annes County on the eastern side of a fresh runn of Tuckahoe Creek. *Note 1: This is a certification. No patent was found. Note 2: This certification was issued by Talbot County.*

Brimington 6/20/1677 – 300a's. L19/490 SR7360
<u>Location</u>: Queen Annes County on the southern side of the Chester River in the woods. Adjoins **George Read's** tract of land called Readbourne. *Note: This patent was issued by Talbot County.*

The Adventure 1679 - 1,700a's. L21/286 SR7362
<u>Location</u>: Queen Annes County on the Chester River at the head of the Northeast Branch. *Note 1: This is a certification. No patent was found. Note 2: This patent was issued by Talbot County.*

The Beginning 9/10/1681 – 500a's. CB2i/250 SR7366
<u>Location</u>: Queen Annes County on the southern side of the Chester River at the head of the Northwest Branch beginning at a marked Chesnutt.
<u>Other persons mentioned</u>: Land rights assigned by **William Bishop.** *Note: This patent was issued by Talbot County.*

Chesterfield 9/15/1681 – 500a's. CB2i/251 SR7366

Location: Queen Annes County at the southern side at the head of the Chester River on the Northwest Branch in the woods. Adjoins his own tract of land called The Addition.
Other persons mentioned: Land rights assigned by **Henry Parker** assignee of **Anthony Maile.** *Note: This patent was issued by Talbot County.*

The Addition 9/16/1681 - 500a's. CB2i/253 SR7366
Location: Queen Annes County on the southern side of the Chester River on the Northwest Branch at the head. Adjoins his own tract of land called Chesterfield.
Other persons mentioned: Land rights assigned by **William Bishop.** *Note: This patent was issued by Talbot County.*

Expectation 4/11/1683 – 300a's. CB3i/207 SR7367
Location: Queen Annes County on the southern side of the Chester adjoining His Lordships Manor. *Note: This certification was issued by Talbot County.*

Slaughterton 5/1/1683 – 500a's. CB3i/218 SR7367
Location: Queen Annes County on the southern side of the Chester River on Rousebys Branch. Adjoins **Christopher Rouseby's** tract of land called Rousebys Discovery.
Other persons mentioned: Land rights assigned by **George Conely** assignee of **John Slaughter** *(former owner). Note: This patent was issued by Talbot County.*

Lowes Arcadia 8/10/1683 – 1,000a's. CB3i/377 SR7367
Location: Queen Annes County on the southern side of the Chester River on the southwest side of Island Creek. Adjoins **Robert Smith's** tract of land called Stoke. *Note: This patent was issued by Talbot County.*

Unnamed Patent 8/10/1684 - 300a's. SDA/504 SR7369
Location: Queen Annes County on the southern side of the Chester River beginning at a marked Oake of the Lord Proprietor's tract of land called His LOPS Manor. *Note: This patent was issued by Kent County.*

Lowes Desire 8/10/1683 - 1,500a's. CB3i/292 SR7367
Location: Queen Annes County on the southern side of the Chester River on the northern side of Red Lyon Branch beginning at a bound tree of **John Slater's** tract of land. *Note: This patent was issued by Talbot County.*

Lundy, John
Johns Forrest 4/7/1687 – 200a's. L22/340 SR7363
Location: Queen Annes County on the southern side of the Chester River on the western side of Unicorn Branch beginning at a bound tree of **Thomas Smithson's** tract of land called Reviving Springs.

Other persons mentioned: Land rights assigned by **Robert Ellis**. *Note 1: This is a certification. The tract was patented by **Henrietta Maria Lloyd** in 1695 (C3i/406 SR7377). Note 2: This certification was issued by Talbot County.*

Batchellors Plaines 5/13/1687 – 216a's. L22/340 SR7363
Location: Queen Annes County on the southern side of the Chester River on the eastern side of Unicorn Branch. Adjoins **Thomas Collins'** tract of land called Kellmanam.
Other persons mentioned: Land rights assigned by **Robert Smith**. *Note 1: This is a certification. The tract was patented by **Henrietta Maria Lloyd** in 1695 (C3i/4078 SR7377). Note 2: This certification was issued by Talbot County.*

Lundy 9/1/1687 – 200a's. NS2i/462 SR7371
Location: Queen Annes County on the southern side of the Chester River on the southern side of Red Lyon Branch by the branchside. *Note: This patent was issued by Talbot County.*

Macklin/Macklyn, Robert
Macklin 1/7/1658 - 100a's. LQ/255 SR7345
Location: Queen Annes County on the southern side of the Chester River on the eastern side of Courseys Creek beginning at the northernmost bound tree of **James Bowling's** tract of land called Bowlingsley. Also adjoins **Robert Smith's** tract called The Adventure. *Note 1: Land rights based on Macklin transporting **himself** into this Province here to inhabit as appears on record. Note 2: This patent was issued by Kent County.*

The Reward 1/17/1658 - 400a's. LQ/305 SR7345
Location: Queen Annes County on the eastern side of the Chester River on the southern side of Corsica Creek of the Eastern Bay on Bogues Branch beginning at a marked Cedar. Adjoins **John Boage's** tract of land called Boagley. *Note: This patent was issued by Kent County.*

Macklinburg 1/4/1659 - 400a's. L4/296 SR7346
Location: Queen Annes County on the eastern side of the Chester River beginning at a bound tree standing at the mouth of Herring Creek it being the northeast bound tree of **George Read's** tract of land.
Other persons mentioned: Land rights assigned by **John Baxter** due him for transporting **himself** and his **wife** into this Province here to inhabit as appears on record. Additional rights assigned by **William Jackson** and **Nicholas Gwyther**. *Note: The patent document does not specify the patenting county.*

Macklins Fancy 12/14/1682 – 500a's. L10/495 SR7352

Location: Queen Annes County on the southern side of the Chester River in the woods on Red Lyon Branch beginning at a marked White Oak.
Other persons mentioned: Land rights assigned by **Richard Peacocke.** *Note 1: This is a certification. No patent was found. Note 2: This certification was issued by Talbot County.*

Yarmouth 12/14/1682 – 100a's. L21/492 SR7362
Location: Queen Annes County on the southern side of the Chester River on the southern side of the Main Branch of Corsica Creek.
Other persons mentioned: Land rights assigned by **Richard Peacocke.** *Note: This patent was issued by Talbot County.*

Macklins Beginning 11/13/1683 - 400a's. NSBi/66 SR7370
Location: Queen Annes County on the southern side of the Chester River on the southern side of Red Lyon Branch beginning at a marked White Oak.
Other persons mentioned: Land rights assigned by Deputy Surveyor **Richard Peacocke.** *Note: This patent was issued by Talbot County.*

Ashburys Addition 5/25/1696 – 35a's. BB3B/433 SR7374
Location: Queen Annes County on the easternmost side of Kent Island at the head of Piney Creek. Adjoins **Francis Ashbury's** tract of land called Pascoes Adventure.
Other persons mentioned: Land rights assigned by **Philemon Hemsley.** *Note: This patent was issued by Talbot County.*

Macklyne, Robert, Jr.
Macklynes Addition 4/26/1695 – 36a's. C3i/136 SR7377
Location: Queen Annes County on the southern side of the Chester River on the southern side of Corsica Creek at Macklynes Cove. Begins at a marked Cedar of his own tract of land called The Reward. *Note 1: Another patent showing the owners name as Macklin was found (WD/101 SR7372 - 11/10/1685). Note: This patent was issued by Talbot County.*

Magregor, James, Planter
The Welsh Ridge 7/24/1673 – 500a's. L17/197 SR7358
Location: Queen Annes County on the southern side of the Chester River at the head of Corsica Creek beginning at a marked Poplar of **William Smith's** tract of land called Smiths Ridge. Also adjoins **Humphrey Davenport's** tract called Welsh Ridge Addition.
Other persons mentioned: Magregor transported **himself, Hugh Magregor, William Magregor** *(no relationships indicated),* **James Lovell, Thomas Smith, William Host, Hugh Owens, James Morgan,** and **Thomas Ashley** into this Province here to inhabit as appears on record. *Note: This patent was issued by Talbot County.*

Marsh, Thomas, Deceased
Poplar Neck 5/12/1664 - 300a's. L6/313 SR7348
Location: Queen Annes County on Kent Island at the head of Smiths Branch of Poplar Creek. *Note 1: This is a certification. No patent was found. Note 2: The certification document does not specify the certifying county. The tract is included because MSA Patent Index #55 places it in Queen Annes County.*

Marshes Forbearance 10/1/1677 - 150a's. L19/572 SR7360
Location: Queen Annes County on Kent Island on Beaver Neck Creek extending to Phillpotts Creek.
Other persons mentioned: Marsh transported **Sammuell Freeman, Curtis Long,** and **Thomas Heckman** into this Province here to inhabit as appears on record. *Note: The patent document does not specify the patenting county.*

Marshall, Thomas, Mariner of Byford in the kingdom of England.
Purchase 8/1/1701 – 86a's. DD5i/031 SR7378
Location: Queen Annes County at the head of the Wye River at the head of a branch of Cabbin Creek. Adjoins **William Young's** tract of land called Youngs Chance. *Note: This patent was issued by Talbot County.*

Martin, Robert
Martins Neck 8/8/1650 - 100a's. AB&H/332 SR7344
Location: Queen Annes County on Kent Island on Pigg Quarter Creek extending to Martins Creek. *Note 1: Land rights based on Martin having transported **himself** into this Province here to inhabit in 1649, as appears on record. Note 2: This patent was issued by St. Marys County.*

Masters, Charles, Planter
The Bone Yard 1/26/1671 – 200a's. L13/99 SR7355
Location: Queen Annes County on the Wye River in the woods. Adjoins **Henry Hawkins'** tract of land.
Other persons mentioned: Land rights assigned by **John Pitt.** *Note: This patent was issued by Talbot County.*

Vine Yard 7/10/1671 – 250a's. L13/102 SR7355
Location: Queen Annes County on the Wye River in the woods beginning at a bound tree of **Henry Hawkins'** tract of land.
Other persons mentioned: Land rights assigned by **John Pitt.** *Note: This patent was issued by Talbot County.*

Maxwell, Alexander
Maxby 10/27/1665 – 100a's. L9/136 SR7351
Location: Queen Annes County on the southern side of the Chester River on the western side of Corsica Creek. Adjoins **William Hill's** tract of land

called Gunners Harbour. *Note1: This is a certification. No patent was found. Note 2: This certification was issued by Talbot County.*

Meconakin, John
George Codd 6/20/1688 - 100a's. AB&H/2 SR7354
Location: Queen Annes County on Kent Island on Eastern Creek. Adjoins **Robert Vaughan's** tract of land. *Note: This patent was issued by Kent County.*

The Eastern Island 6/20/1688 - 100a's. AB&H/1 SR7354
Location: Queen Annes County on Long Creek of Kent Island at the Wading Place Bay. *Note: This patent was issued by Kent Island.*

Medcalfe, William & Yewell/Yowell, Thomas, Planters
Goose Hill 9/25/1640 - 90a's. AB&H/85 SR7344
Location: Queen Annes County on the eastern side of Kent Island on New Hogpen Neck on the northern side of Pine Bay bounded by Coxes *(aka Long)* Creek and Ordinary Creek. *Note 1: This is an original **William Clayborn** grant (see forward). Note 2: This patent was issued by St. Marys County.*

Mattapax Neck 9/25/1640 - 220a's. AB&H/85 SR7344
Location: Queen Annes County on the eastern side of Kent Island on Mattapax Neck bound by Piney Creek, Mattapax Creek, Medcalf Branch, Cedar Branch, and Goose Harbor. *Note 1: Land rights based on **Medcalf** having transported **himself** into this Province here to inhabit as appears on record. Rights to 50 acres more assigned by **Yowell** due him for completing his time of service in this Province. Note 2: This is an original **William Clayborn** grant (see forward). Note 3: This patent was issued by St. Marys County.*

Goose Harbor - 9/26/1640 - 130a's. L1/81 SR7341
Location: Queen Annes County on Kent Island on Medcalf Branch of Mattapax Creek to the east of Goose Harbor. *Note 1: Land rights based on **Medcalf** having transported **himself** into this Province here to inhabit as appears on record and **Yewell** having completed his time of service in this Province. Note 2: This is a **William Clayborne** grant (see forward). Note 3: This patent was issued by St. Marys County.*

New Hogpen Neck 9/26/1640 - 150a's. L1/81 SR7341
Location: Queen Annes County on Kent Island on Pine Bay bounded by Coxes and Ordinary Creeks. *Note 1: Land rights based on **Medcalf** having transported **himself** into this Province here to inhabit as appears on record and **Yewell** having completed his time of service in this Province. Note 2:*

*This is a **William Clayborne** Grant (see forward). Note 3: This patent was issued by St. Marys County.*

Mitchell, John

Mitchells Addition 10/16/1670 – 200a's. L13/52 SR7355
Location: Queen Annes County on the southern side of the Chester River on the eastern side of Island Creek beginning at a bound tree of **Samuel Winslow's** tract of land called Tottenham. Also adjoins **Stephen Tully's** tract called Tullys Delight. *Note: This patent was issued by Talbot County.*

Mitchell, Will

Rich Neck 10/20/1651 - 1,000a's. LAB&H/143 SR7344
Location: Queen Annes County on Kent Island respecting Island Neck and Rich Neck beginning at marked Oak standing by Marshy Point. *Note 1: This is a certification issued by Kent County. The tract was patented by **Phillip Land** and **Gregory Fox** in 1651 (LAB&H/397 SR7344).*

Wading Place Neck 10/21/1651 - 1,000a's. AB&H/143 SR7344
Location: Queen Annes County on Wading Place Isle near Kent Island beginning at a marked Pine standing at the mouth of Marshy Creek. *Note: This is a certification issued by Kent County. No patent was found*

Moore, Alexander & Vaughan, William

Moorefields 10/1/1687 – 94a's. NS2i/594 SR7371
Location: Queen Annes County on a branch of the Wye River on the northern side of **John Dunn's** tract of land called Dunns Range beginning at a marked Hickory standing by Pokady Road Path. Also adjoins their own tract of land called Moorefields Addition.
Other persons mentioned: Land rights assigned by **Thomas Smithson.** *Note 1: This is a certification. No patent was found. Note 2: This certification was issued by Talbot County.*

Moorefields Addition 6/12/1688 – 30a's. NS2i/624 SR7371
Location: Queen Annes County on a branch of the Wye River on the northern side of **John Dunn's** tract of land called Dunns Range beginning at a marked Hickory standing by Pokady Road Path. Also adjoins their own tract of land called Moorefields.
Other persons mentioned: Land rights assigned by **Thomas Smithson.** *Note 1: This is a certification. No patent was found. Note 2: This certification was issued by Talbot County.*

Morgan, Evan, Planter

Cold Harbour 5/17/1666 – 100a's. L10/238 SR7352

Location: Queen Annes County on the northern side of the Wye River on a point by the riverside in the woods. *Note 1: This is a certification. No patent was found. Note 2: This certification was issued by Talbot County.*

Morgan, Henry
Indian Spring 8/17/1650 - 100a's. AB&H/131 SR7344
Location: Queen Annes County on Kent Island adjoining his dwelling plantation. *Note 1: Land rights based on Morgan having transported **himself** into this Province here to inhabit in 1637. Note 2: This is a seldom-used form of abbreviated patent document that minimizes or excludes location information. This is included in the certification which, in this instance, was not found. Note 3: This patent was issued by St. Marys County.*

Unnamed Patent 8/17/1650 - 300a's. AB&H/108 SR7344
Location: Queen Annes County on Kent Island beginning at a bound Oak standing by the head of Long Creek in the woods. Adjoins his own unnamed 100-acre tract and **John Medcalfe's** land.
Other persons mentioned: **Morgan** transported his **wife** and servant **Henry Thomas** into this Province here to inhabit in 1649, as appears on record. *Note 1: This may have been an original **William Clayborn** grant (see forward). Note 2: This patent was issued by St. Marys County.*

Unnamed Patent 8/17/1650 - 100a's. AB&H/108 SR7344
Location: Queen Annes County on Kent Island at the head of Matapeck Creek. Adjoins his own unnamed 300-acre tract of land. *Note 1: This may have been an original **William Clayborn** grant (see forward). Note 2: This patent was issued by St. Marys County.*

Morgans Neck 1/26/1658 - 300a's. LQ/360 SR7345
Location: Queen Annes County on the eastern side of the St. Michaels River on Morgans Creek respecting Parsons Point on Kent Island.
Other persons mentioned: Morgan transported **Saith** *(a manservant),* **Francis Malyn,** and **Francis Ash** into this Province here to inhabit as appears on record. *Note: The patent document does not specify the patenting county. The tract is included because MSA Patent Index #55 places it in Queen Annes County.*

Morgan St. Michaels 1/26/1658 - 300a's. LQ/362 SR7345
Location: Queen Annes County on the eastern side of the St. Michaels River on the eastern side of Morgans Creek on Griffins Branch. Respects Parsons Point on Kent Island.
Other persons mentioned Morgan transported **Edward Park, John Watts,** and **Ann Grasse** into this Province here to inhabit as appears on record. *Note: The patent document does not specify the patenting county. The tract is included because MSA Patent Index #55 places it in Queen Annes County.*

Bluff Point 1/9/1659 - 200a's. L4/307 SR7346
Location: Queen Annes County on Marshy Creek of Kent Island. Adjoins **William Mitchell's** tract of land called The Wading Place. *Note: This patent was issued by Kent County.*

Marron 1/9/1659 - 430a's. L4/309 SR7346
Location: Queen Annes County on the northern side of the St. Michaels River on Champes Creek adjoining his own tract of land. *Note: The patent document does not specify the patenting county. The tract is included because MSA Patent Index #55 places it in Queen Annes County.*

Morgan, Herbert
Morgans Enlargement 6/1/1700 – 260a's. IB&ILC/353 SR7368
Location: Queen Annes County on Kent Island on the northern side of Hogg Pen Creek near the road. Adjoins **William Lawrence's** tract of land called The Forlorn Hope.
Other persons mentioned: Land rights assigned by **Richard Skinner.** *Note: This patent was issued by Talbot County.*

Morgan, John, Planter
Hopewell 1662 - 100a's. L5/132 SR7347
Location: Queen Annes County on the eastern side of the Chester River on the northern side of Reads Creek beginning at a marked Oak of **Edmond Sims** tract of land called Broad Neck. Also adjoins **John Winchester's** tract called Winchester. *Note: This patent was issued by Kent County.*

Unnamed Patent 1662 - 100a's. L5/139 SR7347
Location: Queen Annes County on the eastern side of the Chester River on the northern side of Reads Creek beginning at a bound Oak standing by a marsh. Adjoins **John Winchester's** tract of land called Winton. *Note: This patent was issued by Kent County.*

Morgans Neglect 3/10/1695 – 150a's. BB3B/328 SR7374
Location: Queen Annes County at the head of the Wye River on Beaver Branch. Adjoins **Moses Harris'** tract of land called Harrisses Range and **John Dunn's** tract called Dunns Range.
Other persons mentioned: Land rights assigned by **John Davis** assignee of **William Taylard.** *Note: This patent was issued by Talbot County.*

The Adventure 6/19/1665 - 100a's. L7/616 SR7349
Location: Queen Annes County on the eastern side of the Chester River on Reads Creek. Adjoins **John Winchester's** tract of land called Winton and his own unnamed tract. *Note: This patent was issued by Kent County.*

Change 9/11/1674 – 200a's. L18/238 SR7359
Location: Queen Annes County on the western side of Tuckahoe Creek in the woods. Adjoins a tract of land called Partnership.
Other persons mentioned: Land rights assigned by **George Robotham** assignee of **Richard Keene,** attorney for **John Abbington.** *Note: This patent was issued by Talbot County.*

Morgan, Martin
Morgans Hope 1/15/1665 - 400a's. L9/78 SR7351
Location: Queen Annes County on the southern side of the Chester River on the southern side of the Eastern Branch. *Note 1: This is a certification. No patent was found. Note 2: This certification was issued by Talbot County. The tract is included because MSA Patent Index #55 places it in Queen Annes County.*

Morris, Robert, Mariner
Mill Mount 9/12/1665 – 400a's. L8/237 SR7350
Location: Queen Annes County at the head of the Northeast Branch of the Wye River. Adjoins **Thomas Tristram's** tract of land called Tristram Resurveyed, **James Sedgwick's** tract called Hackneys Marsh Resurveyed, and **Jacob Smith's** tract called The Addition.
Other persons mentioned: Morris transported **Ann Smith, Richard Edmund, Judith Musick, Richard Long, Edmond Cox, Bridgett Cox** *(no relationship indicated),* **Katherine Gould,** and **John Henderson** into this Province here to inhabit as appears on record. *Note: This patent was issued by Talbot County*

Myles. Thomas, Planter
Unnamed Patent 8/22/1650 - 150a's. AB&H/333 SR7344
Location: Queen Annes County on the eastern side of Kent Island on Cox Creek beginning at a marked Cedar. *Note 1: Land rights are based on Myles having transported **himself** and his **wife** into this Province here to inhabit in 1649, as appears on record. Note 2: This patent was issued by St. Marys County.*

Newman, John
Newmans Lott 9/10/1665 – 200a's. L8/262 SR7350
Location: Queen Annes County at the head of the Wye River in the woods. Adjoins **William Jones** and **Peter Sides'** tract of land called Planters Delight and **Robert Noble's** tract of land called Nobles Chance.
Other persons mentioned: Land rights assigned by **Robert Burle.** Additional rights assigned by **Henry Hawkins** assignee of **Ralph Hawkins** *(no relationship indicated). Note: This patent was issued by Talbot County.*

Noble, Robert

Noble Chance 9/14/1665 – 300a's. L8/270 SR7350
Location: Queen Annes County at the head of the Wye River in the woods.
Adjoins **John Newman's** tract of land called Newmans Lott.
Other persons mentioned: Land rights assigned by **Robert Burle** assignee of
Edward Lloyd. *Note: This patent was issued by Talbot County.*

Nobles Range 7/1/1679 – 200a's. L21/218 SR7362
Location: Queen Annes County on the Wye River on a forke of Williams
Branch. Adjoins **William Young's** tract of land called Carpenters Square.
Also adjoins **Richard Carter's** tract called Carters Forrest.
Other persons mentioned: Land rights assigned by **John Pemberton**
assignee of **William Sharpe.** *Note 1: This is a certification. No patent was
found. Note 2: This certification was issued by Talbot County.*

Nobles Addition 5/8/1683 – 150a's. SDA/253 SR7369
Location: Queen Annes County on the Wye River in the woods. Adjoins
William Jones and **Peter Sides'** tract of land called Planters Delight,
George Cowley's tract called Normanton, and **Christopher Santee's** tract
called Knaves Island.
Other persons mentioned: Land rights assigned by **Henry Parker.** *Note:
This patent was issued by Talbot County.*

Norrest, Robert

The Long Runne 9/10/1685 - 100a's. NS2i/164 SR7371
Location: Queen Annes County on the southern side of the Chester River in
the woods. Begins at a bound tree of **Thomas Todd's** tract of land called
Darwan.
Other persons mentioned: Land rights assigned by **Robert Smith.** *Note:
This patent was issued by Talbot County.*

Mount Malicke 6//1/1686 – 150a's. NSBi/336 SR7370
Location: Queen Annes County on the southern side of the Chester River on
the western side of the Main Branch beginning at a marked Oak.
Other persons mentioned: Land rights assigned by **Robert Smith.** *Note:
This patent was issued by Talbot County.*

Norrests Addition 6/12/1688 – 100a's. NS2i/653 SR7371
Location: Queen Annes County on the southern side of the Chester River on
the northern side of Corsica Creek beginning at a bound Hickory of **Richard
Jones'** tract of land called Jones Park. *Note: This patent was issued by
Talbot County.*

Norris, Robert

Claxton Hill 8/10/1683 – 150a's. CB3i/332 SR7367

Location: Queen Annes County on the southern side of the Chester River on the northern side of Coursegalls Branch beginning at a bound tree of **Robert Smith's** tract of land called The Adventure. Also adjoins **Jonathan Libfey's** land and his own tract called Claxton Hill Addition.

Other persons mentioned: Land rights assigned by **Richard Rearent** assignee of **Michale Turbutt.** *Note: This patent was issued by Talbot County.*

Claxton Hill Addition 6/12/1688 – 80a's. NS2i/636 SR7371
Location: Queen Annes County on the southern side of the Chester River on Corsica Creek adjoining his own tract of land called Claxton Hills. Also adjoins tracts called Jones Parke and Jones Lott.

Other persons mentioned: Land rights assigned by **Vincent Lowe.** *Note: This patent was issued by Talbot County.*

Norris, Thomas
Norrisderry 6/24/1673 – 350a's. L17/148 SR7358
Location: Queen Annes County on the southern side of the Chester River at the head of Island Creek beginning at a bound tree of **Andrew Skinner** and **Nathaniel Evetts'** tract of land called Waterford. Also adjoins **George Read's** tract called Readbourne and **Robert Macklin's** tract called Macklinburg.

Other persons mentioned: Land rights to 200 acres assigned by **Matthew Warde.** Rights to 50 acres assigned by **Henry Peake** due him for completion of his time of service in this Province. *Note: This patent was issued by Talbot County.*

Presbury 4/20/1677 - 150a's. L15/684 SR4327
Location: Queen Annes County on Burris Creek of the Chester River beginning at a bound White Oak standing by a branch. *Note 1: This certification was issued by Kent County. Note 2: This was an original* ***William Clayborn*** *grant (see forward). Note 3: This is a certification. No patent was found.*

Obder, John
Weeke 10/11/1665 - 400a's. L9/87 SR7351
Location: Queen Annes County on the southern side of the Chester River on the eastern side of Courseys Creek on Alder Branch. Adjoins **Robert Holton's** *(deceased) tract of land. Note 1: This is a certification. No patent was found. Note 2: The certification document does not specify the issuing county. The tract is included because MSA Patent Index #55 places it in Queen Annes County.*

Osborne, Thomas, Planter
Timber Neck 10/2/1667 - 100a's. L11/57 SR7353

Location: Queen Annes County on Kent Island at the head of Pigg Quarter Creek beginning at a marked Chesnutt.
Other persons mentioned: Land rights assigned by **John Wright.** *Note: The patent document does not specify the patenting county*

Oulson, John
Oulsons Pasture 8/10/1695 - 20a's. C3i/10 SR7377
Location: Queen Annes County on Kent Island on Coxes Creek beginning at a bound tree of **John Wright** and **Thomas Collins'** tract of land called Wallnut Ridge.
Other persons mentioned: Land rights assigned by **Simon Wilmer.** *Note: This patent was issued by Talbot County.*

Oulsons Relief 10/5/1695 - 100a's. C3i/37 SR7377
Location: Queen Annes County on Kent Isle beginning at a bound tree of a tract of land called Barren Ridge. Also adjoins **John Dine's** tract called Limbrick.
Other persons mentioned: Land rights assigned by **Philemon Hemsley** assignee of **Simon Wilmer.** *Note: The patent document does not specify the patenting county.*

Page, Robert
Ulthorpe 6/10/1683 - 100a's. CB3i/393 SR7367
Location; Queen Annes County beginning at a marked Pine of John **Winchester's** tract of land. Also adjoins the land of **Henry Coursey.**
Other persons mentioned: Land rights assigned by **Matthew Ward** assignee of **George Jolly** and his wife **Isabella** due them for completing their time of service in this Province. *Note 1: The patent document does not specify the patenting county. Note 2: The information in the patent document is not sufficient to determine the location of this tract. However, Maryland State Land Patent Index #55 does indicate that it was located in Queen Annes County.*

Parker, Henry & Winslow, Samuel
Tottenham 5/7/1666 – 600a's. L9/406 SR7351
Location: Queen Annes County on the southern side of the Chester River on the Southeast Branch at the dividing beginning at a marked White Oak. Adjoins **James Heath's** tract of land called Upper Heathworth and **John Mitchell's** tract called Mitchells Addition.
Other persons mentioned: Land rights assigned by **William Hill.** Additional rights assigned by **John Edmondson** assignee of **John Richardson.** *Note: This patent was issued by Talbot County.*

Parker, Henry
Parkers Lott 8/26/1665 – 200a's. L8/177 SR7350

Location: Queen Annes County on the southern side of the Chester River on the Eastern Branch. Adjoins **Michael Hackett's** tract of land called Highgate Lane.

Other persons mentioned: Land rights assigned by **Alexander Ray.** *Note: This patent was issued by Talbot County.*

Woodland Neck 5/8/1666 – 200a's. L0/402 SR7351
Location: Queen Annes County on the southern side of the Chester River on the western side of Corsica Creek beginning at a marked Cedar.

Other persons mentioned: Land rights assigned by **Christopher Rolls.** *Note: This patent was issued by Talbot County.*

Niniveh 4/28/1667 – 600a's. L10/483 SR7352
Location: Queen Annes County on the southern side of the Chester River on the western side of the Southwest Branch of Corsica Creek. Adjoins **Christopher Thomas'** tract of land called Barbados Hall.

Other persons mentioned: Land rights assigned by **Samuel Winslow.** *Note: This patent was issued by Talbot County.*

Ninevehs Addition 8/16/1680 - 200a's. CB2i/26 SR7366
Location: Queen Annes County on the southern side of the Chester River on the western side of the Southwest Branch of Corsica Creek. *Note: This patent was issued by Talbot County.*

Winchester 1683 – 200a's. SDA/127 SR7369
Location: Queen Annes County on the southern side of the Chester River on Red Lyon Creek beginning at a bound tree of **Thomas Collins'** tract of land. Also adjoins **William Hemsley's** tract called Little Brittaine.

Other persons mentioned: Land rights assigned by **Vincent Lowe.** *Note: This patent was issued by Talbot County.*

Broomly 8/10/1683 - 200a's. SDA/47 SR7369
Location: Queen Annes County among the branches of Williams Branch of the Wye River. Adjoins **Thomas Williams'** tract of land and **Henry Costin's** 279-acre tract called Lambeth.

Other persons mentioned; Land rights assigned by **James Sedgwick.**
Note: The patent document does not specify the patenting county. However, MSA Patent Index #55 for Talbot County includes this tract and based on the location description it was located in present day Queen Annes County.

Duns Range Addition 8/10/1683 – 200a's. CB3i/389 SR7367
Location: Queen Annes County at the head of a small branch of a branch of the Wye River called Bruers Branch. Adjoins **John Dunn's** tract of land called Dunns Range.

Other persons mentioned: Land rights assigned by **Vincent Lowe** assignee of **Henry Lowe** *(no relationship indicated). Note: This patent was issued by Talbot County.*

Salisbury 8/10/1683 - 300a's. SDA/233 SR7369
Location: Queen Annes County on the southern side of the Chester River on the northern side of the Southwest Branch of Cousegall Creek beginning at a bound Poplar. Adjoins the land of **John Hawkins.**
Other persons mentioned: Land rights assigned by **Vincent Lowe.** *Note: This patent was issued by Talbot County.*

Parsons, John
Parsons Recovery 12/15/1700 - 22a's. DD5i/92 SR7378
Location: Queen Annes County on the southern side of the Chester River by the riverside. Begins at a bound tree of **Matthew Ward's** tract of land called Mount Pleasure. *Note: This patent was issued by Kent County.*

Parsons His Chance 11/7/1709 - 115a's. DD5i/555 SR7378
Location: Queen Annes County on the southern side of the Chester River on Beckles Creek. Adjoins **Richard Tilghman's** tract of land called Tilghmans Discovery.
Other persons mentioned: Land rights assigned by **Edward Elliott** and **George Haddoway.** *Note: This patent was issued by Kent County.*

Pascall, George, Planter
Pascalls Chance 3/8/1666 - 250a's. L10/407 SR7352
Location: Queen Annes County on the southern side of the Chester River on the eastern side of Corsica Creek. Adjoins **Eschell Crosscomb's** tract of land.
Other persons mentioned: Pascall transported **himself,** wife **Elizabeth, William Neale,** and **Ellen Dobbins** into this Province here to inhabit as appears on record. *Note: This patent was issued by Talbot County.*

Paxton, Hugh
Paxtons Lott 12/5/1682 – 100a's. L21/492 SR7362
Location: Queen Annes County at the head of a branch of the Back Wye River beginning at a bound tree of **Giles Butter's** tract of land called Butterfield.
Other persons mentioned: Land rights assigned by **Richard Peacocke.** *Note 1: This is a certification. No patent was found. Note 2: This certification was issued by Talbot County.*

The Range 6/1/1685 – 200a's. NSBi/327 SR7370
Location: Queen Annes County on a road near a small branch running out of Thomas His Branch of the Wye River.

Other persons mentioned: Land rights assigned by **Robert Swift.** *Note: This certification was issued by Talbot County.*

Peddar, Richard
The Forrest of Windsor 3/20/1681 – 250a's. CB3i/120 SR7367
Location: Queen Annes County at the head of Williams Branch of the Wye River adjoining **John Clymer's** tract of land called Grantham.
Other persons mentioned: Peddar transported **himself**, wife **Mary**, daughter **Mary**, and **Blanche Williams** into this Province here to inhabit as appears on record. *Note: This patent was issued by Talbot County.*

Pemberton, John
Bostons Addition 1/21/1681 - 150a's. CB2i/468 SR7366
Location: Queen Annes County at the head of Tuckahoe Creek in the woods beginning at a bound tree of his own tract of land called Boston.
Other persons mentioned: Land rights assigned by **John Lane** and **Richard Peacock.** *Note: This patent was issued by Talbot County.*

Perry, Daniell, Planter
Shearin 10/10/1707 - 100a's. DD5i/380 SR7378
Location: Queen Annes County on the eastern side of the Chester River on the western side of Unicorn Branch. Begins at a bound tree of **Thomas Hatton's** tract of land. Also adjoins the land of **James Crimp.**
Other persons mentioned: Land rights assigned by **Nicholas Cloud.** *Note: This patent was issued by Kent County.*

Petts/Potts, Thomas
Unnamed Certification 4/30/1640 - 600a's. AB&H/89 SR7344
Location: Queen Annes County on the eastern side of Kent Island in Crayford Manor between the head of Potts Branch and Butlers Creek near Alder Swamp. *Note: This patent was issued by St. Marys County.*

Unnamed Patent 5/7/1641 - 100a's. L1/94 SR7341
Location: Queen Annes County on the eastern side of Kent Island in Crayford Manor on Potts Branch extending to Baxters Creek and Alder Swamp. *Note 1: The patent document addresses a legal matter that should be read by anyone with specific interest in this land or the owner or **Francis Brooks**. Note 2: This patent was issued by St. Marys County.*

Potts Gift 8/2/1650 - 100a's. AB&H/128 SR7344
Location: Queen Annes County on Kent Island beginning at a bound Locust standing by the Chesapeake Bayside. Adjoins **John Winchester's** tract of land called Winchester. *Note 1: Land rights based on **Petts** having transported **himself** into this Province here to inhabit in 1635, as appears on record. Note 2: This is a seldom-used form of abbreviated patent document*

that minimizes or excludes location information. This is included in the certification which, in this instance, was not found. Note 3: This patent was issued in St. Mary's County.

Phillips, John, Planter
Pig Quarter 8/8/1650 - 100a's. AB&H/129 SR7344
<u>Location</u>: Queen Annes County on Kent Island on Pigg Quarter Creek in the woods. *Note 1: Land rights based on Phillips having transported **himself** into this Province here to inhabit in 1650, as appears on record. Note 2: This is a seldom-used form of abbreviated patent document that minimizes or excludes location information. This is included in the certification which, in this instance, was not found. Note 3: This patent was issued by St. Marys County.*

Philpott/Phillpott, Robert
Unnamed Patent 9/7/1640 - 600a's. L1/79 SR7341
<u>Location</u>: Queen Annes County on the eastern side of Kent Island on Phillpotts Creek at the head of the northernmost branch of Long Point Branch. Adjoins **Richard Thompson's** tract of land on South Pine Bay. *Note: This was a **William Clayborn** grant (see forward). Note 2: This patent was issued by St. Marys County.*
Phillpots Neck 12/10/1640 - 350a's. AB&H/131 SR7344
<u>Location</u>: Queen Annes County on the eastern side of Kent Island in Old Fort Manor between the land of **Richard Thompson,** Pig Bay, and the Chesapeake Bay. *Note 1: Land rights based on Phillpott having transported **himself** into this Province here to inhabit as appears on record. Note 2: This patent was issued by Kent County. Note 3: This was an original **William Clayborn** grant (see forward).*

Pierce, John
Pierces Land 6/5/1686 - 200a's. IB&ILC/247 SR7363
<u>Location</u>: Queen Annes County on the southern side of the Chester River on the lower side of a marsh on Hoampey Branch.
<u>Other persons mentioned</u>: Land rights assigned by **Vincent Lowe.** *Note 1: This is a certification. No patent was found. Note 2: This certification was issued by Talbot County.*

Piner, John, son of **Francis Piner**
Piners Hill 6/1/1687 – 200a's. IB&ILC/279 SR7368
<u>Location</u>: Queen Annes County on the southern side of the Chester River by a marsh.
<u>Other persons mentioned</u>: Land rights assigned by **Vincent Lowe.** *Note: This patent was issued by Talbot County.*

Plater, George
Pokehicory Ridge 11/10/1695 - 1,000a's. BB3B/211 SR7374
Location: Queen Annes County at the head of the Chester River in Talsy Meadow.
Other persons mentioned: Land rights assigned by **Robert Smith.** *Note: This patent was issued by Talbot County.*

Ponder, John
Ponderfield 3/6/1688 – 200a's. NSBi/691 SR7370
Location: Queen Annes County on the southern side of the Chester River on the eastern side of Unicorn Branch. Adjoins **Francis Sheppard's** tract of land called Sheppards Forrest.
Other persons mentioned: Land rights assigned by **Robert Devinish** assignee of Francis Sheppard. *Note: This patent was issued by Talbot County.*

Porter, William, Planter
Parsons Neck 8/21/1650 - 200a's. AB&H/333 SR7344
Location: Queen Annes County on Kent Island at the Eastern Marsh by the Chesapeake Bayside. Adjoins **Capt. Vaughan's** tract of land.
Other persons mentioned: Parsons transported himself and his wife here to inhabit in 1649, as appears on reecord. *Note 1: This is a seldom-used form of abbreviated patent document that minimizes or excludes location information. This is included in the certification which, in this instance, was not found. Note 2: This patent was issued by St. Marys County.*

Power, John & Howden, Mary & Judith
Macklinburg Res. 6/22/1683 - 700a's. L21/528 SR7362
Location: Queen Annes County on the southern side of the Chester River on Island Creek. *Note 1: A marginal notation indicated that Judith Howden is the wife of Thomas Wyatt. Note 2: The certification document includes detailed legal information that should be read by anyone interested in this land or in the people named. Note 3: This is a certification issued by Talbot County. No patent was found.*

Power, John
Macklinborough 3/28/1677 - 800a's. L19/449 SR7360
Location: Queen Annes County on the eastern side of the Chester River on Herring Creek in the woods.
Other persons mentioned: Land rights assigned by former owner **Robert Macklin.** *Note: This patent was issued by Talbot County.*

Price, Andrew
The Good Increase 10/29/1679 – 200a's. L21/223 SR7362

Location: Queen Annes County on the southern side of the Chester River on the southern side of the Southeast Branch Island Creek beginning at a bound tree of **Richard Collins'** tract of land called Shotland.
Other persons mentioned: Land rights assigned by **Robert Smith**. *Note 1: This is a certification. No patent was found. Note 2: This certification was issued by Talbot County.*

Margaretts Hill 12/19/1681 – 200a's. CB2i/492 SR7366
Location: Queen Annes County at the head of Tuckahoe Creek on Robothams Branch.
Other persons mentioned: Land rights assigned by **Henry Price** *(no relationship indicated). Note 1: This is a certification. No patent was found. Note 2: This certification was issued by Talbot County.*

Brecknock 3/30/1683 – 100a's. CB3i/206 SR7367
Location: Queen Annes County on the Back Wye River in the woods. Adjoins **Robert Smith's** tract of land and his own tract called Stagwell. *Note: This patent was issued by Talbot County.*

Stagwell 3/5/1701 - 526a's. DD5i/259 SR7378
Location: Queen Annes County by the riverside on the eastern side of the Back Wye River formerly called Morgans Creek beginning at a bound tree of **Robert Smith's** tract of land called Smeath. Also adjoins his own tract called Brecknock. *Note 1: This is a certification. The tract was patented by* **Richard Bennett** *on 12/6/1706 (DD5i/260 SR7378. Note 2: This certification was issued by Talbot County.*

Price, William
    Pentrowey 8/20/1650 - 50a's. AB&H/334 SR7344
    Location: Queen Annes County on Kent Island near Cox Creek. Adjoins **John Deer's** tract of land called Pentregay.
    Other persons mentioned: Land rights assigned by **Thomas Marsh**. *Note: This patent was issued by St. Marys County.*

    Prices Hill 5/9/1666 – 300a's. L9/404 SR7351
    Location: Queen Annes County on the southern side of Island Creek of the Wye River on a point of land at the mouth of Price Cove.
    Other persons mentioned: Land rights assigned by **Henry Parker** assignee of **Thomas Turner**. Additional rights assigned by **Abraham Bishop**. *Note: This patent was issued by Talbot County.*

Proddy, William, Planter
    Unnamed Certification 8/6/1650 - 200a's. AB&H/106 SR7344
    Location: Queen Annes County on the northeast side of Kent Island on Cox Creek extending to the Chesapeake Bay. Adjoins **John Russell's** tract of

land called The Northeast Thickett. *Note: This is a certification issued by St. Marys County. No patent was found.*

Prowse, George
Prout Park 1/20/1667 – 300a's. L11/252 SR7353
Location: Queen Annes County at the head of the North Branch of the Wye River adjoining **Richard Bridges'** tract of land called Detteridge.
Other persons mentioned: Land rights assigned by **Catherine Phelps** and **William Golden** assignees of **Francis Armstrong** assignee of **John Elley**. *Note 1: This is a certification. No patent was found. Note 2: This certification was issued by Talbot County.*

Purlivant, Richard, Barber/Surgeon
Unnamed Patent 9/25/1640 - 100a's. L1/84 SR7341
Location: Queen Annes County on Kent Island on Hogpen Neck of Hogpen Creek extending to Thicketty Creek. *Note 1: This was a **William Clayborn** Grant (see forward). Note 2: The patent document does not specify the patenting county.*

Hogpen Neck 9/26/1640 - 100a's. L1/84 SR7341
Location: Queen Annes County on Kent Island bounded by Hog Pen Creek, Thicketty Creek, and the Chesapeake Bay. *Note 1: Land rights based on Purlivant having transported **himself** into this Province here to inhabit as appears on record. Note 2: This patent was issued by St. Marys County.*

Unnamed Patent 12/1/1640 - 180a's. L1/89 SR7341
Location: Queen Annes County on Beaver Neck Creek in Crayford Manor on Kent Island. Extends to Cane Bite Creek. *Note 1: Land rights based on Purlivant having transported **himself** into this Province here to inhabit as appears on record. Note 2: This patent was issued by St. Marys County. Note 3: Purlivant may have been granted additional rights for practicing his art to the benefit of the inhabitants of Kent Isle.*

Purlivant 12/6/1640 - 200a's. L1/90 SR7341
Location: Queen Annes County on Kent Island on the western side of Beaver Creek at the head of the Northern Branch extending to Cones Bite Creek. *Note: The patent document does not specify the patenting county.*

Rawlings, John (son of **Anthony**), Planter
Rawlings Chance 5/15/1668 – 330a's. L11/399 SR7353
Location: Queen Annes County on the southern side of the Chester River on the eastern side of the dividing on the southern side of Island Creek. Adjoins **Ralph Fishborne's** tract of land called Mount Hope and **John Elliott's** tract called Elliotts Addition. *Note: This patent was issued by Talbot County.*

Read, George
    Readbourne 1/3/1659 - 1,000a's. L4/195 SR7346
    <u>Location</u>: On the eastern side of the Chester River on Herring Creek respecting Sewells Point to the west. *Note: The patent document does not specify the patenting county. The tract is included because MSA Patent Index #55 places it in Queen Annes County.*

Read, Matthew, Planter
    Reading 1/18/1658 - 450a's. LQ/311 SR7345
    <u>Location</u>: Queen Annes County on the southern side of the Chester River on the southern side of Read's Creek extending to Reads Back Branch. Adjoins **Robert Smith's** tract of land called Neglect.
    <u>Other persons mentioned</u>: Land rights assigned by **Francis Bright** due him for transporting **himself** and wife **Ann.** Also Read transported **himself, William Mouse, Ann Slack,** and **Elizabeth Lockett** into this Province here to inhabit as appears on record. *Note: This patent was issued by Kent County.*

    Butts Neck 10/2/1667 - 50a's. L11/58 SR7353
    <u>Location</u>: Queen Annes County on Kent Island on the western side of Coxes Creek beginning at a marked Oak standing by a branch of the said creek. Adjoins **Thomas Miles'** tract of land.
    <u>Other persons mentioned</u>: Land rights assigned by **John Wright.** *Note: The patent document does not specify the patenting county.*

    Unnamed Certification Res. 3/18/1678 - 377a's. L21/305 SR7362
    <u>Location</u>: Queen Annes County on the southern side of the Chester River on Reads Back Creek. *Note 1: This is a certification. The land was formerly surveyed for **Henry Parker.** No patent was found. Note 2: This certification of resurvey was issued by Talbot County.*

Reynolds, John
    Chesterton 3/10/1685 - 150a's. NS2i/162 SR7371
    <u>Location</u>: Queen Annes County at the head of the Chester River on a forke of a branch.
    <u>Other persons mentioned</u>: Land rights assigned by **Richard Royston.** *Note: This patent was issued by Talbot County.*

Ridgely, James, Planter
    Ridgelys Chance 10/1/1687 – 200a's. NS2i/419 SR7371
    <u>Location</u>: Queen Annes County on the southern side of the Chester River on a small runn of Elletts Branch.
    <u>Other persons mentioned</u>: Land rights assigned by **Robert Smith** assignee of **Thomas Collins.** *Note: This patent was issued by Talbot County.*

Robinson, John & Tully, Stephen
   Content 8/10/1683 - 200a's. SDA/107 SR7369
   Location: Queen Annes County on the northern side of a small branch on the western side of Tuckahoe Creek beginning at a marked Poplar.
   Other persons mentioned: Land rights assigned by **Richard Peacock.** *Note: This patent was issued by Talbot County.*

Robinson, John
   Robinsons Farme 8/10/1681 – 200a's. L21/375 SR7362
   Location; Queen Annes County on the southern side of a branch of the Main Branch of Tuckahoe Creek by the branchside.
   Other persons mentioned: Land rights assigned by **Richard Peacock.** *Note 1: This is a certification. No patent was found. Note 2: This certification was issued by Talbot County.*

   Chesnutt Meadow 12/6/1682 - 200a's. L21/493 SR7362
   Location: Queen Annes County on the western side of the Main Branch of Tuckahoe Creek. Adjoins a tract of land called Providence laid out for **Robinson** and **StephenTully.** *Note 1: This patent was issued by Talbot County.*

   The Front Meadow 12/6/1682 – 200a's. L21/493 SR7362
   Location: Queen Annes County on the western side of the northmost branch of Tuckahoe Creek adjoining a tract owned by himself and **Stephen Tully** called Providence.
   Other persons mentioned: Land rights assigned by **Richard Peacocke.** *Note 1: This is a certification. No patent was found. Note 2: This certification was issued by Talbot County.*

   Jamaicas Addition 8/10/1683 – 50a's. SDA/338 SR7369
   Location: Queen Annes County on the southern side of the Chester River on the southern side of Corsica Creek beginning at a bound tree of **Richard Jones'** tract of land called Denby.
   Other persons mentioned: Land rights assigned by **Richard Peacock** assignee of **Michael Turbutt.** *Note: This patent was issued by Talbot County.*

   Robinsons Addition 8/10/1683 – 200a's. SDA/232 SR7369
   Location: Queen Annes County on the southern side of a small branch of Tuckahoe Creek. Adjoins **Stephen Tully's** tract of land called Tullys Addition.
   Other persons mentioned: Land rights assigned by **Richard Peacock.** *Note: This patent was issued by Talbot County.*

Robotham, George
Robothams Parke 6/10/1685 – 500a's. NS2i/213 SR 7371
Location: Queen Annes County on the southern side of the Chester River on the northern side of Unicorn Branch beginning at a great stooping White Oak. Adjoins **William Hemsley's** tract of land called Friendship.
Other persons mentioned: Land rights assigned by **Thomas Vaughan.** *Note: This patent was issued by Talbot County.*

Rodway, John & Rowles, Walter, Planters
Bristoll Marsh 9/6/1670 – 400a's. L14/84 SR7356
Location: Queen Annes County on the southern side of the Chester River at the head of Courseys Creek on Carmans Branch. Adjoins **Michael Vandeford's** tract called St. Pauls and **John Jackson's** tract called Fortune.
Other persons mentioned: Rowles transported **himself, Dorothy Raymond,** and **John Gavenbere.** Rodway transported **himself.** Additional rights assigned by **Owen Howell** due him for transporting **himself** into this Province here to inhabit as appears on record. Additional rights assigned by **John Kye** and **Robert Pennywell.** *Note: This patent was issued by Talbot County.*

Rodway, John
Lentley 9/4/1674 – 450a's. L18/253 SR7359
Location: Queen Annes County on the southern side of the Chester River in a forke of the northernmost fresh runn of Corsica Creek two miles from the creekside. Begins at a marked Beech. *Note: This patent was issued by Talbot County.*

Wellen 9/11/1674 – 750a's. L18/218 SR7359
Location: Queen Annes County on the southern side of the Chester River between the Southeast and Southwest Branches of Island Creek beginning at a bound Poplar. *Note: This patent was issued by Talbot County.*

Rogers, David
Chance 10/1/1687 – 100a's. NS2i/477 SR7371
Location: Queen Annes County on the southern side of the Chester River at the head of Double Creek. Adjoins **James Smith's** tract of land called The Beginning.
Other persons mentioned: Land rights assigned by **Thomas Collins.** *Note: This patent was issued by Talbot County.*

Maryes Dower 11/10/1695 – 200a's. BB3B/406 SR7374
Location: Queen Annes County on Brewers Branch of the Wye River in the woods. Adjoins **Moses Harris'** tract of land called Ramseys Forrest.
Other persons mentioned: Land rights assigned by **William Hemsley.** *Note: This patent was issued by Talbot County.*

Rouseby, Christopher
Rouseby 12/16/1679 – 500a's. L21/22 SR7362
Location: Queen Annes County on the southern side of the Chester River on the northern side of Rousebys Creek in the woods.
Other persons mentioned: Rouseby transported **Hannah Tatwell, Casandra Warburton, William Cleveland, William Share, William Barton, Thomas James, Walter Pardeo, John Perivy, Elizabeth Perivy** *(no relationship indicated),* and **George Lockier** into this Province here to inhabit as appears on record. *Note: This patent was issued by Talbot County.*

Rouseby, John
Sledmar 7/16/1679 - 800a's. L21/004 SR7362
Location: Queen Annes County on the southern side of the Chester River on the eastern side of Rousebys Branch.
Other persons mentioned: Rouseby transported **himself.** Additional rights assigned by **Robert Ridgely** assignee of **Samuel Gibbons** due him for transporting **Robert Kenny, Rose Esprey, Elizabeth Smith, Lettie Coopland, Jake Forrest, Elizabeth Perkinson, Jane** *(could be James)* **Lyon, Elisabeth Winslowe, Ellinor Mackholister, Margarett Grimes, Elizabeth Johnson, Sarah Kennas, Edmond Magee, John Mustard, John Mawland, James Mackaelle,** and **James Kirkwood** into this Province here to inhabit as appears on record. *Note: This patent was issued by Talbot County.*

Rowles, William
Oyer Moyne 9/27/1680 - 200a's. CB2i/66 SR7366
Location: Queen Annes County on the eastern side of Kent Island by a creekside in a swampy marsh. Begins at a bound tree of **Henry Morgan's** tract of land called Beaverton now in the possession of **Edward Coppin.**
Other persons mentioned: Land rights assigned by **Michael Miller.** *Note: This patent was issued by Kent County.*

Royston, Richard
Royston 8/1/1673 - 1,200a's. L15/28 SR4327
Location: Queen Annes County on the southern side of the Chester River at the mouth of a small creek. *Note: This patent was issued by Talbot County.*

Russell, John, Planter
The Northeast Thickett 8/6/1650 - 200a's. AB&H/130 SR7344
Location: Queen Annes County on the northern side of Kent Island by the Chesapeake Bayside. Adjoins **William Proddy's** unnamed 200-acre tract of land. *Note: This patent was issued by St. Marys County.*

Russendall 2/3/1658 - 250a's. L4/378 SR7346
Location: Queen Annes County on the St. Michaels River on Russells Creek
extending to Morgan Creek. Adjoins **Henry Morgan's** tract of land.
Other persons mentioned: Russell transported **Symon Phillips** into this
Province here to inhabit as appears on record. Additional rights assigned by
Phillip Connors and **Robert Vaughan.** *Note 1: This patent was issued by
Kent County. Note 2: The tract is included because MSA Patent Index #55
places it in Queen Annes County.*

Ruth, Thomas
Sandy Hurst 12/10/1701 - 500a's. DD5i/101 SR7378
Location: In the freshes of the Chester River on the southern side near an
island of marsh beginning at a bound tree of **Richard Jones'** tract of land
called Jones Fancy.
Other persons mentioned: Land rights assigned by **James Heath.** *Note 1:
This is a certification. The tract was patented by James Heath on 11/18/1703
(DD5i/101 SR73778). Note 2: This certification was issued by Kent County.*

Sadler, Giles
Sadlers Rest 2/15/1659 - 400a's. L4/264 SR7346
Location: Queen Annes County on the northern side of the St. Michaels
River on the western side of Morgan Creek on Sadlers Cove beginning at a
marked Oak. *Note 1: This is a certification. No patent was found. Note 2:
The certification document does not specify the certifying county. The tract is
included because MSA Patent Index #55 places it in Queen Annes County.*

Salisbury, John
Bradfords Addition 8/10/1683 – 100a's. SDA/121 SR7369
Location: Queen Annes County on the southern side of the Chester River on
Elliotts Branch. Begins as a bound tree of **John Broadrib's** tract of land
called Bradford.
Other persons mentioned: Land rights assigned by **Richard Peacock.** *Note:
This patent was issued by Talbot County.*

Salisbury, William
Bradfords Addition 8/22/1681 – 100a's. L21/377 SR7362
Location: Queen Annes County on the southern side of the Chester River on
the southern side of Elliotts Branch. Adjoins **John Broadrib's** tract of land
called Bradford.
Other persons mentioned: Land rights assigned by **Richard Peacock.** *Note
1: This is a certification. No patent was found. Note 2: This certification was
issued by Talbot County.*

Salter, John
Salters Marsh 1/20/1658 - 100a's. LQ/346 SR7345

Location: Queen Annes County on the eastern side of the St. Michaels River on the northern side of Morgans Creek respecting Parsons Point on Kent Island. *Note: The patent document does not specify the patenting county.*

Beaver Neck 9/20/1658 - 200a's. LQ/194 SR7345
Location: Queen Annes County on Kent Island bounded by Beaver Creek and The Chesapeake Bay. *Note: This patent was issued by Kent County.*

The Addicon 7/10/1705 - 250a's. CDi/248 SR7376
Location: Queen Annes County on the southern side of the Chester River in the woods beginning at a bound Oak of **Anthony Griffin's** tract of land called Prices Hill.
Other persons mentioned: Land rights assigned by **Giles Bond** assignee of **William Taylard.** *Note: This patent was issued by Kent County.*

Santee, Christopher
Knaves Island 4/19/1684 – 500a's. L22/113 SR7363
Location: Queen Annes County on Lloyds Creek in the woods adjoining his own tract of land called Knaves Stand Off.
Other persons mentioned: Land rights assigned by **John Larkin.** *Note 1: This is a certification. No patent was found. Note 2: This certification was issued by Talbot County.*

Knaves Stand Off 5/10/1685 – 50a's. NS2i/145 SR7371
Location: Queen Annes County on Lloyds Creek of the Wye River adjoining his own tract of land called Knaves Island. Also adjoins **Philemon Lloyd's** tract called Long Neglect.
Other persons mentioned: Land rights assigned by **John Larkin.** *Note: This patent was issued by Talbot County.*
Sayer, Peter
Branfield 8/15/1681 - 800a's. CB2i/247 SR7366
Location: Queen Annes County on the northern side of the Chester River adjoining **William Sharpe's** tract of land called Mount Pleasant
Other persons mentioned: Land rights assigned by **William Cross** assignee of **Vincent Lowe.** *Note 1: This patent was issued by Talbot County. Note 2: MSA Patent Index #55 places the tract in Queen Annes County.*

Sayers Range 8/10/1683 – 300a's. L21/352 SR7367
Location: Queen Annes County on the southern side of the Chester River on the southern side of Red Lyon Branch in the woods. Adjoins **John Davis'** tract of land called Davis Range and his own tract called Sayers Range Addition. *Note: This patent was issued by Talbot County.*

Sayers Range Addition 8/10/1685 – 500a's. NSBi/70 SR7370

Location: Queen Annes County on the southern side of the Chester River on the southern side of Red Lyon Branch beginning at a bound Poplar of his own tract of land called Sayers Range. *Note: This patent was issued by Talbot County.*

Sayers Forrest 10/9/1687 – 2,250a's. L22/417 SR7363
Location: Queen Annes County betwixt the Wye River and The Chesapeake Bay including all the cleared land not formerly surveyed on that neck of land commonly called Sayers Neck. Begins at a marshy creek near **Col. Coursey's** land upward to **Richard Jackson's** land and then downward to **Henry Beedle's** tract and down the riverside to **Henry Coursey's** land. Also adjoins tracts owned by **Nicholas Broadway** on Broadways Creek and **Evan Morgan.** *Note 1: This is a certification. No patent was found. Note 2: This certification was issued by Talbot County.*

The Gore 10/9/1687 - 175a's. L22/418 SR7363
Location: Queen Annes County on the Chesapeake Bay respecting Kent Island adjoining **Richard Jackson's** tracts of land called The First Hundred and The Second Hundred and **Jenkins'** tract called The Third Hundred. *Note: This is a certification issued by Talbot County. No patent was found.*

Scott, James

Old Mill 9/15/1664 – 250a's. L7/445 SR7349
Location: Queen Annes County on the Northeast Branch of the Wye River beginning at a bound tree of **John Wright's** tract of land called Bingley. Also adjoins **John Downes'** tract called Hopton and **Elizabeth Bruer's** tract called Widdows Chance at the mouth of Cabbin Branch. *Note: This patent was issued by Talbot County.*

James Lott 10/27/1665 – 150a's. L9/137 SR7351
Location: Queen Annes County on the southern side of the Chester River on the western side of Corsica Creek beginning at a bound tree of **Alexander Maxwell's** tract of land called Maxby. Also adjoins **Richard Burridge's** tract. *Note 1: This is a certification. No patent was found. Note 2: This certification was issued by Talbot County.*

Scott, John

Scotts Chance 10/10/1708 - 100a's. DD5i/500 SR7378
Location: Queen Annes County on a forke of Tuckahoe Creek at Tullys Neck beginning at a bound tree of **Vincent Lowe's** tract of land called Stratton. Also joins the land of **William Coursey.**
Other persons mentioned: Land rights assigned by **Giles Bond.** *Note 1: This patent was issued by Kent County. Note 2: MSA Patent Index #55 places this tract in Queen Annes County.*

Scotton, Thomas
> **Scottons Addition** 7/29/1700 - 60a's. DD5i/26 SR7378
> Location: Queen Annes County on the southern side of the Chester River on the western side of the Main Branch
> Other persons mentioned: Land rights assigned by **Daniel Boaes**. *Note: This patent was issued by Kent County.*

Sedgwick, James
> **Camberwell** 6/25/1681 – 500a's. L21/338 SR7362
> Location: Queen Annes County betwixt the branches of Tuckahoe Creek and Corsica Creek on Scotts Branch beginning at a marked White Oak. *Note 1: This is a certification. No patent was found. Note 2: This certification was issued by Talbot County.*

> **Hackneys Marsh Res.** 6/1/1685 – 300a's. NSBI/99 SR7370
> Location: Queen Annes County on Thomas Branch of the Wye River beginning at a bound tree of **William Young's** tract of land called Middle Plantation. Also adjoins **Robert Morris'** tract called Mount Mill and **Jacob Smith's** tract called The Addition. *Note: This patent was issued by Talbot County.*

> **Stepney** 6/12/1688 – 300a's. NS2i/632 SR7371
> Location: Queen Annes County on the southern side of the Chester River on the southern side of the Red Lyon Branch adjoining **John Hawkins'** tract of land called Contention. *Note: This patent was issued by Talbot County.*

Seth, Jacob
> **The Addition** 4/15/1696 - 50a's. BB3B/321 SR7374
> Location: Queen Annes County at the head of the Wye River adjoining a tract of land called Mount Mile. Also adjoins **William Young's** tract called Middle Plantation.
> Other persons mentioned: Land rights assigned by **Philemon Hemsley**. *Note: This patent was issued by Talbot County.*

Sewell, Nicholas
> **Poplar Ridge** 8/10/1684 – 500a's. NSBi/2 SR7370
> Location: Queen Annes County on the southern side of the Chester River on Red Lyon Branch in the woods. *Note: This patent was issued by Talbot County.*

> **Sewells Forke** 8/10/1684 – 1,000a's. NSBi/1 SR7370
> Location: Queen Annes County on the southern side of the Chester River on the eastern side of the Red Lyon Branch in the woods. *Note: This patent was issued by Talbot County.*

Shepheard, Francis & Tilghman, William
The Partnership 10/1/1682 – 1,000a's. CB3i/187 SR7367
Location: Queen Annes County on the southern side of the Chester River in the woods. Adjoins **Richard Royston's** tract of land called Royston. *Note: This patent was issued by Talbot County.*

Sheppard, Francis & Seward, Thomas, Planters
Molden 6/12/1688 - 283a's. NS2i/654 SR7371
Location: Queen Annes County on Coursegall Creek above Courseys Point by the riverside.
Other persons mentioned: Land rights assigned by **Charles Robinson** assignee of **Vincent Lowe.** *Note: This patent was issued by Talbot County.*

Shepheard/Shepherd/Sheppard, Francis, Planter
Sheppards Discovery 12/19/1682 - 400a's. L21/496 SR7362
Location: Queen Annes County on the southern side of the Chester River on Jones Creek. Begins at a marked Oak of **John** and **William Coursey's** tract of land called Courseys Towne.
Other persons mentioned: Land rights assigned by **Richard Peacock.** *Note: This patent was issued by Talbot County.*

Barefield 4/27/1683 – 200a's. CB3i/259 SR7367
Location: Queen Annes County on the southern side of the Chester River on the northern side of a branch of Britland Creek. Adjoins his own tract of land called Shepherds Fortune.
Other persons mentioned: Land rights assigned by **Robert Smith.** *Note: This patent was issued by Talbot County.*

Shepherds Fortune 8/10/1683 – 500a's. CB3i/339 SR7367
Location: Queen Annes County on the southern side of the Chester River on the northern side of Jones Creek adjoining his own tract of land called Barfield. Also adjoins **John Whittington's** tract of land called Whittingtons Lott.
Other persons mentioned: Land rights assigned by **Simon Wilmer.** *Note: This patent was issued by Talbot County.*

Shepheards Hook 8/10/1683 – 200a's. SDA/246 SR7369
Location: Queen Annes County on the southern side of the Chester River on the southern side of a small branch of Double Creek.
Other persons mentioned: Land rights assigned by **Robert Smith.** *Note: This patent was issued by Talbot County.*

Sheppards Forrest 8/3/1684 – 200a's. NSBi/324 SR7370
Location: Queen Annes County on the southern side of the Chester River on the fork of a branch of the s'd river beginning at a marked White Oak.

Other persons mentioned: Land rights assigned by **William Bishop.** *Note: This patent was issued by Talbot County.*

Ashton 6/5/1685 – 200a's. L22/185 SR7363
Location: Queen Annes County on the southern side of the Chester River in the woods beginning at a bound tree of his own tract of land called Kenningfield. *Note 1: This is a certification. No patent was found. Note 2: This certification was issued by Talbot County.*

Ramseys Folly 4/1/1686 – 200a's. NSBi/300 SR7370
Location: Queen Annes County on the southern side of the Chester River beginning at a marked Oak.
Other persons mentioned: Land rights assigned by **Thomas Collins.** *Note: This patent was issued by Talbot County.*

Ashford 8/1/1686 – 200a's. NSBi/318 SR7370
Location: Queen Annes County on the southern side of the Chester River in the woods beginning at a bound tree of his own tract of land called Hennifield.
Other persons mentioned: Land rights assigned by **Thomas Collins,** planter. *Note: This patent was issued by Talbot County.*

Hennifield 6/1/1687 – 200a's. NS2i/340 SR7371
Location: Queen Annes County on the southern side of the Chester River in a forke of Jones Creek. Adjoins his own tract of land called Ashford.
Other persons mentioned: Land rights assigned by **William Bishop.** *Note: This patent was issued by Talbot County.*

Shaver 3/4/1688 – 200a's. NSBi/672 SR7370
Location: Queen Annes County on the western side of Unicorn Branch of the Chester River. Adjoins **Simon Willmore's** tract of land called Willmores Range.
Other persons mentioned: Land rights assigned by **Robert Devinish.** *Note: This patent was issued by Talbot County.*

Sheppards Forrest 3/6/1688 – 400a's. NSBi/671 SR7370
Location: Queen Annes County on the southern side of the Chester River on Unicorn Branch on the eastern side of the Upper Road. Adjoins **Christopher Rouseby's** tract of land.
Other persons mentioned: Land rights assigned by **Robert Devinish** assignee of **Francis Sheppard.** *Note: This patent was issued by Talbot County.*

Sheppards Folds 6/12/1688 - 400a's. NS2i/665 SR7371
Location: Queen Annes County on the eastern side of the Chester River about a mile above the road.

Other persons mentioned: Land rights assigned by **Thomas Collins** and **William Hackett**. *Note: This patent was issued by Talbot County.*

Sheppards Redoubt 6/12/1688 – 300a's. NS2i/663 SRF7371
Location: Queen Annes County on Red Lyon Branch of the Chester River in the woods. Adjoins **John Slaughter's** tract of land called Slaughterton.
Other persons mentioned: Land rights assigned by **Thomas Truittson**.
Note: This patent was issued by Talbot County.

Shirt, William, Planter
Waterton 9/17/1668 - 660a's. L12/137 SR7354
Location: Queen Annes County.
Other persons mentioned: Land rights assigned by **William Coursey**. *Note 1: This is a seldom-used form of abbreviated patent document that minimizes or excludes location information. This is included in the certification which, in this instance, was not found. Note 2: The patent document does not specify the patenting county. The tract is included because MSA Patent Index #55 places it in Queen Annes County.*

Short, Robert
Mersons Freehold 12/9/1640 - 50a's. L1/89 SR7341
Location: Queen Annes County on the western side of Kent Island in Crayford Manor on Merson Pond in the woods by the Chesapeake Bayside. Adjoins **Edward Commins** 100-acre unnamed tract of land. *Note 1: This is an original **William Clayborn** grant (see forward). Note 2: This patent was issued by St. Marys County.*

Sides, Peter, Planter
Wisbitch 9/9/1667 – 100a's. L11/86 SR7353
Location: Queen Annes County on the eastern side of the Middle Branch of the Wye River. Adjoins his and **William Jones'** tract of land called Dobbs Creek and **Henry Hawkins'** tract called Poplar Hill.
Other persons mentioned: Land rights assigned by **Edward Lloyd** and Henry Hawkins. *Note: This patent was issued by Talbot County.*

Sigley, William
Good Luck 4/24/1701 - 100a's. DD5i/28 SR7378
Location: Queen Annes County on the southern side of the Northeast Branch of the Chester River in the woods. Adjoins **John Parsons'** tract of land.
Other persons mentioned: Land rights assigned by **Lambert Wilmer**. *Note: The patent document does not specify the patenting county.*

Singleton, John & Jones, Richard, Planters
The Forlorn Hope 9/1/1665 – 300a's. L8/198 SR7350

Location: Queen Annes County on the southern side of the Chester River on the Eastern Branch of Hinsontown Creek near a swamp. *Note: This patent was issued by Talbot County.*

Goose Quarter 5/12/1676 – 50a's. L19/363 SR7360
Location: Queen Annes County on the southern side of the Chester River on the western side of Hinsontown Creek at the mouth. Adjoins **William Tilghman's** tract of land called Tilghmans Pasture. *Note: This patent was issued by Talbot County.*

The Addition 9/4/1665 – 50a's. L8/205 SR7350
Location: Queen Annes County on the southern side of the Chester River on the southern side of Hinsontown Creek adjoining **Thomas Hinson's** tract of land. *Note: This patent was issued by Talbot County.*

Skinner, Andrew, Winslow, Samuel, & Parker, Henry
Providence 5/8/1666 – 600a's. L9/394 SR7351
Location: Queen Annes County on the southern side of the Chester River on the eastern side of the Southwest Branch of Corsica Creek at a fork by the first dividing.
Other persons mentioned: Land rights assigned by **William Hill, Alexander Larrimore,** and **Henry Cate.** *Note: This patent was issued by Talbot County.*

Skinner, Andrew & Evett, Nathaniel
Waterford 5/9/1666 - 400a's. LQ/411 SR7345
Location: Queen Annes County on the southern side of the Chester River on the western side of Island Creek beginning at a marked Oak. Adjoins **Thomas Norris'** tract of land called Norrisderry.
Other persons mentioned: Land rights assigned by **Christopher Dennis.**
Note: This patent was issued by Talbot County.

Skinner, Andrew, Planter
St. Michaels Fresh Runn Res. 9/13/1664 – 1,150a's. SDA/436 SR7349
Location: Queen Annes County on the eastern side of the Main Branch of the Wye River in the woods. Adjoins **John King's** tract of land called Bettys Dowry and **Richard Carter's** tract called Carters Skonce.
Other persons mentioned: Land rights assigned by **William Bretta.** *Note 1: This resurvey was undertaken to consolidate Skinner's rights to 500 acres of land with his own tract called Addicon. Note 2: This patent was issued by Talbot County,*

The Triangle 9/13/1664 – 125a's. SDA/434 SR7349

Location: Queen Annes County at the head of the Middle Branch of the Wye River in the woods at the mouth of Quarter Cove. Adjoins **Thomas Williams'** tract of land called Wilton.
Other persons mentioned: Land rights assigned by **William Bretta.** *Note: This patent was issued by Talbot County.*

Forked Neck 8/26/1665 - 50a's. L8/92 SR7350
Location: Queen Annes County on the northern side of the St. Michaels River at the head of Morgans Creek. *Note: The patent document does not specify the patenting county. The tract is included because MSA Patent Index #55 places it in Queen Annes County.*

Slaughter, John
Slaughterton 12/7/1675 – 500a's. L19/405 SR7360
Location: Queen Annes County on the southern side of the Chester River on Rousebys Branch. Adjoins **Christopher Rouseby's** tract of land called Rousebys Recovery.
Other persons mentioned: Land rights assigned by **George Conely.** *Note: This patent was issued by Talbot County.*

Smith, Catherine/Katherine
Unnamed Patent 12/10/1640 – 250a's. L1/86 SR7341
Location: Queen Annes County on Kent Island bound by Katherines Creek, Little Creek and Broad Creek. *Note 1: Catherine Smith is the infant daughter of **John Smith** and the heir of **Henry Crowley** (deceased). Note 2: This patent was issued by St. Marys County. Note 3: The certification, which shows the certified acres as 150 (AB&H/866 SR7344,) includes the following statement dated 9/26/1640: "To Mr. Secretary: I would have (you) to draw a patent in freehold to Catherine Smith of the land lost her for yearly rent of half a bushel of corn (unsigned)."*

Smith, Jacob
The Addition 4/15/1696 – 40a's. BB3B/321 SR7374
Location: Queen Annes County at the head of the Wye River adjoining **Robert Morris'** tract called Mill Mount and **James Sedgwick's** tract called Hackneys Marsh Resurveyed.
Other persons mentioned: Land rights assigned by **Philemon Hemsley.**
Note: This patent was issued by Talbot County.

Smith, James
Smiths Beginning 12/13/1682 - 200a's. L21/495 SR7362
Location: Queen Annes County on the southern side of the Chester River on Matsons Branch. Adjoins **John Breme's** tract of land called Jamaica and his own tract called Smiths Delight.

Other persons mentioned: Land rights assigned by **Richard Peacock.** *Note 1: This is a certification. No patent was found. Note 2: This patent was issued by Talbot County.*

Smiths Delight 11/15/1683 - 300a's. SDA/499 SR7369
Location: Queen Annes County on the southern side of the Chester River at the head of Double Creek. Adjoins his own tract of land called Smiths Beginning and **John Breme's** tract called Jamaica. *Note: The patent document does not specify the patenting county.*

Smithfield 4/1/1686 – 200a's. NSBi/322 SR7370
Location: Queen Annes County on the southern side of the Chester River in the woods on Red Lyon Branch beginning at a marked Red Oak.
Other persons mentioned: Land rights assigned by **Robert Smith** *(no relationship indicated). Note: This patent was issued by Talbot County.*

Smiths Addition 6/12/1688 - 106a's. NS2i/633 SR7371
Location: Queen Annes County on the southern side of the Chester River in a forke of Hambletons Branch. Adjoins **John Gilbert's** tract of land called Jamaica.
Other persons mentioned: Land rights assigned by **Vincent Lowe.** *Note: This patent was issued by Talbot County.*

Smith, John, Planter
Unnamed Certification 9/7/1640 - 50a's. L1/85 SR7341
Location: Queen Annes County on Kent Island near his dwelling house in Crayford Manor. *Note 1: This is a **William Clayborne** grant (see forward). Note 2: The certification document does not specify the patenting county.*

Smiths Lott 2/26/1666 - 200a's. L10/397 SR7352
Location: Queen Annes County on the south side of the Chester River on Winchester Creek. Adjoins **Nathaniel Evett's** tract of land called Wintons Addition.
Other persons mentioned: Smith transported **himself,** wife **Hanna,** daughter **Hannah,** and **Elizabeth Chambers** into this Province here to inhabit as appears on record. *Note: This patent was issued by Talbot County.*

Smith, Robert
Smeath 1659 - 600a's. L4/193 SR7346
Location: Queen Annes County on the northern side of the St. Michaels River on the eastern side of Morgans Creek on Smiths Cove of Smiths Creek.
Other persons mentioned: Smith transported himself and later married **Rose,** Widow of **Richard Gilbert,** thereby assuming rights due Gilbert for transporting **himself,** wife Rose, her **daughter,** and Gilbert's servants

Walter Waterlings and **Thomas Thomas.** *Note: The patent document does not specify the patenting county. The tract is included because MSA Patent Index #55 places it in Queen Annes County.*

Bradburnes Delight 8/20/1676 -200a's. L21/544 SR7362
Location: Queen Annes County on the eastern branch of a cove of a small branch running out of Coursegal Creek. Begins at a marked tree standing by the branch side.
Other persons mentioned: Land rights assigned by **John Stanley.** *Note: This is a certification. No patent was found. Note 2: The patent document does not specify the patenting county.*

Batchellors Plaine 12/18/1676 - 300a's. L21/544 SR7362
Location: Queen Annes County on the eastern side of the Chester River on Unicorn Branch beginning at the easternmost bound tree of **Richard Tilghman's** tract of land called Tilghmans Addition.
Other persons mentioned: Land rights assigned by **Ellis Umphries.** *Note 1: This is a certification. No patent was found. Note 2: This patent was issued by Talbot County.*

Normanton 5/10/1677 – 800a's. L20/60 SR7361
Location: Queen Annes County on Nobles Branch of the Wye River adjoining **Henry Costin's** tract of land called Lambeth and **Robert Noble's** tract called Nobles Addition.
Other persons mentioned: Land rights assigned by former owner **George Cowley** due him for transporting **John Hartley, Grace Turner, John Denunes, Thomas Roe, Stephen Pegg, William Holland, Thomas Chane, Edward Smith,** and **William Atkinson** into this Province here to inhabit as appears on record. *Note: This patent was issued by Talbot County.*

Jamaica 7/27/1678 - 100a's. L21/133 SR7362
Location: Queen Annes County on the southern side of the Chester River in the woods beginning at a marked Red Oak. Adjoins a tract of land called Staples Choice. *Note 1: This is a certification. The tract was patented by **Richard Jones** in 1686 (NSBi/303 SR7370). Note 2: This certification was issued by Kent County.*

Fishingham 5/7/1679 – 200a's. L21/30 SR7362
Location: Queen Annes County on the southern side of the Chester River on the eastern side of Coursegall Creek beginning at a bound tree of **Robert Ellis'** tract of land called Wrexains Plaines. Also adjoins his own tract called Smiths Reserve. *Note: This patent was issued by Talbot County.*

Neglect 5/7/1679 – 100a's. L21/025 SR7362

Location: Queen Annes County on the southern side of the Chester River in the woods on Reads Creek. Begins at a marked Oak of **Matthew Read's** tract of land called Reading. *Note: This patent was issued by Talbot County.*

Smiths Lott 5/7/1679 – 100a's. L21/37 SR7362
Location: Queen Annes County on the southern side of the Chester River on the western side of Coursegall Creek beginning at a marked Red Oak. *Note: This patent was issued by Talbot County.*

Tell Tale Loss 5/7/1679 – 100a's. L21/35 SR7362
Location: Queen Annes County on the southern side of the Chester River by a marsh near The Wading Place. *Note: This patent was issued by Talbot County.*

The Adventure 5/7/1679 - 200a's. L21/36 SR7362
Location: Queen Annes County on the southern side of the Chester River on Coursegall Creek. Adjoins **William Hemsley's** tract of land. Also adjoins **Robert Norrest's** tract called Clarken Hall. *Note: This patent was issued by Talbot County.*

Pleasant Spring 1/19/1680 – 300a's. CB2i/442 SR7366
Location: Queen Annes County on the southern side of the Chester River on the northern side of the easternmost branch of Corsica Creek beginning at a marked Poplar. *Note: This patent was issued by Talbot County.*

Powells Fancy 1/11/1681 – 300a's. CB2i/444 SR7366
Location: Queen Annes County on a branch of the Wye River. Adjoins **Matthew Mason** and **Hugh Croft's** tract of land called Batchellors Choice. *Note: This patent was issued by Talbot County.*

Smiths Addition 1/19/1681 - 300a's. L14/476 SR7366
Location: Queen Annes County on the northern side of Hinson's Creek. Adjoins **Thomas Hinson Jr.'s** tract of land called Hinsons Addition, **Richard Jones'** tract called Labor in Vain, and a tract called Hinson Town. *Note: This patent was issued by Talbot County.*

Smiths Forrest 6/25/1681 – 300a's. L21/341 SR7362
Location: Queen Annes County on the southern side of the Chester River on a small branch of the Eastern Branch of Corsica Creek on the northern side of a great meadow. Adjoins **Charles Hollingsworth's** tract of land called Smiths Forrest. *Note 1: This is a certification. No patent was found. Note 2: This certification was issued by Talbot County.*

Smiths Reserve 2/21/1682 – 84a's. L21/593 SR7362

Location: Queen Annes County on the southern side of the Chester River beginning at a marked Pine of a tract of land called Berlands Addition. Also adjoins **John Jackson's** tract called Fortune, **Desborough Bennett's** tract called Bennetts addition and the land of **Michael Powell.** *Note: This is a certification. No patent was found. Note: This certification was issued by Talbot County.*

Smiths Range 7/3/1682 - 300a's. CB3i/174 SR7367
Location: Queen Annes County on the southern side of the Chester River on the northern side of the Southeast Branch beginning at a marked Poplar. *Note: This patent was issued by Talbot County.*

Triangle 7/3/1682 - 100a's. CB3i/176 SR7367
Location: Queen Annes County on the southern side of the Chester River beginning at a bound tree of **George Pascall's** tract of land. Also adjoins **William Hemsley's** tract called Chesterfield. *Note: This patent was issued by Talbot County.*

Smithfield 5/8/1683 - 200a's. SDA/298 SR7369
Location: Queen Annes County on the southern side of the Chester River on the eastern side of Fishing Creek. Begins at a marked Oak of **Richard Jones'** tract of land called Jamaica.
Other persons mentioned: Land rights assigned by **Henry Parker.** *Note: This patent was issued by Talbot County*

Chance 8/10/1683 – 200a's. CB3i/409 SR7367
Location: Queen Annes County on the southern side of the Chester River on Prato Branch. Adjoins **Stephen Tully's** tract of land. *Note: This patent was issued by Talbot County.*

Smiths Inlet 8/10/1683 – 200a's. SDA/327 SR7369
Location: Queen Annes County on the southern side of the Chester River on the southern side of Corsica Creek adjoining **George Holland's** tract of land called Denton and **James Scott's** tract called Mackwell. *Note: This patent was issued by Talbot County.*

Golden Grove 9/10/1683 - 116a's. CB3i/304 SR7367
Location: Queen Annes County on the Northwest Branch of the Wye River in the woods. Adjoins **William Turlo's** tract of land called Emerys Addition. *Note: This patent was issued by Talbot County.*

Compton 10/10/1686 - 135a's. L22/297 SR7363
Location: Queen Annes County on the southern side of the Chester River in the woods on Cleets Branch. Begins at a bound tree of his own tract of land

now in the possession of **Daniel Demsay.** *Note: This is a certification issued by Talbot County. No patent was found.*

Lampton 10/10/1686 – 185a's. L22/277 SR7363
Location: Queen Annes County on the upper side of Elletts Branch of the Chester River in the woods. *Note 1: This is a certification. No patent was found. Note 2: This certification was issued by Talbot County.*

Milland 10/10/1686 – 60a's. L22/308 SR7363
Location: Queen Annes County on the upper side of the Southeast Branch of the Chester River beginning at a bound tree of **Daniel Jenifer's** tract of land called Land of the Prophecy. Also adjoins **John Rodway's** tract. *Note 1: This is a certification. No patent was found. Note 2: This patent was issued by Talbot County.*

Astrick 10/11/1686 – 225a's. L22/307 SR7363
Location: Queen Annes County on the southern side of the Chester River on a branch of Corsica Creek. Begins at a bound tree of his own tract of land. Also adjoins **Stephen Tully's** tract called Ripely and **John Whittall's** tract called Whittall. *Note 1: This is a certification. No patent was found. Note 2: This certification was issued by Talbot County.*

Manton 6/11/1686 – 300a's. L22/307 SR7363
Location: Queen Annes County on the southern side of the Chester River. Adjoins **Richard Royston's** tract of land now in the possession of **William Allen.** *Note 1: This is a certification. No patent was found. Note 2: This certification was issued by Talbot County.*

Plaines 1685 – 105a's. NS2i/489 SR7371
Location: Queen Annes County on the southern side of the Chester River on the northern side of Winchester Branch adjoining a tract of land owned by **John Lewis** and **John Clairen.**
Other persons mentioned: Land rights assigned by **Henry Parker.** *Note: This patent was issued by Talbot County.*

Smiths Chance 10/1/1687 – 50a's. NS2i/453 SR7371
Location: Queen Annes County on the southern side of the Chester River on the southern side of Corsica Creek beginning at a bound Oak of **James Scott's** tract of land. Also adjoins the land of **John Boage.** *Note: This patent was issued by Talbot County.*

Smiths Polygon 10/1/1687 – 400a's. NS2i/479 SR7371
Location: Queen Annes County on the southern side of the Chester River on the southern side of Corsica Creek extending to the branches of Fishing Creek beginning at a bound tree of **William Smith's** tract of land. Also

adjoins **Nathaniell Evett's** tract called Winton, **Henry Parker's** tract called Woodland Neck, and tracts owned by **John Clairer, Richard Jones,** and **Thomas Heglin.** *Note: This patent was issued by Talbot County.*

Outrange 3/2/1688 – 400a's. NSBi/693 SR7370
Location: Queen Annes County on the southern side of the Chester River on Hambleton Creek. Adjoins **Steven Tully's** tract of land called Ripely.
Other persons mentioned: Land rights assigned by **Daniel Toes.** *Note: This patent was issued by Talbot County.*

Condon 6/12/1688 – 320a's. NS2i/646 SR 7371
Location: Queen Annes County on the southern side of the Chester River on Red Lyon Branch beginning at a bound tree of **John Winchester's** tract of land called Winchester. *Note: This patent was issued by Talbot County.*

Malton 9/26/1686 – 389a's. L22/364 SR7363
Location: Queen Annes County on the southern side of the Chester River on Unicorn Branch. Adjoins **John Mitchell's** tract of land called Mitchells Addition.
Other persons mentioned: Land rights assigned by **Michael Miller.** *Note 1: This is a certification. No patent was found. Note 2: This certification was issued by Talbot County.*

Smiths Reserve 10/1/1689 - 250a's. NS2i/481 SR7371
Location: Queen Annes County on the southern side of the Chester River on the Eastern Branch of Corsica Creek beginning at a bound tree of his own tract of land called Fishingham. *Note: This patent was issued by Talbot County.*

Double Hills 11/10/1695 – 160a's. BB3B/30 SR7374
Location: Queen Annes County on the southern side of the Chester River on Double Creek adjoining **Seth Foster's** tract of land called Standish Wood. Also adjoins **Matthew Ward's** tract called Wards Parke. *Note: This patent was issued by Talbot County.*

Emerys Fortune Addition 11/10/1695 – 270a's. BB3B/27 SR7374
Location: Queen Annes County on a branch of the Wye River adjoining **William Turlo's** tract of land called Emerys Fortune. Also adjoins **Michael Powels Vandefort's** tract called Vandefort and **Matthew Ward's** tract called The Green Spring. *Note: This patent was issued by Talbot County.*

The Forlorn Hope 11/10/1695 – 935a's. BB3B/396 SR7374
Location: Queen Annes County at the head of the Chester River on the eastern side of Sheades Branch one mile from Duck Creek. Adjoins his own

tract of land called Rearegard. *Note: This patent was issued by Talbot County.*

The Reason 11/10/1695 – 360a's. BB3B/29 SR7374
Location: Queen Annes County on the western side of Thomas Branch. Adjoins **Richard Budge's** tract of land called Petteridge. *Note 1: The information in the patent document is not sufficient to determine the location of this tract. However, Maryland State Land Patent Index #55 does indicate that it was located in Queen Annes County. Note 2: This patent was issued by Talbot County.*

Smiths Range Addition 3/31/1696 – 290a's. BB3B/436 SR7374
Location: Queen Annes County on the southern side of the Chester River on the Southeast Branch beginning at a marked Oak of **Steven Partly's** tract of land called Phipply. Also adjoins **Thomas Collins'** tract called Kellmanan Plaines. *Note: This patent was issued by Talbot County.*

The Contention 5/31/1696 - 100a's. BB3B/435 SR7374
Location: Queen Annes County on the southern side of Island Creek. Adjoins **John Broadrib's** tract of land called Freshford. *Note: This patent was issued by Talbot County.*

The Adventure 5/31/1696 - 160a's. BB3B/437 SR7374
Location: Queen Annes County on the southern side of the Chester River on the southern side of Courseys Creek beginning at a bound tree of **Patrick Forrest's** tract of land called Forrests Lodge. Also adjoins **Robert Macklin** and **Thomas Francis'** tract called Francis Enlargement. *Note: This patent was issued by Talbot County.*

The Addicon 10/10/1701 - 180a's. CDi/215 SR7376
Location: Queen Annes County on the easternmost end of Kent Island beginning at a bound tree of **Pascha Dunns'** tract of land called Parsons Neck.
Other persons mentioned: Land rights assigned by **Philemon Hemsley.**
Note: This patent was issued by Talbot County.

Dispute 10/17/1705 - 240a's. FF7i/295 SR7360
Location: Queen Annes County on the southern side of the Chester River on the western side of a branch beginning at a bound tree of **William Bishop's** tract of land. *Note 1: This is a certification. No patent was found. Note 2: This patent was issued by Talbot County.*

Stoke 4/10/1709 - 100a's. DD5i/567 SR7378
Location: Queen Annes County on the southern side of the Chester River on the western side of the Southwest Branch of Island Creek *(also known as*

110

Elliotts Branch). Adjoins **Vincent Lowe's** tract of land called Lowes Arcadia and **Thomas Collins'** tract called Collins His Land. *Note: This patent was issued by Talbot County.*

Smith, William
Poplar Neck 9/12/1665 – 100a's. L8/247 SR7350
Location: Queen Annes County on the North Branch of the Wye River adjoining **John Wright's** tract of land. Also adjoins **Roger Grosses** tract called Abbington, **William Snaggs'** tract called Batchellors Delight, and **William Jones** and **Peter Sides'** tract called Dobbs Creek.
Other persons mentioned: Land rights assigned by **Edward Lloyd.** *Note: This patent was issued by Talbot County.*

Smiths Ridge 5/9/1666 - 100a's. L9/438 SR7351
Location: Queen Annes County on the southern side of the Chester River at the head of the Southwest Branch of Corsica Creek beginning at a bound Poplar of **James Magregor's** tract of land called The Welsh Ridge. *Note: This patent was issued by Talbot County.*

Kelding 8/13/1666 – 500a's. L10/31 SR7352
Location: Queen Annes County at the head of the Eastern Branch of the Wye River beginning at a bound tree of **Henry Dabney's** tract of land called Buckingham. *Note: This patent was issued by Talbot County.*

Sexton 8/13/1666 - 500a's. L10/21 SR7352
Location: Queen Annes County on the southern side of the Chester River on the western side of Corsica Creek. Adjoins **Nathaniell Evett's** tract of land.
Other persons mentioned: Land rights assigned by **Charles Calvert.** *Note: This patent was issued by Talbot County.*

Bocking 3/20/1705 – 500a's. WD/507 SR7372
Location: Queen Annes County at the head of a branch of the Wye River beginning at a bound tree standing in the eastern line of **George Prowse's** tract of land called Prout Park.
Other persons mentioned: Land rights assigned by **Robert Smith.** *Note: This patent was issued by Talbot County.*

Smithson, Thomas
Reviving Springs 6/12/1688 - 500a's. NS2i/629 SR7371
Location: Queen Annes Branch on the eastern side of the Chester River on the lower side of the Main Branch of Unicorn Creek by the Upper Road. Adjoins **James Clayland's** tract of land called Bridgewater and **John Lundy's** tract called Johns Forrest. *Note: This patent was issued by Talbot County.*

Snaggs, William, Planter
  Batchellors Delight 9/12/1665 – 100a's. L8/249 SR7350
  Location: Queen Annes County on the northern side of the Wye River in the
  woods. Adjoins **William Smith's** tract of land called Poplar Neck.
  Other persons mentioned: Land rights assigned by **Thomas Bradley.** *Note:*
  This patent was issued by Talbot County.

Snowden, Henry, Planter
  Shoreditch 10/1/1687 – 150a's. NS2i/589 SR7371
  Location: Queen Annes County on Williams Branch of the Wye River in the
  woods.
  Other persons mentioned: Land rights assigned by **Thomas Smithson.** *Note:*
  This patent was issued by Talbot County.

Southerne, Valentine
  Southernes Addition 10/5/1695 - 84a's. - C3i/24 SR7377
  Location: Queen Annes County on Kent Island. Begins at a bound Oake of
  John Phillips' tract of land called Pigg Quarter. Also adjoins **Peter**
  Johnson's tract called Hills Cabbin.
  Other persons mentioned: Land rights assigned by **Simon Wilmer.** *Note:*
  This patent was issued by Kent County.

Sparkes/Sparks, William
  Sparkes Own 6/21/1683 – 100a's. L21/527 SR7362
  Location: Queen Annes County on the eastern side of the Chester River on
  the northern side of Island Creek adjoining his own tract of land called
  Sparkes Choice. Also adjoins **Henry Wilcocks'** tract called Mount Hope and
  the land of **Michael Hackett.**
  Other persons mentioned: Land rights assigned by **William Coursey**
  assignee of **Vincent Lowe.** *Note: This patent was issued by Talbot County.*

  Sparks Choice 9/10/1684 - 100a's. SDA/507 SR7369
  Location: Queen Annes County on the Eastern side of the Chester River on
  the northern side of Island Creek adjoining a tract of land that was sold by
  Michael Hackett to **Captain Hide.** Also adjoins **John Michael's** tract of
  land.
  Other persons mentioned: Land rights assigned by **William Coursey, Jr.,**
  assignee of **Vincent Lowe.** *Note: This patent was issued by Talbot County.*

  Sparkes Outlett 6/12/1688 – 114a's. NS2i/625 SR7371
  Location: Queen Annes County on the Chester River in Chester Manor
  between **John Hawkins'** tract called Contention and **William Parker's** tract.
  Other persons mentioned: Land rights assigned by **Thomas Smithson.** *Note:*
  This patent was issued by Talbot County.

Spriggs, Thomas
  Sprigley 1/10/1658 - 600a's. LQ/309 SR7345
  Location: Queen Annes County on the eastern side of the Chester River on
  Spriggs Creek on Muddy Point. Adjoins **John Coursey's** tract of land called
  Cedar Branch at the northernmost bound tree.
  Other persons mentioned: Spriggs transported **himself,** wife **Catherine,**
  Virlinder Ropey, Edward Bushell, Nathaniel Spriggs *(no relationship
  indicated), and **Hugh Johnson** into this Province here to inhabit as appears
  on record. Note: This patent was issued by Kent County.*

Sprye, Christopher
  Spryly 10/1/1687 – 200a's. NS2i/568 SR7371
  Location: Queen Annes County on the southern side of the Chester River on
  the next branch above the Red Lyon Branch extending to Prowses Branch by
  the Lower Road.
  Other persons mentioned: Land rights assigned by **Thomas Smithson.** *Note:
  This patent was issued by Talbot County.*

Stagwell, Thomas
  Stagwell 1/3/1659 - 300a's. L4/297 SR7346
  Location: Queen Annes County on the northern side of the St. Michaels
  River on the eastern side of Morgans Creek. Adjoins **Robert Smith's** tract of
  land called Long Point.
  Other persons mentioned: Stagwell transported **himself,** wife **Ruth,** and son
  Thomas into this Province here to inhabit as appears on record. *Note: The
  patent document does not specify the patenting county. The tract is included
  because MSA Patent Index #55 places it in Queen Annes County.*

Stephens, Charles
  Stephens Lott 1688 – 19a's. IB&ILC/183 SR7365
  Location: Queen Annes County on the Wye River.
  Other persons mentioned: Land rights assigned by **William Hemsley.** *Note:
  The information in the patent document is not sufficient to determine present
  day location. MSA Land Index # 55 shows that it was patented in Talbot
  County. It is included because it was probably located in what is present day
  Queen Annes County.*

Stephenson, Simon & Noble, Robert
  Nobles Ridge 7/9/1674 – 150a's. L15/372 SR4327
  Location: Queen Annes County on a fresh runn of the Eastern Runn of the
  Wye River in the woods. *Note 1: This is a certification. No patent was
  found. Note 2: This certification was issued by Talbot County.*

Stevens, Francis
  Jones Plott 5/10/1695 - 90a's. C3i/16 SR7377

Location: Queen Annes County on the eastern side of Kent Island by Great Thickett Creek extending to the eastern side of Eastern Creek beginning at a bound Spanish Oak. Adjoins **William Joyner's** tract of land.
Other persons mentioned: Land rights assigned by former owner **John Jones.** *Note: This patent was issued by Kent County.*

Stevens Adventure 11/10/1695 - 255a's. C3i/143 SR7377
Location: Queen Annes County on Kent Island at the head of Pigg Quarter Creek by a bridge. Adjoins **John Phillips'** tract of land called Pigg Quarter, **Peter Johnson's** tract called Hills Cabbin, and **Vincent Lowes'** tract called Timber Ridge.
Other persons mentioned: Land rights assigned by **Simon Wilmer** assignee of **Philemon Hemsley.** *Note: This patent was issued by Kent County.*

Stevens, Simon
Addition 8/10/1685 – 75a's. NS2i/79 SR73 71
Location: Queen Annes County on the northern side of the Back Wye River beginning at a bound tree of **Richard Sweatman's** tract of land called Sweatmans Hope. Also adjoins **Robert Whetstone's** tract of land now in the possession of **John Emmerson.**
Other persons mentioned: Land rights assigned by **William Coursey.** *Note: This patent was issued by Talbot County.*

Stevens, William, Planter
Stevens Choice 4/8/1662 - 1,000a's. L5/61 SR7347
Location: Queen Annes County on the western side of an island in Morgans Creek beginning at a marked Oak of **John Felton's** tract of land called Drum Point. *Note: The patent document does not specify the patenting county. The tract is included because MSA Patent Index #55 places it in Queen Annes County.*

Stevenson, Ann
Anns Chance 6/1/1685 – 50a's. NS2i/160 SR7371
Location: Queen Annes County on the eastern side of the Middle Branch of the Wye River on Halfmoon Cove. Adjoins **William Shirt's** tract of land called Waterton. *Note: This patent was issued by Talbot County.*

Stint, Thomas
Crawford 1641 – 100a's. AB&H/95 SR7344
Location: Queen Annes County on the eastern side of Kent Island on Smith's Branch in Butlers Marsh extending to Coxes Bay. *Note: This is an original* **William Clayborn** *grant (see forward). Note: This patent was issued by St. Marys County.*

Stoope, Henry & Gibson, John
Stoopley Gibson 2/1/1658 -150a's. LQ/374 SR7345
Location: Queen Annes County on the northeast side of Kent Island
beginning at a marked Pokehikery standing by the Eastern Bay near the
mouth of Great Thicketty Creek. Adjoins **Alexander Waters'** tract of land
called Piney Neck.
Other persons mentioned: Land rights assigned by **Charles Stowere.** *Note:*
This patent was issued by St. Marys County.

Sullivant, Florence
Dungarnam 6/12/1688 – 300a's. NS2i/664 SR7371
Location: Queen Annes County on the southern side of the Chester River
beginning at a bound tree of **Isaac Winchester's** tract of land called Sarahs
Portion. Also adjoining the land of **Thomas Collins.**
Other persons mentioned: Land rights assigned by **Thomas Smithson.** *Note:*
This patent was issued by Talbot County.

Sybrey, Jonathan
Inkercell 4/1/1672 - 200a's. L16/526 SR7357
Location: Queen Annes County on the northern side of the Eastern Branch of
Corsica Creek. Adjoins **George Pascall's** tract of land called Pascalls
Choice. *Note: This patent was issued by Talbot County.*

Wickersly 4/1/1672 - 500a's. L14/493 SR7356
Location: Queen Annes County on the southern side of the Chester River on
the Southeast Branch. Adjoins a tract of land laid out for the Lord Proprietor.
Note: This patent was issued by Talbot County.

Tanner, Thomas
Tanners Advantage 10/10/1703 – 39a's. DD5i/110 SR7378
Location: Queen Annes County on Sparkes Point of Kent Island by a cove.
Other persons mentioned: Land rights assigned by **William Coursey.** *Note:*
This patent was issued by Talbot County.

Thomas, Christopher
Barbados Hall 9/10/1665 – 350a's. L8/297 SR7350
Location: Queen Annes County on the southern side of the Chester River on
the southern side of Corsica Creek beginning at a bound tree standing at the
dividing near Thomas Cove.
Other persons mentioned: Thomas transported **himself,** wife **Susan,** his
children, Katherine Higgins, John Edu, William Codd, and Codd's wife
Jane into this Province here to inhabit as appears on record. *Note: This*
patent was issued by Talbot County.

Thomas, Gabrielle

Conoway 5/18/1687 – 470a's. L22/339 SR7363
Location: Queen Annes County on the southern side of the Chester River at
the mouth of Unicorn Branch beginning at a bound tree of **Robert Smith's**
tract of land called Walton.
Other persons mentioned: Land rights assigned by Robert Smith. *Note: This
patent was issued by Talbot County.*

Thompson, Richard, Planter

Poplar Island Manor 11/6/1640 - 1,480a's. AB&H/85 SR7344
Location: Queen Annes County with 1,000 acres on Poplar Island (to the
south of Kent Island) near his dwelling plantation and 480 acres on Kent
Island next to Kent Fort between Howards Creek, Thompsons Marsh, and the
Chesapeake Bay.
Other persons mentioned: Thompson transported **himself,** his **wife,** one
**child, John Lee, William Smith, William Brockby, John Cook, Donsabell
Gladden, John Thompson,** and **Herbert Smith** into this Province here to
inhabit in 1636, as appears on record. *Note 1: This is described as a
"pretended"* **William Clayborn** *grant. Immediately before the certification
(same reference) there is a written statement presumably entered by the Lord
Proprietor stating, " I would have you lay out for Richard Thompson 1,000
acres lying nearest together about his plantation according to a pretended
grant made to him by Capt. Clayborn and to annex to the s'd Manor Poplar
Island and to draw a patent to the s'd Manor and Island by the Conditions of
Plantation. And for doing on this shall be your warrant." Note 2: This patent
was issued by St. Marys County.*

Tilghman, Mary

Recovery 1/19/1681 - 100a's. B23i/441 SR7365
Location: Queen Annes County on the southern side of the Chester River
beginning at a marked Red Oak of **Richard Tilghman's** tract of land called
Poplar Hill. Also adjoins **William Hemsley's** tract called Brittland.
Other persons mentioned: Land rights assigned by **John Swaine.** *Note: This
patent was issued by Talbot County.*

Tilghman, Richard, Chirugeon

Tilghmans Hermitage 4/1/1667 - 400a's. L10/449 SR7352
Location: Queen Annes County on the Eastern Branch of Tilghmans Creek
extending to Spriggs Creek. *Note: This is a Patent of Confirmation issued by
Talbot County. The land was formerly patented by* **John Coursey** *as Cedar
Branch (400a's) in 1658.*

Tilghmans Farme 1/10/1670 - 900a's. L14/149 SR7356
Location: Queen Annes County on the Chester River on George Lingans
Creek.

<u>Other persons mentioned</u>: Tilghman transported **Thomas Ridgely, James Smith, Elizabeth Tilghman** *(no relationship indicated),* **Joseph Shepherd, Edward Butler, James Riggs, Laplin Hendrick, Mary Wright, Evan Thomas, David Williams,** and **Benjamin Sladden.** Three hundred fifty additional acres assigned by **Richard May** assignee of **John Blomfield** and **Thomas Doxey.** *Note: This patent was issued by Talbot County.*

Tilghmans Lott 6/10/1671 – 500a's. L16/254 SR7357
<u>Location</u>: Queen Annes County on the eastern side of the Chester River on Island Creek in the woods. Adjoins **Robert Macklin's** tract of land called The Reward and **Stephen Tully's** tract called Tullys Delight.
<u>Other persons mentioned</u>: Land rights assigned by **James Jackson** due him for transporting **Jeremiah Copely, Elizabeth Pole, Richard Jackmore, Richard Thomas,** and **George House** into this Province here to inhabit as appears on record. *Note: This patent was issued by Talbot County*

Wintons Addition 6/10/1671 - 25a's. L16/213 SR7357
<u>Location</u>: Queen Annes County on the Chester River at the head of Macklins Branch of Wintons Creek. Adjoins tracts owned by **Robert Macklin** and **Nathaniell Evetts.** *Note 1: The reference page is badly torn and difficult to read. Note 2: This patent was issued by Talbot County.*

Tilghmans Addition 7/10/1671 - 400a's. L14/310 SR7356
<u>Location</u>: Queen Annes County on Hinsons Creek of the Chester River on the northern side of his own tract of land called Forlorn Hope. *Note: This patent was issued by Talbot County.*

Poplar Hill 6/1/1673 - 600a's. L17/141 SR7358
<u>Location</u>: Queen Annes County on the eastern side of the Chester River on Fishing Creek beginning at a marked White Oak standing by the creekside. Adjoins **John Whittington's** tracts called Chesnutt Neck and Whittingtons Lott, and **Mary Tilghman's** tract called Recovery. *Note: This patent was issued by Talbot County.*

Tilghmans Discovery 6/1/1673 – 850a's. L17/140 SR7358
<u>Location</u>: Queen Annes County on the southern side of the Chester River on the eastern side of Double Creek in the woods. Adjoins **John Parson's** tract of land called Parsons His Chance.
<u>Other persons mentioned</u>: Land rights to 200 acres assigned by **Richard Jones.** *Note: This patent was issued by Talbot County.*

Tilghmans Range 11/10/1695 - 98a's. C3i/215 SR7377
<u>Location</u>: Queen Annes County by the Eastern Bay on Tilghmans Creek adjoining a tract of land called Kensington. Also adjoins his own tract called Hermitage and tracts owned by **Thomas Spriggs** and **Stephen Denny.**

Other persons mentioned: Land rights assigned by **Philemon Hemsley** assignee of **William Aldom**. *Note: This patent was issued by Talbot County.*

Tilghman, William

Tilghmans Pasture 2/12/1706 – 500a's. DD5i/244 SR7378
Location: Queen Annes County beginning at a bound tree of **Thomas Spriggs'** tract of land. Also adjoins **Simon Carpenter's** tract called Carpenters Meadow and **John Singleton** and **Richard Jones'** tract called Goose Quarter.
Other persons mentioned: Land rights assigned by **Simon Wilmer**. *Note 1: The certification (L21/383 SR7362 dated 11/16/168)1 shows the certified acres to be 300. Note 2: This patent was issued by Talbot County.*

Toaes, Daniel

Lower Ford 10/1/1687 - 200a's. NS2i/586 SR7371
Location: Queen Annes County on the eastern side of the Chester River above the mouth of Unicorn Branch on both sides of the Lower Ford near **Thomas Collins'** tract of land called Rings.
Other persons mentioned: Land rights assigned by **Richard Bennett**. *Note: This patent was issued by Talbot County.*

Todd, Thomas, Planter

Todd Upon Darwin 2/15/1659 – 400a's. L4/443 SR7346
Location: Queen Annes County on the northern side of the St. Michaels River on the southern side of Darwan Creek. Adjoins **Thomas Bennett's** tract of land called Bendon and **Robert Norrest's** tract called Long Runne. *Note: This patent was issued by Kent County.*

Todley 9/7/1675 – 700a's. L19/173 SR7360
Location: Queen Annes County on the southern side of the Chester River at the head of the Western Runn of Corsica Creek. *Note: This patent was issued by Talbot County.*

Tristram/Trustram, Thomas

Trustrams Addition 5/1/1672 – 400a's. L16/614 SR7357
Location: Queen Annes County at the head of the Back Wye River on Long Neck Branch in the woods.
Other persons mentioned: Land rights assigned by **William Coursey**. *Note: This patent was issued by Talbot County.*

Tristram Res. 5/20/1681 - 1,300a's. L21/338 SR7362
Location: Queen Annes County on the Back Wye River beginning at a bound tree of **Robert Morris'** tract of land. *Note 1: This resurvey was undertaken to combine two tracts called Tristrum and Tristrums Addition with a combined acreage of 800 acres. An additional 500 acres of surplus land was*

found between the two tracts. Note 2: This certification and resurvey was issued by Talbot County.

Tulley, John
Tulleys Delight 2/12/1665 - 1,000a's. L6/181 SR7348
Location: Queen Annes County on the eastern side of the Chester River on the Eastern Branch at Elke Point. *Note 1: A notation on the margin of the patent documents states that this is a special grant of land forfeited by* **Richard Husband**. *No further explanation provided. Note 2: This patent was issued by Kent County.*

Tully, Stephen & Robinson, John
Providence 5/24/1681 - 600a's. L21/365 SR7362
Location: Queen Annes County on the western side of the northernmost branch of Tuckahoe Creek.
Other persons mentioned: Land rights assigned by **Henry Coursey**. *Note: This is a certification issued by Talbot County. No patent was found.*

Tully, Stephen
Tullington 6/13/1674 – 300a's. L15/374 SR4327
Location: Queen Annes County on the southern side of the Chester River at the head of Tullys Creek beginning at a marked Oak standing in the woods. Other persons mentioned; Land rights assigned by **George Cowley**. *Note 1: This is a certification. No patent was found. Note 2: This certification was issued by Talbot County.*

Tullys Lott 6/15/1674 – 300a's. L15/374SR4327
Location: Queen Annes County on the southern side of the Chester River on the southern side of the Main Branch of Parkers Creek.
Other persons mentioned: Land rights assigned by **George Cowley**. *Note 1: This is a certification. No patent was found. Note 2: This certification was issued by Talbot County.*

Ripely 7/30/1674 - 950a's. L15/304 SR4327
Location: Queen Annes County on the southern side of the Chester River on Hamiltons Branch.
Other persons mentioned: Land rights assigned by **John Tully, Sr.** *(no relationship indicated)* due him for transporting **John Hazard, John Gregory, John Baker, Thomas Stanes, Matthew Smith, Francis Loudern, James Loudall, Ann Ratfield,** and **James Walker**. Additional rights assigned by **Henry Bodle** assignee of **Thomas Hedge** due Hedge for transporting **himself, Thomas Walker, Bridgett Louathberry, Michael Cook,** and **John Thomas Worthington**. Also, **Tully** transported his wife **Elizabeth** into this Province here to inhabit as appears on record. Fifty acres more assigned by **Robert Moulder** and **Nathaniell Heathcott** due them for

completing their time of service in this Province. *Note: This patent was issued by Talbot County.*

Upper Deale 4/14/1677 – 500a's. L19/466 SR7360
Location: Queen Annes County on the southern side of the Chester River at the head of Tullys Creek adjoining his own tract of land called Lords Gift. *Note: This patent was issued by Talbot County.*

Ashton 9/10/1677 - 300a's. L9/466 SR7351
Location: Queen Annes County on the southern side of the Chester River in the woods beginning at a marked Oak of his own tract of land. Also adjoins **Edward Beck's** tract called Barton. *Note: This patent was issued by Talbot County.*

Tullys Reserve 1683 – 300a's. SDA/279 SR7369
Location: Queen Annes County on the southern side of the Chester River on the southern side of Corsica Creek beginning at a marked White Oak. *Note: This patent was issued by Talbot County.*

Lords Guift 5/4/1683 - 300a's. SDA/205 SR7369
Location: Queen Annes County on the southern side of the Chester River on the eastern side of Corsica Creek adjoining his own tract of land called Upper Deale. Also adjoins **Thomas Todd's** tract called Todley. *Note: This patent was issued by Talbot County.*

Tullys Addition 5/18/1683 - 300a's. SDA/168 SR7369
Location: Queen Annes County on the southern side of the Choptank River on the western side of the North Branch of Tuckahoe Creek beginning at a bound Oak standing in a forke. Adjoins his own tract of land called Stepney. *Note 1: MSA Patent Index #55 places this tract in Queen Annes County. Note 2: This patent was issued by Talbot County.*

Stepney 11/13/1683 – 200a's. NSBi/63 SR7370
Location: Queen Annes County on the western side of the northmost branch of Tuckahoe Creek adjoining his own tract of land called Tullys Addition. Other persons mentioned: Land rights assigned by **Richard Peacock.** *Note: This patent was issued by Talbot County.*

Turlo, William
Emerys Fortune 3/10/1695 – 190a's. C3i/457 SR7377
Location: Queen Annes County on Morgans Branch of the Wye River on the western side of the Main Road. Adjoins **Blanges** tract of land above Wye Bridge. Also adjoins **Michael Paulus Vandeford's** tract called Vandeford. **Matthew Ward's** tract called The Green Spring, and **Arthur Emery's** tracts called Emerys Addition and Emerys Neglect.

Other persons mentioned: Land rights assigned by **Philemon Hemsley.**
Note: This patent was issued by Talbot County.

Vandeford/Vandefort/Vanderfort, Michael Paul/Paulas/Poules, Powellson/Powleson, Planter
  Unnamed Patent 8/3/1662 – 200a's. L5/140 SR7347
  Location: Queen Annes County at the head of Courseys Creek beginning at a marked Oak standing on a point of land in the woods. *Note: The patent document does not identify the patenting county.*

  St. Pauls 3/19/1661 - 300a's. L6/11 SR7348
  Location: Queen Annes County. Parcel 1 at the head of Courseys Creek of the Chester River. Parcel 2 on the southern side of Carmens Cove. *Note 1: These are certifications. No patents were found. Note 2: The certification document does not specify the certifying county. These tracts are included in this volume because MSA Patent Index #55 places them in Queen Annes County.*

  Paules Fort 7/4/1663 - 200a's. L5/392 SR7347
  Location: Queen Annes County on the southern side of the Chester River on the eastern side of Courseys Creek extending to Carmens Branch. *Note 1: Land rights based on **Vandeford** having transported several unnamed persons into this Province here to inhabit as appears on record. Note 2: The patent document does not specify the patenting county. The tract is included in this volume because MSA Patent Index #55 places it in Queen Annes County.*

  Charmans Neck 11/10/1666 - 150a's. L10/244 SR7352
  Location: Queen Annes County on a branch of Courseys Creek near Carmens Cove. Adjoins **Patrick Forrest's** tract of land called Forrests Cove. *Note: The patent document does not specify the patenting county.*

  Vandefords Agreement 8/1/1673 - 100a's. L15/24 SR4327
  Location: Queen Annes County at the head of the Western Branch of Courseys Creek beginning at a bound tree of his own tract of land. Also adjoins the land of **Desborough Bennett.**
  Other persons mentioned: Land rights assigned by **James Clayland**. *Note: This patent was issued by Talbot County.*

  Vanderfort 8/1/1673 – 850a's. L17/217 SR7358
  Location: Queen Anne County on the southern side of the Chester River about one mile from the head of Courseys Creek beginning at a marked Poplar. Adjoins **William Turlo's** tract of land called Emerys Fortune.
  Other persons mentioned: Land rights assigned by **William Clayland**. *Note: This patent was issued by Talbot County.*

Vaughan, Thomas
Inclosure 10/24/1681 - 300a's. L21/381 SR7362
Location: Queen Annes County on the western side of the Main Branch of
Tuckahoe Creek. Adjoins **Philemon Lloyd** and **Henry Parker's** tract of land
called Loyd Parke, **William Diggs'** tract called Bradford Land, and **William
Dawson's** tract called Dawsons Neck. *Note 1: This is a certification issued
by Talbot County. No patent was found.*

Vaughans Discovery 10/24/1681 - 400a's. L21/381 SR7362
Location: Queen Annes County on the western side of the Main Branch of
Tuckahoe Creek. Begins at a bound tree of **Philemon Loyd** and **Henry
Parker's** tract of land called Loyds Parke. *Note: This is a certification issued
by Talbot County. No patent was found.*

Vaughn, Robert, Commander of Kent Isle
Parsons Point 8/20/1650 - 500a's. AB&H/126 SR7344
Location: Queen Annes County on Kent Island by the Eastern Marsh by the
Chesapeake Bay.
Other persons mentioned: Vaughan transported **James Courtnay** (1638),
Will Lowder (1642), **Frances Ward** (1640), **Penelope Price** and **Mary
Field** (1644), and **Frances Pink** (1646) into this Province here to inhabit as
appears on record. *Note: This patent was issued by St. Marys County.*

Vaughn, William & Pooly, John
Poolys Discovery 6/12/1688 – 16a's. NS2i/635 SR7371
Location: Queen Annes County on Muddy Branch of the Wye River
adjoining **Robert Noble's** tract of land.
Other persons mentioned: Land rights assigned by **Thomas Smithson**
assignee of **Daniel Walker.** *Note: This patent was issued by Talbot County.*

Wade, Zachary & Hines, Isaac
Beaver Neck 8/18/1650 - 200a's. AB&H/109 SR7344
Location: Queen Annes County on Kent Island on Beaver Creek extending to
the Chesapeake Bayside. *Note 1: This is a certification issued by St. Marys
County. The land was patented by **John Salter** in 1658 (LQ/194 SR7345).
Note 2: A notation in the margin of the certification document says,
"Canceled objected upon **Brooks** titles". No explanation found. Note 3: This
certification was issued by St. Marys County.*

Wade, Zachary, Planter
Wades Point 2/2/1658 - 400a's. LQ/371 SR7345
Location: Queen Annes County on Kent Island respecting Green Point.
Other persons mentioned: Wade transported **himself,** his **wife,** and
Cornelius Haggan into this Province here to inhabit as appears on record.

Additional land rights assigned by **Richard Lloyd.** *Note: The patent document does not specify the patenting county.*

Walker, Daniell

Cheshire 11/21/1676 - 200a's. L19/430 SR7360
Location: Queen Annes County on the southern side of the Chester River on Winchester Creek. Begins at a bound tree of **Thomas Hinson, Jr.'s** tract of land called Grayes Inn.
Other persons mentioned: Land rights assigned by **Francis Bellass** assignee of **John Mitchell** assignee of **Thomas Browne.** *Note: This patent was issued by Talbot County.*

Walker, John

Walkers Square 6/1/1687 – 300a's. IB&ILC/315 SR7368
Location: Queen Annes County at the head of Thomas Branch of the Wye River. Adjoins **Hugh Paxton's** tract of land called Manchester and **Arthur Emery** and Hugh Paxton's tract called Emery Paxton.
Other persons mentioned; Land rights assigned by **Richard Royston.** *Note: This patent was issued by Talbot County.*

Ward/Warde, Matthew

Green Spring 6/1/1673 – 50a's. L17/133 SR7358
Location: Queen Annes County on the southern side of the Chester River at the head of the Main Branch of Double Creek. Adjoins **Matthew Mason** and **Herbert Croft's** tract of land called Batchellors Choice. Also adjoins **Arthur Emery's** tract called Emery's Neglect. *Note 1: The patent document spells the owner's name as Ward and as Warde. Note 2: The certification document (L17/429 SR7358) shows the certified acres as 60. Note 3: This patent was issued by Talbot County.*

Parke 6/1/1673 – 1,000a's. L17/134 SR7358
Location: Queen Annes County on the southern side of the Chester River at the head of the Main Branch of Double Creek in the woods. *Note: This patent was issued by Talbot County.*

Wards Hermitage 10/2/1674 - 400a's. L19/256 SR7360
Location: Queen Annes County on the southern side of the Chester River on the main runn of Corsica Creek. *Note: This patent was issued by Talbot County.*

Waters, Alexander, Planter

Pyney Neck 6/20/1668 - 50a's. L12/3 SR7354
Location: Queen Annes County on the northern side of Kent Island by the bayside. Adjoins **Henry Stoope** and **John Gibson's** tract of land called Stoopley Gibson and his own tract called Waters Addition.

Other persons mentioned: Land rights assigned by **Henry Parker.** *Note: This patent was issued by Kent County.*

Dundee 7/26/1680 – 100a's. L22/14 SR7363
Location: Queen Annes County on Kent Island on the northern side of Kerbys Cove of Long Creek extending to Pyney Creek. Begins at a marked Red Oak standing by the cove side. Adjoins his own tracts of land called Pyney Neck and Waters Addition. *Note: This tract was patented by Kent County.*

Waters Addition 8/1/1682 - 50a's. L22/16 SR7363
Location: Queen Annes County on Kent Island on the Eastern Bay adjoining his own tracts of land called Piney Neck and Dundee. *Note: This patent was issued by Kent County.*

Maidens Choyce 4/10/1698 - 65a's. CC4i/64 SR7375
Location: Queen Annes County on Kent Island near the Wading Place on a branch of Pyney Creek. Adjoins **John Gibson** and **Henry Stoope's** tract of land called Stoopley Gibson.
Other persons mentioned: Land rights assigned by **Richard Skinner.** *Note: This patent was issued by Talbot County.*

The Woodland Neck 6/20/1688 - 50a's. AB&H/5 SR7354
Location: Queen Annes County on Kent Island beginning at a marked Oak standing by the Eastern Creek in the woods.
Other persons mentioned: Land rights assigned by **Henry Parker.** *Note: This patent was issued by Kent County.*

Watts, George, Planter
Meadstone 5/1/1672 – 250a's. L16/607 SR7357
Location: Queen Annes County on the northern side of the Choptank River on Williams Branch of the Back Wye River. Adjoins **Nicholas Lowe** and **Thomas Earle's** tract of land called Discovery. *Note: This patent was issued by Talbot County.*

Weatherall, Thomas
Weatherall 10/18/1651 - 100a's. AB&H/195 SR7344
Location: Queen Annes County on Kent Island on Alder Branch. Adjoins **Robert Martin's** tract of land called Martins Neck and **Richard Blunt's** tract called Great Neck.
Other persons mentioned: Land rights assigned by **Phillip Connor.** *Note: This patent was issued by St. Marys County.*

Weekes, Joseph
Unnamed Patent 1/24/1652 - 400a's. AB&H/240 SR7344

Location: Queen Annes County on the northern side of Kent Island beginning at a bound tree standing on Loves Point at the mouth of Loves Creek. Adjoins **Matthew Ward's** tract of land called Chester Point.
Other persons mentioned: Land rights assigned by **Elizabeth Commins.**
Note 1: This patent was issued by Kent County. Note 2: An earlier St. Marys County patent dated 1/24/1652 was found (AB&H/240 SR7344). The owner's name is spelled Weeks in the earlier patent.

Wells, John, Planter
Trustrum Wells, 4/1/1672 – 450a's. L16/588 SR7357
Location: Queen Annes County at the head of the Back Wye River on Williams His Branch in the woods. Adjoins **Philemon Hemsley's** tract of land called Hemsleys Reserve.
Other persons mentioned: Land rights assigned by **William Coursey.** *Note: This patent was issued by Talbot County.*

Wetherby, Thomas
Plesford 6/4/1685 – 200a's. L22/181 SR7363
Location: Queen Annes County on the southern side of the Chester River on a forke of Double Creek.
Other persons mentioned: Land rights assigned by **Henry Parker** assignee of **Robert Smith.** *Note 1: This is a certification. No patent was found. Note 2: This certification was issued by Talbot County.*

Whetstone, Stephen
Whetstone 9/12/1665 – 300a's. L8/251 SR7350
Location: Queen Annes County on the northernmost branch of the Wye River adjoining the land of **John Wright.** Also adjoins **William Snaggs'** tract of land called Batchellors Delight.
Other persons mentioned: Land rights assigned by **John Shaw.** *Note: This patent was issued by Talbot County.*

Whittall, John
Whittall 4/24/1683 – 100a's. CB3i/246 SR7367
Location: Queen Annes County on the Southeast Branch of the Chester River. Adjoins a tract of land laid out for **William Hemsley** now in the possession of **John Hollingsworth.**
Other persons mentioned: Land rights assigned by **Henry Parker** assignee of **James Barber** assignee of **William Sharpe.** *Note: This patent was issued by Talbot County.*

Whittington, John
Chestnutt Neck 8/3/1683 – 150a's. SDA/328 SR7369

Location: Queen Annes County on the southern side of the Chester River beginning at a bound tree of **Mary Tilghman's** tract of land called The Recovery. Also adjoins **Richard Tilghman's** tract called Poplar Hill.
Other persons mentioned: Land rights assigned by **Michael Turbutt.** *Note: This patent was issued by Talbot County.*

Whittingtons Lott 8/10/1683 – 400a's. SDA/072 SR7369
Location: Queen Annes County on the southern side of the Chester River by the riverside beginning at a bound tree of **William Hemsley's** tract of land called Little Brittaine. Also adjoins **Francis Shepherd's** tract called Shepherds Fortune, **William Tilghman's** tract called Poplar Hill, and **Mary Tilghman's** tract called The Recovery.
Other persons mentioned: Land rights assigned by **Symon Willmer.** *Note: This patent was issued by Talbot County.*

Whittingtons Lott 4/1/1685 – 200a's. NSBi/325 SR7370
Location: Queen Annes County on the southern side of the Chester River beginning at a bound tree of his own tract of land called Whittingtons Addition.
Other persons mentioned: Land rights assigned by **Robert Smith.** *Note: This patent was issued by Talbot County.*

Wilcocks, Henry
Mount Hopes Addition 8/2/1683 – 100a's. SDA/064 SR7369
Location: Queen Annes County on the southern side of the Chester River beginning at a bound tree of **Ralph Fishbourne's** tract of land called Mount Hope.
Other persons mentioned: Land rights assigned by **Michael Turbutt.** *Note: This patent was issued by Talbot County.*

Wilkenson, John
Wilkensons Addition 9/10/1683 – 100a's. SDA/308 SR7369
Location: Queen Annes County on the southern side of the Chester River on the southern side of Reads Back Creek adjoining his own tract of land called Waltham.
Other persons mentioned: Land rights assigned by **Robert Smith.** *Another patent was found dated 6/30/1684 ((NS2i/392 SR7371). Note: This patent was issued by Talbot County.*

Wilkinson, Thomas
Unnamed Patent 8/8/1662 – 150a's. L5/148 SR7347
Location: Queen Annes County on the northern side of the St. Michaels River on the eastern side of Morgans Creek on the northern side of Indian Branch. *Note 1: A notation in the margin of the patent document identifies this tract name as Wilkensons Choice and states that the tract was assigned*

by the Talbot County Court to **Richard Carter.** *Note 2: The patent document does not identify the patenting county.*

Willan, Richard, Planter
Thimbly Grange 2/20/1659 - 500a's. L4/520 SR7346
Location: Queen Annes County on the northern side of the St. Michaels River on the southern side of Morgans Creek at the head on the eastern side of Willans Creek. *Note: The patent document does not specify the patenting county. The tract is included because MSA Patent Index #55 places it in Queen Annes County.*

Williams, Henry
Rotterdam 8/1/1683 - 50a's. SDA 178 ST7369
Location: Queen Annes County on Kent Island at the Wading Place beginning at a bound tree of **Anthony Workman's** tract of land called Workmans Hazard.
Other persons mentioned: Land rights assigned by **Henry Parker.** *Note: This patent was issued by Talbot County.*

Williams, Thomas
The Addition 9/4/1665 – 700a's. L8/223 SR7350
Location: Queen Annes County at the head of a branch of the Wye River beginning at a bound tree of his own tract of land called Wilton.
Other persons mentioned: Williams transported **himself** and eleven unnamed persons into this Province here to inhabit as appears on record. Additional rights to 100 acres assigned by **Nicholas Waterman.** *Note: This patent was issued by Talbot County.*

Wilton 8/25/1665 – 650a's. L8/170 SR7350
Location: Queen Annes County at the head of Dividing Branch extending to the Middle Branch of the Wye River on Cabbin Cove beginning at a bound tree of **Andrew Skinner's** tract of land called Triangle. Also adjoins his own tract called The Addition.
Other persons mentioned: Williams transported **himself, Elizabeth & Thomas Leith** *(relationship not indicated),* **John Williams, Alexander Williams** *(relationships not indicated),* **Jane Ford, Thomas Bradley, Ann Crossley, John Morgen, Thomas Trouse,** and **John Scott** into this Province here to inhabit as appears on record. *Note: This patent was issued by Talbot County.*

Willmore, Simon
Willmore Range 8/10/1683 - 1,000a's. SDA/113 SR7369
Location: Queen Annes County on the eastern side of the Chester River on Unicorn Branch. Adjoins **Nicholas Massey's** tract of land called Masseys

Hazard and **Francis Sheppard's** tract called Shaver. *Note: This patent was issued by Talbot County.*

Wilson/Willson, James, Planter
Willson 8/1/1686 – 100a's. NSBi/304 SR7370
Location: Queen Annes County on the southern side of the Chester River on the eastern side of a branch of Hambletons Branch.
Other persons mentioned: Land rights assigned by **Robert Smith.** *Note: This patent was issued by Talbot County.*

Wilsons Beginning 8/10/1695 – 100a's. BB3B/310 SR7374
Location: Queen Anne County on the southern side of the Chester River on the eastern side of Hambletons Branch.
Other persons mentioned: Land rights assigned by **Robert Smith.** *Note: This patent was issued by Talbot County.*

Wilsons Beginning 11/10/1695 - 250a's. BB3B/311 SR7374
Location: Queen Annes County on the southern side of the Chester River on the western side of Red Lyon Branch between **Wilson's** dwelling plantation and the aforesaid branch.
Other persons mentioned: Land rights assigned by **Philemon Hemsley** assignee of **Robert Smith** assignee of **Samuel Withers.** *Note: This patent was issued by Talbot County.*

Wilson, William
Wilsons Adventure 5/1/1698 - 54a's. CC4i/50 SR7375
Location: Queen Annes County on Kent Island at the head of a branch falling into the Wading Place. Begins at a bound tree of a tract of **John Meconakin's** tract of land called Eastern Island by the Black Swamp. Also adjoins **Roger Baxter's** tract now in the possession of **George Williams.** *Note: This patent was issued by Talbot County.*

Winchester, Isaac
Ericksons Islands 11/10/1680 - 20a's. L21/304 SR7362
Location: Queen Annes County. Two hummocks of small islands including some small islands of marsh off Kent Island at the mouth of the Eastern Creek in the Eastern Bay. Adjoins **Thomas Bradnox's** tract of land called Broad Oak now in the possession of **John Rigby.** *Note: This patent was issued by Kent County.*

Isaacs Addition 3/27/1682 - 50a's. CB3i/108 SR7367
Location: Queen Annes County on Kent Island on Picketts Creek. Adjoins **Robert Purlivant's** tract of land called Purlivant and **Thomas Marsh's** tract called Marsh His Forbearance. *Note: The patent document does not specify the patenting county.*

Sarahs Portion 8/10/1683 – 300a's. CB3i/394 SR7367
Location: Queen Annes County on the southern side of the Chester River on the southern side of Red Lyon Branch in the woods. Adjoins **Florence Sullivant's** tract of land called Dungarnam. *Note: This patent was issued by Talbot County.*

Winchester, John
Winchester 8/2/1650 - 250a's. AB&H/126 SR7344
Location: Queen Annes County on the eastern side of Kent Island near the Wading Place beginning at a marked Pine standing at the mouth of Winchesters Creek.
Other persons mentioned: Winchester transported **himself,** wife **Mary,** and children **John** and **Mary** into this Province here to inhabit as appears on record. *Note: This patent was issued by St. Marys County.*

Winton 1/10/1658 - 300a's. LQ/319 SR7345
Location: Queen Annes County on the eastern side of the Chester River on the southern side of Corsica Creek on Macklins Branch. *Note: The patent document does not specify the patenting county.*

Winckles, Edward, Planter
Virgin Inn 6/1/1673 – 200a's. L17/136 SR7358
Location: Queen Annes County on the easternmost branch of the Wye River beginning at a bound tree of **Elizabeth Brewer's** tract of land called Widdows Chance. Also adjoins **James Scott's** tract called Old Mill.
Other persons mentioned: Land rights assigned by **Ralph Blackhall.** *Note: This patent was issued by Talbot County.*

Winckles Ridge 10/6/1674 – 250a's. L18/239 SR7359
Location: Queen Annes County on Bruers Branch of the Wye River in the woods. Adjoins **Henry Parker's** tract of land. *Note: This patent was issued by Talbot County.*

Winslow, Samuel & Parker, Henry
Niniveh 5/7/1666 - 600a's. L9/400 SR7351
Location: Queen Annes County on the southern side of the Chester River on the southwest side of Corsica Creek beginning at a bound Poplar. Adjoins **Christopher Thomas'** tract of land called Barbados Hall.
Other persons mentioned: Land rights assigned by **William Hill** and **Joseph Winslow.** *Note: This patent was issued by Talbot County.*

Wise, Christopher
Naseby 5/6/1688 - 100a's. NS2i/662 SR7371

Location: Queen Annes County on the southern side of the Chester River on Red Lyon Branch. Adjoins **Peter Dod's** tract of land called Doddington. Other persons mentioned: Land rights assigned by **Thomas Smith** assignee of **Christopher Wise, Sr.** (deceased). *Note: This patent was issued by Talbot County.*

Woolcott, John
Woolcotts Addition 11/26/1667 - 40a's. L11/153 SR7353
Location: Queen Annes County beginning at a bound Red Oak standing at the head of Beavy Neck *(possibly Beaver Neck)* Creek. Adjoins **William Hemsley's** tract of land. *Note: The information in the patent document is not sufficient to determine the location of this tract. However, Maryland State Archives Patent Index #55 indicates that it was located in Queen Annes County.*

Woolman, Rebecca, daughter of **Richard**
Rebeccas Garden 9/25/1675 - 150a's. L19/168 SR7360
Location: Queen Annes County on the Eastern Branch of the Wye River extending to the western side of Nobles Branch.
Other persons mentioned: Land rights assigned by **Philemon Lloyd** assignee of **Henry Hawkins** assignee of **Ralph Hawkins**. *Note: This patent was issued by Talbot County.*

Woolman, Richard, Planter
Woolmans Land 8/8/1662 - 100a's. L5/144 SR7347
Location: Queen Annes County on the northern side of the St. Michaels River on the eastern side of Morgans Creek beginning at a bound tree of **James Scott's** tract of land called James Land on a point of marsh of Doctors Creek. *Note: The patent document does not specify the patenting county. The tract is included because MSA Patent Index #55 places it in Queen Annes County.*

Woolmans Land 8/8/1662 - 150a's. L5/146 SR7347
Location: Queen Annes County on the northern side of the St. Michaels River beginning at a marked Oak. *Note: The patent document does not specify the patenting county. The tract is included because MSA Patent Index #55 places it in Queen Annes County.*

Workeman/Workman, Anthony
Timber Ridge 1/20/1681 - 250a's. CB2i/432 SR7366
Location: Queen Annes County on Kent Island between Pigg Quarter and Coxes Creeks in a swamp.
Other persons mentioned: Land rights assigned by **Bryan Omally**. *Note: This patent was issued by Kent County.*

Workmans Hazard 2/6/1681 - 150a's. CB2i/433 SR7366
<u>Location</u>: Queen Annes County at the Wading Place.
<u>Other persons mentioned</u>: **Workman** transported **himself** into this Province here to inhabit as appears on record. Additional rights assigned by his wife **Elizabeth** due her for completion of her time of service in this Province. Further rights assigned by **Henry Williams** assignee of **John Bullen**. *Note: This patent was issued by Kent County.*

Wright, John & Collins, Thomas
The Barren Ridge 10/2/1667 - 100a's. L11/55 SR7353
<u>Location</u>: Queen Annes County on Kent Island on the eastern side of Coxes Creek beginning at a marked Pine. *Note: The patent document does not specify the patenting county.*

Wallnutt Ridge 10/2/1667 - 100a's. L11/56 SR7353
<u>Location</u>: Queen Annes County on Kent Island on the eastern side of Coxes Creek on the upper side of a cove. *Note: The patent document does not specify the patenting county.*

Wright, John, Planter, Merchant
Middleton 5/5/1665 – 800a's. L9/110 SR7351
<u>Location</u>: Queen Annes County on the Middle Branch of the Wye River at the mouth of Dividing Creek on Halfmoon Cove. Adjoins **Thomas Harwood's** tract of land called Harwoods Lyon and **Henry Hawkins'** tract called Poplar Hill. *Note 1: This is a certification. No patent was found. Note 2: This certification was issued by Talbot County.*

Skipton 1/4/1666 – 300a's. L10/320 SR7352
<u>Location</u>: Queen Annes County at the head of the Eastern Branch of the Wye River beginning at a bound tree of **Elizabeth Bruer's** tract of land called Widdows Chance. Also adjoins **William Finney's** tract called Finneys Hermitage and **William Hemsley's** tract called The Farme.
<u>Other persons mentioned</u>: Land rights assigned by **Richard Blunt** and **Thomas Osborne**. *Note: This patent was issued by Talbot County.*

Bingley 1/9/1666 – 640a's. L10/317 SR7352
<u>Location</u>: Queen Annes County on the Wye River by a cove in the woods. Adjoins **Atwell Bodewell's** tract of land called Corke.
<u>Other persons mentioned</u>: Land rights assigned by **Henry Parker** assignee of **William Smith**. Additional rights assigned by **William Blunt**. *Note: This patent was issued by Talbot County.*

Woodstock 1/9/1666 - 900a's. L10/314 SR7352
<u>Location</u>: Queen Annes County on the easternmost branch of the Middle Branch of the Wye River on the northern side of Halfmoon Cove.

Other persons mentioned: Land rights assigned by **Richard Fitzallen**. *Note: The patent document does not specify the patenting county*

Wrights Point 12/10/1666 – 50a's. L9/441 SR7351
Location: Queen Annes County on the southern side of the Chester River bounded by Hinsontown Creek and the Chesapeake Bay. Adjoins **John Whetstone's** tract of land called Whetstone and the land of **Matthew Read**. Other persons mentioned: Land rights assigned by former owner **Stephen Tully**. *Note: This patent was issued by Talbot County.*

Wrights Choice 6/10/1671 - 200a's. L16/185 SR7357
Location: Queen Annes County on the western side of Kent Island near Broad Creek. Adjoins **Thomas Broadnax's** tract of land. *Note: The patent document does not specify the patenting county.*

The Tarr Kill 7/30/1688 - 150a's. AB&H/48 SR7354
Location: Queen Annes County on Kent Island on Broad Creek extending to Tarr Kill Creek beginning at a bound Oak. Adjoins tracts of land owned by **Edward Clarkson, Richard Blunt,** and **Thomas Broadnax**. *Note: This patent was issued by Kent County.*

Wright, Matthew
Wrights Rest 10/10/1707 - 300a's. DD5i/388 SR7378
Location: Queen Annes County on the southern side of the Chester River on the western side of the northernmost branch of Tuckahoe Creek beginning at a bound Hickory. Adjoins **John Tulley's** tract of land called Tulleys Addition, the land of **John Seargeant,** and a tract called Providence. *Note: This patent was issued by Kent County.*

Wright, Nathan
Guilford 5/14/1694 – 300a's. B23i/178 SR7365
Location: Queen Annes County at the head of a branch of Tuckahoe Creek in the woods. Begins at a marked Oak of **Stephen Tully's** tract of land called Upper Deale. Also adjoins **James Downs'** tract called Downs Forrest. *Note: This patent was issued by Talbot County.*

Wright, Nathaniell/Nathaniele
Wrights Choice 2/7/1682 – 300a's. L21/544 SR7362
Location: Queen Annes County on the southern side of the Chester River on the Southeast Branch of Island Creek adjoining **Robert Smith's** tract of land. Other persons mentioned: Land rights assigned by Robert Smith and **Richard Peacock**. *Note 1: This is a certification. No patent was found. Note 2: This certification was issued by Talbot County.*

Wrights Chance 10/10/1707 - 300a's. DD5i/388 SR7378

Location: Queen Annes County on the southern side of the Chester River on the western side of the Main Branch of Tuckahoe Creek. Adjoins **Stephen Tully's** tract of land called Tullys Addition, the land of **John Seargeant,** and a tract called Providence. *Note: This patent was issued by Kent County.*

Wright, Samuell

Wrights Chance 11/10/1695 – 126a's. WD/107 SR7372
Location: Queen Annes County on the southern side of the Chester River at the head of Winchester Creek adjoining his own tract of land. *Note: This patent was issued by Talbot County.*

Wright, Soloman & Nathaniel

Adventure 8/4/1682 – 100a's. L21/490 SR7362
Location: Queen Annes County on the southern side of the Chester River adjoining **Thomas Jones'** tract of land called Jones Addition and **Richard Jones'** tract called Jones Fortune.
Other persons mentioned: Land rights assigned by **John Lillingston.** *Note: This patent was issued by Talbot County.*

Wright, Soloman

Guilford 8/10/1685 – 300a's. NS2i/149 SR7371
Location: Queen Annes County on the southern side of the Chester River on a branch of Corsica Creek. Begins at a bound tree of **Robert Smith's** tract of land. Also adjoins the land of **John Hawkins.**
Other persons mentioned: Land rights assigned by **Henry Parker.** *Note: This patent was issued by Talbot County.*

Worplesdon 10/1/1687 – 300a's. NS2i//431 SR7371
Location: Queen Annes County on the southern side of the Chester River in a forke of Ellets Branch extending to the Main Branch of the s'd river.
Other persons mentioned: Land rights assigned by **Robert Smith.** *Note: This patent was issued by Talbot County.*

Wyatt, Jane

Jennys Beginning 4/10/1709 - 100a's. DD5i/566 SR7378
Location: Queen Annes County on the southern side of the Chester River on Red Lyon Branch beginning at a bound Red Oak. Adjoins **Charles Lowder's** tract of land called Constantinople.
Other persons mentioned: Land rights assigned by **Elias King.** *Note: This patent was issued by Kent County.*

Yewele. Thomas

Lincolne 3/15/1681 – 200a's. CB3i/119 SR7367
Location: Queen Annes County at the head of Williams Branch of the Wye River in the woods. Adjoins **Henry Costin's** tract of land called Lambeth.

Other persons mentioned: Land rights assigned by **Henry Parker** assignee of **Thomas Collins.** *Note: This patent was issued by Talbot County.*

Young, Richard & Grey, John, Planters
Youngs Chance 9/4/1665 – 450a's. L8/224 SR7350
Location: Queen Annes County at the head of the Middle Branch of the Wye River adjoining **Andrew Skinner's** tract of land called St. Michaels Fresh Runn.
Other persons mentioned: Land rights assigned by **William Durand** and **Thomas Bradley** due Durand for transporting **Sarah Barratt, John Bromfield, Robert Miller, John Green, Alice Smith, Michael Billett, James Foote, John Glover,** and **Edward Swinden** into this Province here to inhabit as appears on record. *Note: This patent was issued by Talbot County.*

Young, William, Planter
Middle Plantation 7/10/1672 – 200a's. L19/404 SR7360
Location: Queen Annes County in the woods by the road from the head of the Wye River to the Chester River. *Note 1: This is a certification. No patent was found. Note 2: This certification was issued by Talbot County.*

Carpenters Square 9/6/1675 – 200a's. L19/170 SR7360
Location: Queen Annes County on Carpenters Branch of the Back Wye River adjoining **John Wells'** tract of land.
Other persons mentioned: Land rights assigned by **William Finney** assignee of **Moses Harris** and **John Greene** due them for completing their time of service. Additional rights assigned by **Gyles Butter** due him for his wife **Elizabeth's** completion of her time of service in this Province. *Note: This patent was issued by Talbot County.*

Hopewell 8/20/1675 – 200a's. L19/404 SR7360
Location: Queen Annes County at the head of the Wye River in the woods. Adjoins **Peter Sides'** tract of land called Wisbitch. *Note 1: This is a certification. No patent was found. Note 2: This certification was issued by Talbot County.*

The Addition 1679 – 50a's. L21/227 SR7362
Location: Queen Annes County on William Creek of the Wye River adjoining his own tract of land called Carpenters Square. Also adjoins the land of **Richard Webb.**
Other persons mentioned: Land rights assigned by **Henry Parker** assignee of **Thomas Collins.** *Note: This is a certification issued by Talbot County. No patent was found.*

Standford 1/19/1681 – 300a's. CB2i/451 SR7366

Location: Queen Annes County on the Thomas His Branch of the Wye River. Adjoins **Thomas Morris'** tract of land called Mount Mill.
Other persons mentioned: Land rights assigned by **Walter Dickenson.**
Note: This patent was issued by Talbot County.

Youngs Adventure 11/4/1682 – 175a's. L21/491 SR7362
Location: Queen Annes County on Thomas Branch of the Back Wye River beginning at a bound tree of **Richard Bridges'** tract of land called Detteridge. Also adjoins **George Prowse's** tract of land called Prowse Park.
Other persons mentioned: Land rights assigned by **Richard Peacocke.** *Note: This is a certification issued by Talbot County. No patent was found.*

Young's Chance 12/7/1682 – 100a's. L21/494 SR7362
Location: Queen Annes County betwixt the branches of the Back Wye River and Thomas Branch. Adjoins **Hugh Baxter's** tract of land called Purchase. Also adjoins **Richard Bridges'** tract of land called Detteridge and a tract called Stepney.
Other persons mentioned: Land rights assigned by **Richard Peacocke.** *Note 1: This is a certification. No patent was found. Note 2: This certification was issued by Talbot County.*

Youngs Fortune 10/11/1683 - 200a's. L22/30 SR7363
Location: Queen Annes County on the Main Branch of the Back Wye River in the woods. Adjoins **Robert Morris'** tract of land called Mount Mill.
Other persons mentioned: Land rights assigned by **William Coursey.** *Note: This is a certification issued by Talbot County. No patent was found.*

Queen Annes County
Landmarks Mentioned in Grant Documents
(aka- Also Known As)

The following is a list of landmarks found in the tract location information contained in patent documents for the grants, certifications, or resurveys included in this Volume. Unless otherwise stated all landmarks listed are located entirely or partially in Queen Annes County. Please understand that this listing can be no better than the source material. There are many duplicate and like sounding names with different spellings. Tract location information is not always complete or specific as to which of the duplicate or like sounding names is applicable to a specific tract. When this occurs without an adjoining tract named of if the adjoining tract cannot be found, the present day location of the tract and landmark cannot be determined with certainty. Also, there was a tendency to name landmarks (creeks,branches, coves, points, necks, etc.) after the owner of the adjoining land. As a result at least some of these are the same landmark with different names. Despite these difficulties I have tried to make this list as accurate and as interesting as possible.

Abbotts Swamp (Kent Isle)
Adams Bite (Kent Isle)
Alder Branch (of Courseys Cr.)
Alder Swam (Kent Isle)
Andover Branch (of the Southwest Branch of the Chester River) QAC
Back River Creek (of St Michaels River)
Back Wye River (formerly Morgans Cr.)
Barron Neck
Bashas Branch (Kent Isle)
Bathers Creek (of Kent Isle)
Baxters Creek (Kent Isle)
Beaver Creek (Kent Isle)
Beaver Dams Marsh (Tuckahoe Creek)
Beaver Neck Creek
Beavy Neck *(possibly Beaver Neck)* Creek (of Chester River)
Beckles Creek (of Chester River)
Benjamin Oyers Creek (of Eastern Bay) Kent County
Black Swamp (Kent Isle)
Black Wallnut Ridge (a place)
Blunt Point Creek (Kent Isle in Crayford Manor)
Bouges Branch (of Corsica Creek)

Boulens/Bowlings Cove (of Courseys Cr.)
Bread and Cheese Cr. (of Wye River)
Brewers/Bruers Branch/Creek (of Wye River
Broad Creek
Broad Creek (Kent Isle)
Broadnax Creek (Kent Isle)
Broadribs Branch (of Island Cr.)
Broadways Cove (of Wye River)
Broadways Creek (of Wye River)
Browns Branch (of the Southeast Creek)
Britland Creek (of Chester River)
Bugbyes Creek (of the Eastern Bay)
Burns Creek (of Chester River) QAC
Butlers Creek (Kent Isle) QAC
Butlers Marsh (Kent Isle)
Cabbin Branch (of Wye River)
Cabbin Branch (of the Eastern Bay)
Cabbin Cove (of the Middle Branch of Wye River)
Canes Bite *(could be Cones Bite)* Creek (Kent Isle)
Carmens Branch (of Courseys Creek)
Carmens Cove
Cedar Branch (Kent Isle Pine Bay
Champes Cr.
Chester Manor (a place)
Chester River (boundary between QA and Kent Counties)
Clay Pot Neck (Kent Isle Coxes Creek)
Cleets Branch (of Chester River)
Cones Bite (Kent Isle)
Connors Creek (Kent Isle)
Coar Sara Creek (by the road from Tuckahoe Bridge)
Corsica Creek (of Chester River)
Coursefield Creek (Back Wye River)
Coursefield Road (Back Wye River area)
Coursegall Creek (of Chester River)
Coursey Creek
Courseys Back Creek
Courseys Point (Cousegall Creek)
Coursfield Cr. of Chester River
Coxes Creek (Kent Isle)
Craney Creek (Kent Isle)
Crayford Manor (Kent Isle)
Crany Pond (Kent Isle)
Darwan Creek (of the St, Michaels River
Delaware Road (The)
Dividing Branch (of Wye River)

Dividing Creek (of Chester River)
Dividing Creek (of Courseys Creek
Doctors Branch/Creek (of Wye River)
Double Creek (of Chester River)
Duck Creek (of Chester River)
Eastern Bay (The)
Eastern Branch (of Chester River)
Eastern Branch (of Tilghmans Cr.)
Eastern Cr. (Kent Isle)
Easrtern Marsh (Kent Isle)
Eastern Neck (mouth of Chester River)
Elder Branch (Kent Isle of Long Creek)
Elke Point (on the Eastern Branch of the Chester River)
Elletts/Ellets Branch (of the Chester River)
Elliotts Branch (aka Southwest Branch of Island Creek)
Ericksons Branch (of Stints Creek) Kent Isle
Ericksons Island (near Kent Island)
Fishing Creek (of Chester River)
French Womans Br. (westernmost Branch of Tuckahoe Cr.)
Finell Hill (near Unicorn Branch of Chester River)
George Lingans Creek
Gibson Branch (of Tuckahoe Creek)
Giles Branch (Kent Island)
Goose Harbor (Kent Isle)
Great Hinkel Creek (Kent Isle)
Great Thickett/Thickety Creek (Kent Isle)
Green Swamp (of Chester River)
Greens Point (Kent Isle)
Gregorys Cove (of Eastern Bay)
Griffins Branch (of Morgans Cr.)
Gross Branch (of Morgans Cr.of St.Michaels River)
Halfmoon Cove (of Wye River)
Hambleton Creek/Branch (of Chester River)
Hamiltons Creek (of Chester River)
Harwoods Branch/Creek (of the Wye River)
Hattons Branch (Kent Isle)
Hawkinses Creek (of Chester River)
Herring Creek (of Chester River)
Hines Swamp (by Coxes Creek on Kent Isle)
Hinsontown Creek (of Chester River)
Hoampey Creek (of Chester River)
Hobbs Branch (of Wye River)
Hogpen Creek (Kent Isle)
Hogpen Neck Creek (Kent Isle)
Homes Byte (Kent Island)

Honeston Creek (of Chester River)
Horse Road (between Wye and Chester Rivers)
Howards Creek (Kent Isle)
Howards Marsh (Kent Isle)
Howells Branch (Kent Isle)
Indian Branch/Creek (of the Wye River)
Indian Bridge (near Bread & Cheese Creek)
Island Creek (aka the Southwest Branch of the Chester River)
Island Neck (Kent Isle)
Jenkins Creek
Jones Branch (Kent Isle)
Jones Creek (of Chester River)
Katherines Creek (Kent Isle)
Kent Fort Manor (Kent Isle)
Kent Mill (Kent Isle)
Kerbys Cove (of Long Creek on Kent Isle)
Little Creek (Kent Isle)
Little Piney Creek (Kent Isle)
Little Thickett (Kent Isle)
Lloyds Creek (of Wye River)
Longbows Creek (of Wye River)
Long Creek (Kent Isle)
Long Marsh (of Tuckahoe Creek)
Long Neck (on a fork of Tuckahoe Creek)
Long Neck Branch (of Back Wye River)
Long Neck Branch/Creek (of Tuckahoe Creek)
Long Toms Creek (of Wye River)
Lord Phillips Forrest (on the eastern side of the Chester River)
Love Bay (Kent Isle)
Loves Creek (Kent Isle)
Lower Ford (of the Chester River
Lower Road (to Delaware)
Macklins Branch (of Courseys Cr.)
Macklin/Macklyns Cove
Main Road (near Morgans Branch of Wye River)
Manour Branch (of Chester River)
Marshy Point (Kent Isle)
Martin Roads Creek (of Chester River)
Martins Creek (Kent Isle)
Matson's Branch
Mattapax Creek (Kent Isle)
Matthew Reads Creek (of Chester River)
Medcalf Branch (of Mattapax Creek on Kent Isle)
Merson Point (Kent Isle)
Michael Rinon Island (in Wye River)

Middle Branch (of Wye River)
Mill Branch (of Corsica Creek)
Morgans Branch/Creek(of Wye River)
Muddy Branch (of Wye River)
Muddy Point (of Spriggs Creek)
New Ordinary Bay (Kent Isle)
Newells Creek
New Work Island (Wye River)
Nobles Branch (of Wye River
Northeast Bay (of the Eastern Bay)
Northeast Creek (Kent Isle)
Northwest Creek (Kent Isle)
Old Fort Manor (Kent Isle)
Old Schoolhouse (near Wye Mill)
Ordinary Creek (Kent Isle)
Oyster Creek (Kent Isle)
Parkers Creek (of Chester River)
Parsons Point (Kent Isle)
Pearles Creek (of Chester River)
Philpotts Creek (Kent Isle)
Picards Branch/Creek (Kent Isle)
Picketts Creek (Kent Isle)
Pig Bay (Kent Isle)
Pigg Quarter Creek (Kent Isle)
Pine Creek (Kent Isle)
Pine Bay (Kent Isle)
Pokady Road (Wye River area)
Poplar Creek (Kent Isle)
Poplar Isle (to the south of Kent Isle)
Poplar Neck (Kent Isle)
Potts Branch (Kent Isle)
Prato Branch (of Chester River)
Prices Hill
Priors Creek (Kent Isle)
Prowse Branch (of Chester River)
Pyney Creek (Kent Isle)
Pyney Swamp (of Tuckahoe Cr.)
Quarter Cove (of Wye River)
Reads/Reeds Back Branch/Creek (of Chester River)
Reads Creek (of Chester River)
Red Lyon Branch (of Chester River)
Marked Road from the head of Wye River to the Chester River
Road to Wye Mill
Robothams Branch (of Tuckahoe Creek)
Roland Creek (of Chester River)

Rousebys Branch (of Chester River)
Russels Creek (of St. Michaels River)
Sadlers Cove (of Morgans Creek)
Salisbury Plaine (a place)
Sassafras Road
Sayers Neck (between Wye River and The Chesapeake Bay)
Scotts Branch
Sewells Point (Herring Creek)
Sheades Creek (of Chester River)
Shirts Branch (Coxes Bay on Kent Isle)
Smiths Branch (of Poplar Creek on Kent Isle)
Smiths Cove (Kent Isle)
Smiths Cove (of Morgan Creek)
Smiths Creek (of St. Michaels River)
Southeast Branch/Creek of the Chester River (aka Island Creek)
South Pine Bay (Kent Isle)
Southwest Branch (of Island Creek –aka Elliotts Branch)
Sparks Point (Kent Island)
Spriggs Creek (of Chester River)
Stints Creek (Kent Isle)
St. Giles Branch (of Hogpen Creek on Kent Isle)
St. Catherines Branch (Kent Isle)
St. Michaels River –Talbot County
Swan Creek
Talsey Meadow (a place)
Tapahanna Marsh
Tarr Kill Creek (Kent Isle)
Tarr Kill Field (Kent Isle)
Thickety Creek (Kent Island)
Thickety Neck Creek (Kent Island)
Thomas Branch (of Back Wye River)
Thomas Cove (of Corsica Creek)
Thompsons Branch (of Howards Creek on Kent Isle)
Thompsons Marsh (Kent Isle)
Tilghmans Cove (of Corsica Creek)
Tilghmans Creek
Tuckahoe Bridge
Tuckahoe Road (Back Wye River area)
Tullys Neck (by Tuckahoe Creek)
Unicorn Branch/Creek (of the Chester River)
Upper Ford (of the Chester River)
Upper Point (at the mouth of Unicorn Branch of the Chester River)
Upper Road (The) (near Unicorn Branch)
Vaughan Bay (Kent Isle)
Wading Plac3e (of Chester River)

Wading Place (Kent Isle)
Wading Place Bay (Kent Isle)
Wading Place Isle (near Kent Isle)
Wading Place Neck
Wallsey Creek
Western Branch (of Coursey Creek)
Western Branch (of Wye River)
Western Runn (of Corsica Creek)
Williams Branch/Creek/Williams His Creek (head of Wye River)
Wilmers Fork (Unicorn Branch of Chester River)
Wilmers Point (on Chester River)
Winchester Creek (of Chester River)
Winchesters Creek (Kent Isle)
Wolf Trap Bridge (Long Toms Creek of Wye River)
Woolmans Back Creek (of Wye River)
Wye Branch (of Tuckahoe Creek
Wye Bridge (of Wye River)
Wye River

Queen Anne County Index of People

To facilitate the search for immigrant information, the names of persons transported to Maryland by others (or by themselves) who were subsequently claimed as rights for acreage under the Maryland "headright" system are shown in bold type and persons completing their periods of indentured service are shown in italics. At the risk of some redundancy, the same names found in a non-immigrant context are shown separately. Individuals are shown in bold type each time they were claimed by themselves or by anyone else for rights to land in Queen Annes County. Either there were many persons with the same name or a number of individuals (and family members as well) were claimed more than once. The truth is probably a mixture of the two possibilities. For more information on the headright system or the Conditions of Plantation, please see the Introduction to this volume.

A

Abbington, John, 79
Abbott/ Abott, John, 1
Abbott, Andrew, 3
Abington, Andrew, 1, 9, 46
Abraham, Alexander, 10
Adams, Thomas, 1
Aldom, William, 117
Aldridge, Ann (wife of George), 1
Aldridge Children (four unnamed), 1
Aldridge, George, 1
Allen, Henry, 11
Allen, Thomas, 2
Allen, William, 2, 107
Armstrong, Francis, 56, 89
Arrount, Elizabeth (widow & executirx of James), 36
Arrount, James, 36
Ashbury, Francis, 2, 73

Ash, Francis, 77
Ashley, Henry, 2
Ashley, Henry, 2
Ashley, Henry, 36
Ashley, Thomas, 73
Askin, John, 18
Atkinson, William, 104

B

Baker, John, 11
Baker, John, 118
Bally, Ambrose, 53
Baltimore, Lord, 3
Barber, Henry, 42
Barber, James, 42, 124
Barefoote, Mary, 37
Barracliffe, Edward, 3
Barratt, Sarah, 133
Barton, William, 93
Basha, Andrew, 1, 3, 24

146

Codd, **William**, 114
Collins, Richard, 20, 45, 49, 88
Collins, Thomas, 3, 15, 16, 20(2),
    59(2), 61, 64(2), 67, 72, 82, 83,
    90, 92, 99, 100, 109, 110, 114,
    116, 117, 130, 133
Comegys, Cornelius, 18, 19, 22, 31,
    44, 56
Comegys, William, 23
Commins, Edward, 23, 52, 65, 100,
    124
Commins, Elizabeth, 10, 23, 53
Conely, George, 71, 102
Conners/Connor/Connors, Phillip, 2,
    10(2), 17, 23, 53
Connor/Connors, Phillip, 24(2)
Connor/Connors, Phillip, 35, 38, 94,
    123
Connor/Connors, Phillip, Sr., 24(3)
Connor, Mary Wrright (widow of John
    Wright & wife of Phillip), 24
Connor, Phillip, Jr., 24
Connor, William, 44
Cook. Edward, 40
Cook, John, 115
Cook, Michael, 118
Cooper, Robert, 3, 24
Coopland, Lettie, 93
Copely, Jeremiah, 116
Coppage, John, 24
Copper, George, 26
Coppin, Edward, 93
Copping, Edward, 25
Costin, Henry, 25, 52, 56, 67, 69, 83,
    104, 132
Coursey, 26
Coursey, Col., 96
Coursey, Henry, 4, 6(3), 13, 14, 26, 27,
    35, 47, 56, 82, 96
Coursey, Henry, Jr., 26, 27(2)
Coursey, John, 27
Coursey, John, 27
Coursey, John, 50(2), 55, 98, 112, 115
Coursey, Judith (wife of William), 50
Coursey, William, 4, 16, 19, 27(2), 49

Coursey, William, 50
Coursey, William, 50, 55(2), 67, 96, 98,
    100, 111, 113, 114, 117, 124,
    134
Coursey, William, Jr/, 111
Courtnay, James, 121
Courtney, Thomas, 18
Courtney, Thomas, 65
Cowley, George, 26, 29, 80, 104,
    118(2)
Cox. Bridgett, 79
Cox, Edmond, 79
Cox, Edward, 29
Cox, Thomas, 11
Cox, William, 29
Crimp, James, 85
Croft, Herbert, 29, 122
Croft, Hugh, 105
Cross, Captain, 15
Crosscomb, Eschell, 84
Crossley, Ann, 126
Cross, William, 30, 95
Crowley, Henry, 102
Crue, John, 35
Crump, Nicholas, 30
Crump, William, 30(3), 49, 70
Cunning, Andrew, 11

D

Dabney, Henry, 110
Dail, John, 31
Dalton, john, 36
Davenport, Humphrey, 31, 70
Davis, John, 8, 32, 51, 78, 95
Davis, Thomas, 32
Dawson, William, 32
Day, Nicholas, 39
Deane, William, 33
Deer, John, 33
Deer, John, 88
Deer, Mrs. (wife of John), 33
Deffecoate, Dernoot, 58
Demsay, Daniel, 107
Dennis, Christopher, 101
Dennis, Richard, 38

Reynolds, John, 9, 90
Richardson, John, 82
Richbrooke, Mary, 69
Ridgely, James, 90
Ridgely, Robert, 93
Ridgely, Thomas, 116
Rigbie, James, 63
Rigbie/Rigby, John, 127
Rigby, James, 38
Riggs, James, 116
Ringold, James, 33
Ringold, John, 33
Road, Walter, 1
Robinson, Charles, 98
Robinson, Christopher, 38
Robinson, John, 62, 91(2)
Robotham, George, 2, 22, 51, 64, 79, 92
Rodway, John, 57, 61
Rodway, John, 92
Rodway, John, 92, 107
Roe, Thomas, 104
Rogers, David, 47, 92
Rolls, Christopher, 83
Ropey, Virlinder, 112
Rouseby, Christopher, 71, 93, 99, 102
Rouseby, John, 93
Rowells/Rowles, Walter, 57
Rowells/Rowles, Walter, 92
Rowles, William, 93
Royston, Mary, 31
Royston/Roystone, Richard, 14, 18, 31, 46(2), 90, 93, 98, 107, 122
Russell, John, 28, 88, 93
Ruth, Thomas, 94

S

Sadler, Giles, 94
Saith (manservant of William Morgan), 77
Salisbury, John, 94
Salisbury, William, 94
Salter, John, 94, 121
Salvage, Joseph, 42
Santee, Christopher, 67, 69, 95

Sayer, Peter, 13, 29, 32
Scott, James, 13, 96, 106, 107, 128, 129
Scott, John, 28, 96
Scott, John, 126
Scotton, Thomas, 97
Sealy, William, 5
Seargeamt, John, 131, 132
Sedgwick, James, 47, 79, 83, 97, 102
Serjent, John, 29
Seth, Jacob, 97
Sewell, Nicholas, 48, 97
Share, William, 93
Sharpe, William, 42, 80, 95, 124
Shaw, John, 124
Sheers, Elizabeth, 24
Shepheard/Shepherd, Sheppard, Francis, 33, 87, 98(3), 125, 127
Shepherd, Joseph, 116
Shingleton, John, 65
Shingleton, Mary (wife of John), 65
Shirt, William, 100, 113
Short, Robert, 100
Sides, Peter, 41, 42, 47, 62, 79, 80, 100, 110, 133
Sigley, William, 100
Simmins, John, 12
Sims, Edmond, 78
Singleton, John, 54, 61, 100, 117
Skinner, Andrew, 8, 13, 16, 58, 81, 101(3), 126, 133
Skinner, Richard, 25, 35, 60, 78, 123
Slack, Ann, 90
Sladen, Benjamin, 116
Slater, John, 71
Slaughter, John, 100, 102
Slaughter, Joseph, 41
Smith, Alice, 133
Smith, Ann, 79
Smith, Catherfine/Katherfine, 102
Smith, Edward, 104
Smith, Elizabeth, 93
Smith, Francis, 42
Smith, Hannah (dau of John), 103
Smith, Herbert, 115

156

Weekes, Joseph, 123
Welch, Jahaine, 58
Welch, Morris, 58
Wells, John, 42, 124, 133
Wells, Toby, 24
West, Elizabeth, 40
Wetherby, Thomas, 124
Whaley. John, 16
Whetstone, John, 131
Whetstone, Robert, 113
Whetstone, Stephen, 32, 51, 124
Whitaker, George, 40
Whitson, Stephen, 37
Whittall, John, 107, 124
Whittington, John, 98, 116, 124
Wigley, Thomas, 12
Wilcocks, Henry, 40, 111, 125
Wilkenson, Thomas, 8, 12, 16, 37, 61, 125
Willan, Richard, 126
Williams, Blanche, 85
Williams, David, 116
Williams, Dorothy (wife of Morgan), 53
Williams, Edward, 10
Williams, George, 127
Williams, Henry, 40, 130
Williams, Morgan, 53
Williams, Nicholas, 10
Williams, Simon, 64
Williams, Thomas, 19, 25, 63, 83, 102
Williams, Thomas, 126**(2)**
Willoughby, Elizabeth, 37
Wilmer, Lambert, 100
Wilmer/Wilmore, Simon, 11, 34(2), 38, 60, 66, 82(2), 98, 99, 111, 113, 117, 125(2)
Wilson, William, 127
Wilson/Willson, James, 127(2)
Wilton, Robert, 52
Winchester, 13
Winchester, Isaac, 38, 43, 114, 127
Winchester, John, 78(3), 82, 85, 108
Winchester, John, 128
Winchester, John (son of John), 128

Winchester, Mary (dau of John), 128
Winchester, Mary (wife of John), 128
Winckles, Edward, 13
Winclkes, Edward, 128
Wingood, Thomas, 53
Winslowe, Elisabeth, 93
Winslow, Joseph, 128
Winslow, Samuel, 12, 40, 49, 52, 76, 82, 83, 101, 128
Wiseback, Abraham, 34
Wise, Christopher, 128
Wise, Christopher, Sr., 129
Withers, Samuel, 127
Woolcott, John, 129
Woolman, 26
Woolman, Revecca (dau of Richard), 129
Woolman, Richard, 25, 129
Workeman/Workman, Anthony, 126, 129
Workeman/Workman, Anthony, 130
Workeman/Workman, Elizabeth (wife of Anthony), 130
Worthington, John Thomas, 118
Wright, John, 7, 13, 16, 24, 37, 39, 42, 46, 47, 51, 59, 63, 82(2), 90, 110, 124, 130
Wright, Mary, 116
Wright, Matthew, 131
Wright, Nathan/Nathaniel, 61, 62, 131(2), 132
Wright, Samuel, 13, 62, 132
Wright, Soloman, 61, 132(2)
Wyatt, Jane, 132
Wyatt, Richard, 53
Wyatt, Thomas, 87

Y

Yewele/Yewell/Yowell, Thomas, 26
Yewele/Yewell/Yowell, Thomas, 75(2)
Yewele/Yewell/Yowell, Thomas, 132
Young, Richard, 133
Young, William, 11, 41, 80, 97(2), 133

Queen Annes County
Index of Tracts

Abbreviations Used

UNP – Unnamed Patent
UNC – Unnamed Certification
Res. – Resurvey
U – Undated

Tract Name	Owners' Name	Year	Page
Abbington	Gross, Roger	1665	42
Abbotts Ash	Abott, John	1640	1
Abington Square	Abington, Andrew	1684	1
Abington Square	Bowles, James	1702	9
Addicon (The)	Salter, John	1705	95
Addicon (The)	Smith, Robert	1701	109
Addition	Stevens, Simon	1685	113
Addition (The)	Hawkins, Henry	1668	47
Addition (The)	Hemsley, William	1688	51
Addition (The)	Hinson, Thomas	1669	53
Addition (The)	Lloyd, Philemon	1680	68
Addition (The)	Lowe, Vincent	1681	71
Addition (The)	Seth, Jacob	1696	97
Addition (The)	Singleton, John & Jones, Richard	1665	101
Addition (The)	Smith, Jacob	1696	102
Addition (The)	Williams, Thomas	1665	126
Addition (The) (C)	Young, William	1679	133
Adventure	Wright, Soloman and Nathaniel	1682	132
Adventure (C)	Jones, Richard	1681	61
Adventure (The)	Hailings, Thomas	1683	45
Adventure (The)	Jones, Richard, Jr.	1683	62
Adventure (The)	Morgan, John	1665	78
Adventure (The)	Smith, Robert	1679	105
Adventure (The)	Smith, Robert	1696	109

Adventure (The) (C)	Legg, William	1680	65
Adventure (The) (C)	Lowe, Vincent	1679	70
Alberts Delight	Johnson, Albert	1683	58
Allens Neck	Allen, Thomas	1640	2
Allens Neck	Allen, William	1686	2
Andover	Comegys, Cornelius	1685	23
Anns Chance	Stevenson, Ann	1685	113
Anthrapp	Hemsley, William	1674	50
Ashburys Addition	Macklin, Robert	1696	73
Ashford	Shepheard, Francis	1686	99
Ashford (C)	Kerby, Walter	1680	63
Ashton	Tully, Stephen	1677	119
Ashton (C)	Shepheard, Francis	1685	99
Astrick (C)	Smith, Robert	1686	107
Aulder Branch	Houlton, Robert	1658	55
Barbados Hall	Thomas, Christopher	1665	114
Barbaras Choyce	Jackson, Thomas	1695	57
Barbers Delight	Bonham, William	1684	8
Barefield	Shepheard, Francis	1683	98
Baron Necke	Hawkins, John	1695	48
Barren Ridge (The)	Wright, John & Collins, Thomas	1667	130
Barron Ridge Addition	Jones, John	1695	60
Barron Ridge Addition (C)	Jones, John	1682	59
Barton	Hackett, William	1682	44
Basha	Basha, Andrew & Cloughton, James	1640	3
Bastable Hill (C)	Dobbs, John	1682	34
Batchellors Chance	Croft, Herbert & Mason, Matthew	1673	29
Batchellors Delight	Snaggs, William	1665	111
Batchellors Hope	Haillings, Thomas	1683	45
Batchellors Plaine (C)	Smith, Robert	1676	104
Batchellors Plaines	Lloyd, Henrietta Maria	1695	67
Batchellors Plaines (C)	Lundy, John	1687	72
Batchelors Adventure	Chaires, John	1683	17
Bath	Broadrib, John	1676	12
Bath Addition	Davenport, Humphrey	1684	32
Beaver Neck	Salter, John	1658	95
Beaver Neck (C)	Wade, Zachary & Hines, Isaac	1650	121
Beaverton	Copping, Edward	1651	25
Beedles Outlett	Beedle, Henry	1673	4
Beginning (The)	Hollingsworth, William	1709	55
Beginning (The)	Lowe, Vincent	1681	70
Belcher	Belcher, Thomas	1652	4
Bendon	Bennett, Thomas	1659	5

Bennetts Addition	Bennett, Desborough	1668	5
Berkes	Lillingstone, John	1683	66
Bingley	Wright, John	1666	130
Bishops Addition	Bishop, William	1662	6
Bishops Field	Bishopp, William	1677	6
Bishops Outlett	Bishop, William	1681	6
Bishopton	Bishop, William	1677	6
Bluff Point	Morgan, Henry	1659	78
Boagley	Boage, John	1658	7
Bocking	Smith, William	1705	110
Bodwell	Bodwell, Atwell	1664	8
Bonaventure	Forbes, Alexander	1700	40
Bone Yard (The) (C)	Masters, Charles	1671	74
Bonnams Addition	Bonnam, William	1685	8
Boothbys Fortune	Boothby, Edward	1685	8
Bostons Addition	Pemberton, John	1681	85
Boulingley	Boulen, James	1662	9
Bowes Range	Bowes, George	1697	9
Bowlingsley	Bowling, James	1658	9
Bradburnes Delight (C)	Smith, Robert	1676	104
Bradford	Broadrib, John	1679	12
Bradfords Addition	Salisbury, John	1683	94
Bradfords Addition (C)	Salisbury, William	1681	94
Braintons Addition	Hawkins, John	1695	48
Brampton	Hemsley, William	1670	50
Branfield	Sayer, Peter	1681	95
Branford (C)	Diggs, William	1681	33
Brecknock	Price, Andrew	1683	88
Bridgewater	Clayland, James	1688	18
Brimington	Lowe, Vincent	1677	70
Bristoll Marsh	Rodway, John & Rowles, Walter	1670	92
Broad Neck	Broadway, Nicholas	1667	12
Broad Oak	Bradnox, Thomas	1658	10
Bromton (C)	Hemsley, William	1669	50
Broomly	Parker, Henry	1683	83
Buck Hill	Bennem, Matthew & Mason, Hugh	1683	5
Burroughs Bridge (C)	Burroughs, John	1685	14
Burton Upon Wallsey	Burton, Edmond	1658	14
Burtons Lott	Burton, Edward	1670	14
Butlers Marsh	Butler, Thomas	1647	15
Butlers Neck	Butler, John	1640	14
Butterfield (C)	Butter, Gyles	1673	15
Butts Neck	Read, Matthew	1667	90

Cabbin Neck (The)	Lombard, Francis & Jones, William	1650	69
Camberwell (C)	Sedgwick, James	1681	97
Carmen and Burton	Carmen, Thomas & Burton, William	1683	15
Carpenters Meadow	Carpenter, Simon	1668	15
Carpenters Outlett	Carpenter, William	1685	15
Carpenters Square	Young, William	1675	133
Carters Addicon	Carter, Richard	1707	16
Carters Addition	Carter, Henry	1695	16
Carters Forrest	Carter, Richard	1695	16
Carters inheritance	Carter, Richard	1667	16
Carters Inheritance Res.	Lloyd, Philemon	1709	69
Castle Miles	Collins, Thomas	1685	21
Cedar Bradnox	Bradnox, Thomas	1658	10
Cedar Branch	Coursey, Joihn	1658	27
Cedar Point (C)	Lloyd, Philemon	1684	68
Chaires Addition	Chaires, John	1687	17
Chance	Granger, Christopher	1683	41
Chance	Lowder, Charles	1709	70
Chance	Rogers, David	1687	92
Chance	Smith, Robert	1683	106
Chance (The)	Carter, Henry	1695	16
Change	Morgan, John	1674	79
Charleville	Lane, John	1681	65
Charmans Neck	Vandefort, Michael Powellson	1666	120
Cheshire	Walker, Daniell	1676	122
Chesnutt Meadow	Robinson, John	1682	91
Chester	Coursey, John & William	1659	27
Chesterfield	Hemsley, William	1670	50
Chesterfield	Hemsley, William	1672	50
Chesterfield	Lowe, Vincent	1681	70
Chesterton	Reynolds, John	1685	90
Chestnutt Neck	Whittington, John	1683	124
Churnells Neck	Churnell, Joseph	1665	17
Claxton Hill	Norris, Robert	1683	80
Claxton Hill Addition	Norris, Robert	1688	81
Clay Bankes	Hollingsworth, John	1664	54
Claypot Neck (C)	Himes, Isaac	1652	53
Clockerton	Clocker, Daniel	1674	18
Clouds Adventure	Cloud, Nicholas	1685	18
Clouds Hermitage	Cloud, Nicholas	1707	19
Clouds Range	Cloud, Nicholas	1707	19
Clowdent	Denton, Henry	1688	33
Cold Harbour (C)	Morgan, Evan	1666	76

Collington	Collins, Thomas	1670	20
Collins His Lott	Collins, Richard	1684	20
Collins Own	Collins, Thomas	1694	22
Collins Range	Collins, Thomas	1683	20
Collins Refusal Res.	Heath, James	1703	49
Colliston	Collins, Thomas	1688	22
Compton (C)	Smith, Robert	1686	106
Condon	Smith, Robert	1688	108
Coney Hall	Gynn, Arthur	1672	43
Connors Neck	Conner, Phillip, Jr.	1670	24
Connors Neck	Connor, Phillip,	1640	23
Conoway	Thomas, Gabrielle	1687	115
Conquest	Cloud, Nicholas	1686	19
Constantinople	Lowder, Charles	1701	70
Content	Robinson, John & Tully, Stephen	1683	91
Content (The)	Hackett, William	1687	45
Contention	Hawkins, John	1682	48
Contention (C)	Hawkins, John	1681	47
Contention (The)	Smith, Robert	1696	109
Cooper (C)	Cooper, Robert	1640	24
Coopers Hill	Joyner, William	1680	63
Coopers Quarter	Cox, Edward	1684	29
Copartnership	Carter, Valentine & John	1699	16
Coppages Ridge	Coppage, John	1700	24
Corke	Lane, John	1683	65
Corke House	Collins, Thomas	1685	21
Costins Hope	Hurlock, George & Costin, Henry	1670	56
Coursey Upon Wye	Coursey, William	1695	29
Courseys Addition	Coursey, Henry	1688	27
Courseys Neck	Coursey, William	1658	27
Courseys Point	Coursey, Henry	1658	26
Courseys Rainge	Coursey, Henry	1665	26
Cove Point	Evetts, Nathaniel	1677	38
Coxs Neck	Cox, William	1640	29
Crany Neck	Huett, Robert & Bellamy, Henry	1640	56
Crany Neck	Lee, Hugh & Hanna	1651	65
Crany Neck (C)	Hewitt, Robert	1651	52
Crawford	Stint, Thomas	1641	113
Crosscombes Pillar (C)	Edenbrook, Edward	1665	35
Crumps Forrest	Crump, William	1688	31
Crumps Chance	Crump, William	1683	30
Crumpton	Crump, William	1683	30
Crumpton	Crump, William	1688	31

Dangerfield (C)	Bishop, William	1684	7
Darland	Lloyd, Philemon	1681	69
Davenport	Davenport, Humphrey	1678	31
Davis Outlett	Davis, John	1683	32
Davis Phenelia	Davis, John	1699	32
Davis Range	Davis, John	1685	32
Dawsons Neck (C)	Dawson, William	1665	32
Dellmore End	Impey, Thomas	1686	56
Denby	Jones, Richard	1683	62
Denbyes Addition	Johnson, John	1687	59
Detteridge	Bridges, Richard	1665	11
Devenishs Chance	Devenish, Robert	1688	33
Discovery	Collins, Thomas & Knowles, Lawrence	1695	20
Dispute (C)	Smith, Robert	1705	109
Dixons Gift	Horney, Geffrey	1709	55
Dobbs Adventure	Dobbs, John	1695	34
Dobbs Creek	Jones, William & Sides, Peter	1665	63
Doctors Gift (The)	Costin, Henry	1681	25
Doddington	Dodd, Peter	1688	34
Double Hills	Smith, Robert	1695	108
Downes Forrest	Downs, James	1683	34
Drum Point	Felton, John	1662	39
Dullidge (C)	Costin, Henry	1687	26
Dundee	Waters, Alexander	1680	123
Dungarnam	Sullivant, Florence	1688	114
Dunns Range	Dunn, John	1683	35
Duns Hazard	Dun, Pasco	1664	34
Duns Range Addition	Parker, Henry	1683	83
Eastern Island (The)	Meconakin, John	1688	75
Elke Point Manor	Husbands, Richard	1659	56
Elliotts Addition	Elliott, John	1683	36
Emery Paxton	Emery, Arthur & Paxton, Hugh	1687	36
Emerys Addition	Emery, Arthur	1686	37
Emerys Fortune	Turlo, William	1695	119
Emerys Fortune Addition	Smith, Robert	1695	108
Emerys Neglect (C)	Emery, Arthur	1682	36
Enjoyment (The)	Lillingstone, John	1684	66
Ericksons Islands	Erickson, Matthew	1683	38
Ericksons Islands	Winchester, Isaac	1680	127
Expectation	Lowe. Vincent	1683	71
Fare Play	Hemsley, Phillemon	1695	49
Fare Play (C)	Coursey, William	1695	28

Farme (The)	Hemsley, William	1688	51
Farrington	Farrington, Robert	1673	39
Finneys Hermitage	Finney, William	1672	39
Finneys Hermitage Res.	Finney, William	1674	39
Finneys Range	Finney, William	1671	39
Fishingham	Smith, Robert	1679	104
Foole Play	Collins, Thomas	1695	22
Forke (The)	Lowder, Charles	1709	70
Forked Neck	Skinner, Andrew	1665	102
Forlorn Hope	Lawrence, William	1683	65
Forlorn Hope (The)	Singleton, John & Jones, Richard	1665	100
Forlorn Hope (The)	Smith, Robert	1695	108
Forrest of Windsor (The)	Peddar, Richard	1681	85
Forrests Lodge	Forrest, Patrick	1658	40
Forsetts Planes	Forsett, Thomas	1673	40
Fortune	Jackson, John	1683	57
Fox Harbor	Hollingsworth, John	1683	54
Fox Hill (C)	Bishop, William	1684	7
France	Blongy, Lewis	1683	7
Frankford (C)	Collins, Thomas	1686	21
Freshford	Broadrib, John	1674	11
Freshford Addition	Collins, Richard	1684	20
Friendship	Hemsley, William	1695	51
Front Meadow (The) (C)	Robinson, John	1682	91
George Codd	Meconakin, John	1688	75
Gleaves Lott	Gleaves, John	1713	41
Glocester	Comegys, William	1685	23
Golden Grove	Smith, Robert	1683	106
Good Increase (The) (C)	Price, Andrew	1679	87
Good Luck	Sigley, William	1701	100
Goose Harbor	Medcalfe, William & Yowell, Thomas	1640	75
Goose Hill	Medcalfe, Wiliiam & Yowell, Thomas	1640	75
Goose Quarter	Singleton, John & Jones, Richard	1676	101
Gore (The) (C)	Sayer, Peter	1687	96
Grantham	Clymer, John	1683	19
Grayes Inn	Hinson, Thomas, Jr.	1668	54
Great Neck	Blunt, Richard	1650	7
Great Neck	Boddy, William	1650	8
Green Spring	Ward, Matthew	1673	122
Greens Adventure	Green, John	1683	41
Griffins Adventure	Griffin, Matthew	1708	42
Gross Addition	Gross, William	1685	42
Gross Coat	Gross, Roger	1658	42

Guiders Lott (C)	Guider, Thomas	1685	43
Guiders Range (C)	Guider, Thomas	1685	43
Guilford	Wright, Nathan	1694	131
Guilford	Wright, Soloman	1685	132
Guithers Lott	Guither, Thomas	1686	43
Gunners Harbour	Hill, William	1672	52
Gwythers Range	Gwyther, William	1686	43
Hackers Forrest	Hacker, John	1707	43
Hackets Delight	Hacket, Michael	1683	44
Hacketts Chance	Hackett, Michael	1683	44
Hacketts Lott	Hackett, Michael	1686	44
Hackneys Marsh Res.	Sedgwick, James	1685	97
Haddon	Hatton, William	1658	47
Hales Neck	Hales, Thomas	1640	45
Halls Harbour	Hall, James	1685	46
Hambleton Parke	Hambleton, Wm. & Parker, Henry	1667	46
Hambletons Hermitage	Hambleton, William	1673	46
Hamers Choice	Hamer, John	1685	46
Hammers Lott	Hammer, John	1708	46
Hammonton	Bastin, Henry	1685	4
Harriss Range	Harris, Moses	1687	46
Harwoods Lyon	Harwood, Thomas	1663	47
Hawkins Farme (C)	Hawkins, John	1679	47
Hazard	Broadway, Robert	1695	13
Heaths Discovery	Heath, James	1701	48
Heaths Forrest Res.	Heath, James	1700	48
Heathworth Res.	Heath, James	1700	48
Hemsley	Hemsley, William	1676	50
Hemsleys Arcadia	Hemsley, William	1695	52
Hemsleys Britania	Hemsley, William	1694	51
Hemsleys Britland	Hemsley, William	1674	50
Hemsleys Brittland	Hemsley, William	1696	52
Hemsleys Choice	Hemsley, William	1663	50
Hemsleys Reserve	Hemsley, Phillemon	1707	49
Hennifield	Sheppard, Francis	1687	99
Higate	Hackett, Michael	1683	44
Highgate Lane	Hacket, Michael	1683	44
Hills Lott (C)	Hill, William	1666	52
Hinson Town	Hinson, Thomas	1659	53
Hinsons Hills	Hinson, Thomas	1675	54
Hinsons Towne Addition	Hinson, John	1667	53
His LOPS Manor	Baltimore, Lord	1684	3
Hogpen Neck	Keyne, Thomas	1647	64

Hogpen Neck	Purlivant, Richard	1640	89
Hope	Johnson, Odbert	1683	59
Hope (The) (C)	Glover, Daniel	1684	41
Hopewell	Morgan, John	1662	78
Hopewell (C)	Young, William	1675	133
Hopton	Hopkinson, Jonathan	1668	55
Horne Island	Barracliffe, Edward	1686	3
Inclosure	Coursey, William	1683	28
Inclosure (C)	Vaughan, Thomas	1681	121
Indian Neck	Aldridge, George	1668	1
Indian Spring	Morgan, Henry	1650	77
Inkercell	Sybrey, Jonathan	1672	114
Isaacs Addition	Winchester, Isaac	1682	127
Jacksons Choice	Jackson, Richard	1664	57
Jacksons Choice	Jackson, Richard	1677	57
Jamaica	Breme, John	1681	11
Jamaica	Jones, Richard	1686	62
Jamaica (C)	Smith, Robert	1678	104
Jamaicas Addition	Robinson, John	1683	91
James Lott (C)	Scott, James	1665	96
James Choice	James, Edward	1699	58
Jasper Lott	Hawkins, John	1695	48
Jenkins Neck	Jenkins, John	1665	58
Jennys Beginning	Wyatt, Jane	1709	132
Jerusalem	Hollingsworth, John	1686	54
Joanes Plackett	Jones, Richard	1675	60
Johns Forrest	Lloyd, Henrietta Maria	1695	67
Johns Forrest (C)	Lundy, John	1687	71
Johnsons Adventure	Johnson, Henry	1696	59
Jones Addition (C)	Jones, Richard	1681	61
Jones Armour	Jones, John	1697	60
Jones Delight	Jones, Thomas	1681	62
Jones Fancy	Jones, Richard	1683	61
Jones Fortune	Jones, Richard	1683	62
Jones Hall	Jones, Richard	1680	60
Jones Park	Jones, Richard	1683	61
Jones Plackett Addition (C)	Jones, Richard	1679	60
Jones Plott	Stevens, Francis	1695	112
Jones Plott (C)	Jones, John	1689	59
Kelding	Smith, William	1666	110
Kelding and Buckingham Res.	Emmerson, John	1697	37
Kelmanam Plaines	Collins, Thomas	1688	22
Kelmannan Plaines (C)	Collins, Thomas	1687	22

Kent Fort Manor	Brent, Giles	1640	11
Kerbeys Prevention (C)	Kerbey, Walter	1695	64
Kerbys Addition (C)	Kerby, Walter	1681	63
Kille Kenney	Collins, Thomas	1685	21
Kinvar Heath (C)	Impey, Thomas	1686	56
Knaves Island (C)	Santee, Christopher	1684	95
Knaves Stand Off	Santee, Christopher	1685	95
Knowles Range	Knowles, Lawrence	1685	64
Labor in Vain	Jones, Richard	1673	60
Lambeth	Costin, Henry	1684	25
Lambeth	Costin, Henry	1685	26
Lambeth	Devenish, Robert	1688	33
Lambeth Fields	Costin , Henry	1673	25
Lampton (C)	Smith, Robert	1686	107
Lancaster	Lancaster, John	1709	64
Land of the Prophecy	Jenefer, Daniel	1666	58
Larrington	Broadrib, John	1679	12
Leicester Fields	Cross, William	1688	30
Lentley	Rodway, John	1674	92
Lewis Chance	Lewis, Thomas	1683	66
Lillingstons Castle	Lillingston, John	1683	66
Lillingstons Castle Addition	Lillingston, John	1684	66
Limbuck	Dine, John	1695	33
Lincolne	Yewele, Thomas	1681	132
Little Ease	Gouldhawke, George	1665	41
Little Thickett	Basha, Giles	1640	4
Lloyd Town	Lloyd, Philemon	1684	68
Lloyds Meadows	Lloyd, Alice	1703	67
Long Neglect	Coursey, William	1696	29
Long Neglect	Lloyd, Edward	1697	67
Long Neglect (C)	Lloyd, Philemon	1687	69
Long Point	Emmerson, Thomas	1665	37
Long Runne (The)	Norrest, Robert	1685	80
Lords Gift	Coursey, Henry	1658	26
Lords Guift	Tully, Stephen	1683	119
Lovely	Lovely, Deliverance	1659	69
Lower Foord	Toaes, Daniel	1687	117
Lower Fords (The)	Jones, Daniel	1687	59
Lowes Arcadia	Lowe, Vincent	1683	71
Lowes Desire	Lowe, Vincent	1683	71
Loyds Costin	Lloyd, Philemon & Costin, Henry	1685	67
Loyds Freshes (C)	Loyd, Philemon	1679	68
Loyds Meadows	Loyd, Philemon	1680	68

Lundy	Lundy, John	1687	72
Macklin	Macklin, Robert	1658	72
Macklinborough	Power, John	1677	87
Macklinburg	Macklyn, Robert	1659	72
Macklinburg Res. (C)	Power, John & Howden, Mary & Judith	1683	87
Macklins Beginning	Macklin, Robert	1683	73
Macklins Fancy (C)	Macklin, Robert	1682	72
Macklynes Addition	Macklyne, Robert, Jr.	1695	73
Maidens Choyce	Waters, Alexander	1698	123
Malton (C)	Smith, Robert	1686	108
Mangy Porkey	Cleeve, Nathaniel	1709	18
Manton (C)	Smith, Robert	1686	107
Margaretts Hill (C)	Price, Andrew	1681	88
Marron	Morgan, Henry	1659	78
Marshes Forbearance	Marsh, Thomas	1677	74
Martins Neck	Martin, Robert	1650	74
Maryes Dower	Rogers, David	1695	92
Marys Portion	Erickson, Matthew	1684	38
Mattapax Neck	Medcalfe, William & Yewell, Thomas	1640	75
Matthews Enlargement	Erickson, Matthew	1695	38
Maxby (C)	Maxwell, Alexander	1665	74
Meadstone	Watts, George	1672	123
Mears Gate	Hemsley, William	1714	52
Meersgate Addition	Lloyd, Edward	1697	67
Meersgate Addition (C)	Lloyd, Philemon	1684	68
Mersons Freehold	Short, Robert	1640	100
Middle Branch (The)	Deane, William	1686	33
Middle Plantation (C)	Young, William	1672	133
Middleton (C)	Wright, John	1665	130
Mill Mount	Morris, Robert	1665	79
Mill Range Res. (C)	Bishop, William	1680	6
Milland (C)	Smith, Robert	1686	107
Mistake (The)	Bishop, Richard	1695	6
Mitchells Addition	Mitchell, John	1670	76
Molden	Sheppard, Francis & Seward, Thomas	1688	98
Moorefields	Moore, Alexander & Vaughan, William	1687	76
Moorefields Addition (C)	Moore, Alexander & Vaughan, William	1688	76
Morgan St. Miichaels	Morgan, Henry	1658	77
Morgans Enlargement	Morgan, Herbert	1700	78
Morgans Hope (C)	Morgan, Martin	1665	79

Morgans Neck	Morgan, Henry	1658	77
Morgans Neglect	Morgan, John	1695	78
Mount Hope	Fishborne, Ralph	1670	39
Mount Hopes Addition	Wilcocks, Henry	1683	125
Mount Malicke	Norrest, Robert	1686	80
Musketoe Range	Broadway, Robert	1696	13
Naseby	Wise, Christopher	1688	128
Nathaniells Point	Clave, Nathaniell	1664	18
Neglect	Smith, Robert	1679	104
Neglect (The)	Coursey, Henry, Jr.	1688	27
Neglect (The) (C)	Coursey, Henry	1687	27
New Hogpen Neck	Medcalfe, William & Yowell, Thomas	1640	75
Newmans Lott	Newman, John	1665	79
Ninevehs Addition	Parker, Henry	1680	83
Niniveh	Parker, Henry	1667	83
Niniveh	Winslow, Samuel & Parker, Henry	1666	128
Noble Chance	Noble, Robert	1665	80
Nobles Addition	Noble, Robert	1683	80
Nobles Range (C)	Noble, Robert	1679	80
Nobles Ridge (C)	Stephenson, Simon & Noble, Robert	1674	112
Nollars Desire (C)	Cloud, Nicholas	1665	18
Normanton	Smith, Robert	1677	104
Normanton (C)	Cowley, George	1673	29
Norrests Addition	Norrest, Robert	1688	80
Norrisderry	Norris, Thomas	1673	81
Northeast Thickett (The)	Russell, John	1650	93
Northumberland	Brostrick, Thomas	1709	13
Notlans Delight	Cloud, Nicholas	1695	19
Notlans Enjoyment	Cloud, Nicholas	1685	19
Okutharpe (C)	Lowe, Vincent	1673	70
Old Mill	Scott, James	1664	96
Oulsons Pasture	Oulson, John	1695	82
Oulsons Relief	Oulson, John	1695	82
Outrange	Smith, Robert	1688	108
Outrange (The) (C)	Bishop, William	1684	7
Oyer Moyne	Rowles, William	1680	93
Padan Aran (C)	Impey, Thomas	1686	56
Parke	Ward, Matthew	1673	122
Parkers Lott	Parker, Henry	1665	82
Parsons His Chance	Parsons, John	1709	84
Parsons Neck	Dunn, Pasco	1665	35
Parsons Neck	Porter, William	1650	87
Parsons Point	Vaughn, Robert	1650	121

Parsons Recovery	Parsons, John	1700	84
Partners Help	Knowles, Lawrence & Collins, Thomas	1695	64
Partnership (The)	Knowles, Lawrence & Collins, Thos.	1695	64
Partnership (The)	Shepheard, Francis & Tilghman, Wm.	1682	98
Pascalls Chance	Pascall, George	1666	84
Pascoes Adventure	Dunn, Pasco	1664	35
Pascos Adventure	Ashbury, Francis	1681	2
Paules Fort	Vandefort, Michael Powleson	1663	120
Paxtons Lott (C)	Paxton, Hugh	1682	84
Peares Plantation	Basha, Giles	1640	4
Peares Plantation (C)	Basha, Giles	1641	3
Pentregay (C)	Deer, John	1650	33
Pentrowey	Price, William	1650	88
Phillpotts Neck	Philpott, Robert	1640	86
Pierces Land (C)	Pierce, John	1686	86
Pig Quarter	Phillips, John	1650	86
Piners Hill	Piner, John	1687	86
Plain Dealing	Crump, Nicholas	1682	30
Plain Dealing	Crump, William	1683	31
Plain Dealing	Hemsley, William	1695	52
Plain Dealing (C)	Hemsley, William	1681	51
Plaines	Smith, Robert	1685	107
Plaines (The)	Broadway, Robert	1695	13
Planters Delight	Jones, William	1673	63
Planters Delight (C)	Jones, William & Sides, Peter	1665	62
Planters Encrease (The)	Francis, Thomas	1676	40
Pleasant Spring	Smith, Robert	1680	105
Pleasant Spring (C)	Boothby, Edward	1685	9
Plesford (C)	Wetherby, Thomas	1685	124
Point Love	Commins, Elizabeth	1650	23
Pokehicory Ridge	Plater, George	1695	87
Ponderfield	Ponder, John	1688	87
Poolys Discovery	Vaughn, William & Pooly, John	1688	121
Poplar Hill	Hawkins, Henry	1677	47
Poplar Hill	Tilghman, Richard	1673	116
Poplar Island Manor	Thompson, Richard	1640	115
Poplar Neck	Smith, William	1665	110
Poplar Neck (C)	Marsh, Thomas	1664	74
Poplar Plaine	Comegys, Cornelius	1685	23
Poplar Ridge	Sewell, Nicholas	1684	97
Porters Lodge	Lillingston, John	1683	66
Potts Gift	Potts Thomas	1650	85

Powells Fancy	Smith, Robert	1681	105
Presbury (C)	Norris, Thomas	1677	81
Prices Hill	Griffin, Anthony	1659	42
Prices Hill	Price, William	1666	88
Primus	Forbes, Alexander	1700	40
Priors Manor	Adams, Thomas	1640	1
Prout Park (C)	Prowse, George	1667	89
Providence	Skinner, A, Winslow, S.& Parker, H.	1666	101
Providence (C)	Davis, Thomas	1683	32
Providence (C)	Tully, Stephen & Robinson, John	1681	118
Purchase	Marshall, Thomas	1701	74
Purchase (The)	Cary, Thomas	1664	16
Purlivant	Purlivant, Richard	1640	89
Pyney Neck	Waters, Alexander	1668	122
Ramseys Folly	Shepheard, Francis	1686	99
Range (The)	Paxton, Hugh	1685	84
Rawlings Chance	Rawlings, John	1668	89
Readbourne	Burk, Richard	1684	13
Readbourne	Read, George	1659	90
Reading	Read, Matthew	1658	90
Reareguard	Chaires, John	1683	17
Reason (The)	Smith, Robert	1695	109
Rebeccas Garden	Woolman, Rebecca	1675	129
Recovery	Tilghman, Mary	1681	115
Reviving Springs	Smithson, Thomas	1688	110
Reward (The)	Macklin, Robert	1658	72
Rich Neck	Mitchell, Will	1651	76
Rich Neck (The)	Land, Phillip & Fox, Gregory	1651	64
Ridgeleys Chance	Ridgely, James	1687	90
Rings	Collins, Thomas	1687	21
Rings End (C)	Collins, Thomas	1686	21
Ripely	Tully, Stephen	1674	118
Roadley	Hemsley, William	1694	51
Robinsons Addition	Robinson, John	1683	91
Robinsons Farme (C)	Robinson, John	1681	91
Robothams Parke	Robotham, George	1685	92
Rosseth	Lloyd, Philemon	1681	68
Rotterdam	Williams, Henry	1683	126
Rouseby	Rouseby, Christopher	1679	93
Royston	Royston, Richard	1673	93
Rumsey Forrest	Harris, Moses	1688	46
Russendall	Russell, John	1658	94
Sadlers Rest (C)	Sadler, Giles	1659	94

Salisbury	Cloud, Nicholas	1685	19
Salisbury	Parker, Henry	1683	84
Salters Marsh	Salter, John	1658	94
Sandy Hurst	Heath, James	1703	49
Sandy Hurst (C)	Ruth, Thomas	1701	94
Sarahs Lott	Costin, Henry	1681	25
Sarahs Portion	Erickson, Matthew	1681	37
Sarahs Portion	Winchester, Isaac	1683	128
Saw Pitt (The)	Bright, Francis	1695	11
Sayers Forrest (C)	Sayer Peter	1687	96
Sayers Range	Sayer, Peter	1683	95
Sayers Range Addition	Sayer, Peter	1685	95
Scottons Addition	Scotton, Thomas	1700	97
Scotts Chance	Scott, John	1708	96
Sewells Forke	Sewell, Nicholas	1684	97
Sexton	Smith, William	1666	110
Shaver	Sheppard, Francis	1688	99
Shearin	Perry, Daniell	1707	85
Shelington	Hinson, Thomas	1666	53
Shepheards Hook	Shepheard, Francis	1683	98
Shepherds Fortune	Shepherd, Francis	1683	98
Sheppards Discovery	Sheppard, Francis	1682	98
Sheppards Folds	Sheppard, Francis	1688	99
Sheppards Forrest	Sheppard, Francis	1684	98
Sheppards Forrest	Sheppard, Francis	1688	99
Sheppards Redoubt	Sheppard, Francis	1688	100
Ship Point	Ingram, Thomas	1668	57
Shoreditch	Snowden, Henry	1687	111
Shotland	Collins, Richard	1684	20
Shrewsbury	Crump, William & Jones, Richard	1685	30
Sintra	Elina, Andrew	1658	35
Skipton	Wright, John	1666	130
Slaughterton	Lowe, Vincent	1683	71
Slaughterton	Slaughter, John	1675	102
Sledmar	Rouseby, John	1679	93
Smeath	Smith, Robert	1659	103
Smithfield	Smith, James	1686	103
Smithfield	Smith, Robert	1683	106
Smiths Addition	Smith, James	1688	103
Smiths Addition	Smith, Robert	1681	105
Smiths Beginning (C)	Smith, James	1682	102
Smiths Chance	Smith, Robert	1687	107
Smiths Delight	Smith, James	1683	103

Smiths Forrest (C)	Smith, Robert	1681	105
Smiths Forrest Addicon	Hollingsworth, Charles	1695	54
Smiths Inlet	Smith, Robert	1683	106
Smiths Lott	Smith, John	1666	103
Smiths Lott	Smith, Robert	1679	105
Smiths Polygon	Smith, Robert	1687	107
Smiths Range	Smith, Robert	1682	106
Smiths Range Addition	Smith, Robert	1696	109
Smiths Reserve	Smith, Robert	1689	108
Smiths Reserve (C)	Smith, Robert	1682	105
Smiths Ridge	Smith, William	1666	110
Solomans Friendship	Hollingsworth, William	1695	55
South Hampton	Hackett, William	1687	45
Southernes Addition	Southerne, Valentine	1695	111
Sparkes Choice	Hackett, Michael	1683	44
Sparkes Outlett	Sparkes, William	1688	111
Sparkes Own (C)	Sparkes, William	1683	111
Sparkes Point	Ashbury, Francis	1681	2
Sparks Choice	Sparks, William	1684	111
Spread Eagle	Jenefer, Daniel	1671	58
Sprigley	Spriggs, Thomas	1658	112
Spring Branch	Jones, Richard	1683	61
Spryly	Sprye, Christopher	1687	112
St. Michaels Fresh Runn Res.	Skinner, Andrew	1664	101
St. Pauls (C)	Vandefort, Michael Paul	1661	120
Stagwell	Bennett, Richard	1706	5
Stagwell	Stagwell, Thomas	1659	112
Stagwell (C)	Price, Andrew	1701	88
Standford	Young, William	1681	133
Standishwood	Foster, Seth	1673	40
Stephens Lott	Stephens, Charles	1688	112
Stepney	Sedgwick, James	1688	97
Stepney	Tully, Stephen	1683	119
Stevens Adventure	Stevens, Francis	1695	113
Stevens Choice	Stevens, William	1662	113
Stinson Erickson	Erickson, , John	1658	37
Stoke	Broadrib, John	1679	12
Stoke	Smith, Robert	1709	109
Stoopley Gibson	Stoope, Henry & Gibson, John	1658	114
Suttons Delight	Boulton, William	1709	9
Syllin	Hinson, Nathaniel	1698	53
Tanners Advantage	Tanner, Thomas	1703	114
Tarre Kill (The)	Wright, John	1688	131

Tell Tale Loss	Smith, Robert	1679	105
Thimbly Grange	Willan, Richard	1659	126
Tilghmans Addition	Tilghman, Richard	1671	116
Tilghmans Discovery	Tilghman, Richard	1673	116
Tilghmans Farme	Tilghman, Richard	1670	115
Tilghmans Hermitage	Tilghman, Richard	1667	115
Tilghmans Lott	Tilghman, Richard	1671	116
Tilghmans Pasture	Tilghman, William	1706	117
Tilghmans Range	Tilghman, Richard	1695	116
Timber Forke	Comegys, Cornelius	1685	22
Timber Neck	Osborne, Thomas	1667	81
Timber Ridge	Workeman, Anthony	1681	129
Todd Upon Darwin	Todd, Thomas	1659	117
Todley	Todd, Thomas	1675	117
Tottenham	Parker, Henry & Winslow, Samuel	1666	82
Triangle	Smith, Robert	1682	106
Triangle (C)	Hemsley, William	1694	51
Triangle (The)	Crump, William	1686	31
Triangle (The)	Skinner, Andrew	1664	101
Tristram Res.	Tristram, Thomas	1681	117
Trustrams Addition	Trustram, Thomas	1672	117
Trustrum	Coursey, William	1665	28
Trustrum Wells	Wells, John	1672	124
Tulleys Delight	Tulley, John	1665	118
Tullington (C)	Tully, Stephen	1674	118
Tulllys Reserve	Tully, Stephen	1683	119
Tullys Addition	Tully, Stephen	1683	119
Tullys Lott (C)	Tully, Stephen	1674	118
Ulthorpe	Page, Robert	1683	82
UNC Bradnox	Bradnox, Thomas	1650	10
UNC Butler (C)	Butler, John	1640	15
UNC Dunn (C)	Dunn, Robert	1651	35
UNC Elliott (C)	Elliott, William	1651	36
UNC Gresham	Gresham, John	1640	42
UNC Potts	Potts, Thomas	1640	85
UNC Proddy	Proddy, William	1650	88
UNC Res. Read	Read, Matthew	1678	90
UNC Smith	Smith, John	1640	103
UNP Abbott	Abbott, John	1640	1
UNP Ashley	Ashley, Henry	1650	2
UNP Basha & Cloughton	Basha, Andrew & Cloughton, James	1640	3
UNP Belcher	Belcher, Thomas	1652	5
UNP Boddy	Boddy, Will	1650	8

UNP Bradnox	Bradnox, Thomas	1650	10
UNP Bradnox	Bradnox, Thomas	1652	10
UNP Clapton	Clapton, Edward	1650	17
UNP Comins	Comins, Edward	1640	23
UNP Coursey	Coursey, William	1662	28
UNP Coursey	Coursey, William	1662	28
UNP Jackson	Jackson, Richard	1664	57
UNP Kent	Kent, Thomas	1641	63
UNP Lowe	Lowe, Vincent	1684	71
UNP Morgan	Morgan, Henry	1650	77
UNP Morgan	Morgan, Henry	1650	77
UNP Morgan	Morgan, John	1662	78
UNP Myles	Myles, Thomas	1650	79
UNP Petts	Petts, Thomas	1641	85
UNP Phillpott	Phillpott, Robert	1640	86
UNP Purlivant	Purlivant, Richard	1640	89
UNP Purlivant	Purlivant, Richard	1640	89
UNP Smith	Smith, Catherine/Katherine	1640	102
UNP Vandefort	Vandefort, Michael Powleson	1662	120
UNP Weekes	Weekes, Joseph	1652	123
UNP Wilkinson	Wilkinson, Thomas	1662	125
Upper Blunt Point	Baxter, Roger	1650	4
Upper Deale	Tully, Stephen	1677	119
Upper Heathworth	Heath, James	1702	49
Vandefords Agreement	Vandeford, Michael Paulas	1673	120
Vanderfort	Vanderfort, Michael Poules	1673	120
Vaughans Discovery (C)	Vaughan, Thomas	1681	121
Vaughns Discovery	Coursey, William	1683	28
Vine Yard	Masters, Charles	1671	74
Virgin Inn	Winckles, Edward	1673	128
Wades Point	Wade, Zachary	1658	121
Wading Place (The)	Land, Phillip & Fox, Gregory	1651	65
Wading Place Neck (C)	Mitchell, Will	1651	76
Wading Place Neck (The)	Connor, Phillip	1658	24
Walkers Square	Walker, John	1687	122
Wallnutt Ridge	Wright, John & Collins, Thomas	1667	130
Waltham	Hynson, Thomas, Jr.	1665	54
Wards Hermitage	Ward, Matthew	1674	122
Warminister	Broadrib, John	1679	12
Waterford	Londey, John	1688	69
Waterford	Skinner, Andrew & Evett, Nathaniel	1666	101
Waters Addition	Waters, Alexander	1682	123
Waterton	Shirt, William	1668	100

Waxford	Dail, John	1707	31
Weatherall	Weatherall, Thomas	1651	123
Weeke (C)	Obder, John	1665	81
Wellen	Rodway, John	1674	92
Welsh Ridge (The)	Magregor, James	1673	73
Welsh Ridge Addition	Davenport, Humphrey	1684	32
Whetstone	Whetstone, Stephen	1665	124
Whittall	Whittall, John	1683	124
Whittingtons Lott	Whittington, John	1683	125
Whittingtons Lott	Whittington, John	1685	125
Wickersly	Sybrey, Jonathan	1672	114
Widdows Chance	Bruer, Elizabeth	1664	13
Wilkensons Addition	Wilkenson, John	1683	125
Willmore Range	Willmore, Simon	1683	126
Willson	Willson, James	1686	127
Wilsons Adventure	Wilson, William	1698	127
Wilsons Beginning	Wilson, James	1695	127
Wilsons Beginning	Wilson, James	1695	127
Wilton	Williams, Thomas	1665	126
Winchester	Parker, Henry	1683	83
Winchester	Winchester, John	1650	128
Winckles Ridge	Winckles, Edward	1674	128
Winters Field	Comegys, William	1708	23
Winton	Evetts, Nathaniel	1667	38
Winton	Winchester, John	1658	128
Wintons Addition	Evetts, Nathaniel	1667	38
Wintons Addition	Tilghman, Richard	1671	115
Wisbitch	Sides, Peter	1667	100
Woodhouse	Londey, John	1688	69
Woodland Neck	Parker, Henry	1666	83
Woodland Neck (The)	Waters, Alexander	1688	123
Woodstock	Wright, John	1666	130
Woodyard Thickett (The)	Connor, Phillip	1650	24
Woodyard Thickett Res.	Conner, Phillip, Jr.	1670	24
Woolcotts Addition	Woolcott, John	1667	129
Woolhampton	Hackett, William	1683	45
Woolmans Land	Woolman, Richard	1662	129
Woolmans Land	Woolman, Richard	1662	129
Workmans Hazard	Workman, Anthony	1681	130
Worplesdon	Wright, Soloman	1687	132
Wrexains Plaines	Ellis, Robert	1683	36
Wrights Chance	Wright, Nathaniell	1707	131
Wrights Chance	Wright, Samuell	1695	132

Wrights Choice	Wright, John	1671	131
Wrights Choice (C)	Wright, Nathaniele	1682	131
Wrights Point	Wright, John	1666	131
Wrights Rest	Wright, Matthew	1707	131
Yarmouth (C)	Macklin, Robert	1682	73
Yarntown (C)	Hurlock, George	1685	56
Youngs Adventure (C)	Young, William	1682	134
Youngs Chance	Young, Richard, & Grey, John	1665	133
Youngs Chance (C)	Young, William	1682	134
Youngs Fortune (C)	Young, William	1683	134

www.ingramcontent.com/pod-product-compliance
Lightning Source LLC
Chambersburg PA
CBHW060505290526
45791CB00001B/272